LEGACY $PORT

HOW TO WIN AT THE BUSINESS OF SPORT IN THE AGE OF SOCIAL GOOD.

NEILL DUFFY, FABIEN PAGET, & JO RAMSAY

SUNBURY PRESS

Mechanicsburg, PA USA

Published by Sunbury Press, Inc.
Mechanicsburg, Pennsylvania

www.sunburypress.com

For information about special discounts for bulk purchases, please contact Sunbury Press Orders Dept. at (855) 338-8359 or orders@sunburypress.com.

To request one of our authors for speaking engagements or book signings, please contact Sunbury Press Publicity Dept. at publicity@sunburypress.com.

FIRST SUNBURY PRESS EDITION: October 2020

Set in Adobe Garamond | Interior design by Crystal Devine | Cover by Halina Myers | Edited by Abigail Henson.

Publisher's Cataloging-in-Publication Data
Names: Duffy, Neill, author | Paget, Fabien, author | Ramsay, Jo, author.
Title: Legacy sport : how to win at the business of sport in the age of social good / Neill Duffy, Fabien Paget, & Jo Ramsay.
Description: First trade paperback edition. | Mechanicsburg, PA : Sunbury Press, 2020.
Summary: *Legacy Sport* is an accessible and informative guide to helping you navigate the sports business world while teaching you how to execute strategies that could make your organization thrive and instill positive change in this age of social good.
Identifiers: ISBN 978-1-620064-03-0 (softcover).
Subjects: SPORTS & RECREATION / Business Aspects | BUSINESS & ECONOMICS / Strategic Planning | BUSINESS & ECONOMICS / Business Ethics | BUSINESS & ECONOMICS / Leadership.

Product of the United States of America
0 1 1 2 3 5 8 13 21 34 55

Continue the Enlightenment!

DEDICATION

With gratitude for those of you who inspire me every day and give me the courage to take the road less traveled.

—NEILL DUFFY

I will always be thankful to all the people who have contributed to shaping the person I am today, those that keep inspiring me every day, and the ones who share this journey with me. My deepest gratitude to all of you!

—FABIEN PAGET

To all those who are committed to using their voice and influence to make the world a better place.

—JO RAMSAY

CONTENTS

Thank You – We Could Not Have Done It Without You ix

Foreword. xii

How to Win at the Business of Sport in the Age of
Social Good xiii

**PART 1: THE PURPOSE REVOLUTION AND WHY
IT MATTERS** 1

1. The Ever-evolving Relationship Between Them and Us 3

2. How Business is Responding to the Shifting Moral
   Landscape. 13
   Leading Thoughts: 20
   *Alan Jope, CEO at Unilever PLC; Hubert Joly, Executive
   Chairman, and former CEO at Best Buy; Sebastian Buck,
   Co-Founder and Strategic Lead at enso; Dr. John Izzo,
   Author, Speaker, and Executive Coach; Carol Cone, CEO
   at Carol Cone ON PURPOSE; Ricardo Fort, Head of
   Global Sponsorships at The Coca-Cola Company; Clementine
   Painter, Senior Manager Strategic Planning at adidas*

3. The Global Goals – A Shared Vision For Success 35

4. Personal Purpose – You Are More Than What You May
   Have Become 42
   Leading Thoughts: 48
   *Kirk Souder, Co-Founder at enso; Lisa Arie, Founder at
   The Vista Caballo*

**PART 2: DOING GOOD WHILE DOING WELL
THROUGH SPORT.** 51

5. Athletes – A Mirror On Society. 53
   Leading Thoughts: 77
   *Lisa Zimouche, Freestyle soccer star; Kevin Anderson,
   Professional tennis player*

6. The Olympic Movement - From Los Angeles and
   Back Again 81
   Leading Thoughts: 93
   Marie Sallois, Director Corporate & Sustainable
   Development at the IOC; Tania Braga, Head of Legacy at
   the IOC

7. Stories From the Frontline of Purpose and Sport. 97
   Case Study: The 34th America's Cup 104
   Case Study: ESPN: The World's Most Purposeful
   Sports Channel. 113
   Leading Thoughts: 127
       Alan Jope, CEO at Unilever PLC; Allen Hershkowitz,
       Founding Director at Sport & Sustainability International;
       Anne-Cecile Turner, Sustainability Director at The Ocean
       Race; Julia Pallé, Senior Sustainability Consultant at
       Formula E; Anna Isaacson, Senior Vice President at the NFL;
       Scott Jenkins, Board Chair at Green Sports Alliance and
       General Manager at Mercedes-Benz Stadium; Ricardo Fort,
       Head of Global Sponsorships at The Coca-Cola Company;
       Joanne Pasternack, Former Warriors & 49ers Foundation
       Executive Director and President & Chief Impact Director at
       Oliver Rose; Clementine Painter, Senior Marketing Manager
       Strategic Planning at adidas; Kely Nascimento-DeLuca,
       Filmmaker

8. Sport For Good Comes of Age 148
   Leading Thoughts: 152
       Tim Shriver, Chairman of the Special Olympics; Benita
       Fitzgerald Mosley, former CEO at Laureus Sport for Good
       USA; Olga Harvey, Chief Strategy and Impact Officer at
       Women's Sports Foundation; Dean Kamen, Founder at
       FIRST; Ben Astin, Managing Director at Lionsraw

9. Where Sport and Purpose Are Heading and Why It
   Matters. What's Next?. 167
   Leading Thoughts: 176
       Sebastian Buck, Co-Founder and Strategic Lead at enso;
       Matthew Campelli, Founder and Editor of The
       Sustainability Report; Lew Blaustein, Founder of Green
       Sports Blog and EcoAthletes; Kevin Martinez, VP Corporate

Citizenship at ESPN; Lucien Boyer, Founder, and Chairman at Global Sports Week; Claude Atcher, CEO at Rugby World Cup France 2023; John Balkam, Author and Social Entrepreneur; Dr. John Izzo, Author, Speaker, and Executive Coach; Carol Cone, CEO at Carol Cone ON PURPOSE

10. Sport's Initial Response to the COVID-19 Pandemic of 2020. 192

PART 3: BRINGING PURPOSE TO LIFE. 199

11. What Purpose Is, and What It Is Not 201
    Leading Thoughts: 207
    Edreece Arghandiwal, CMO and Co-founder at Oakland Roots; Mike Geddes, Chief Purpose Officer at Oakland Roots

12. Defining Your Organizational Purpose 210

13. Identifying and Building Collaborative Partnerships 215

14. Aligning Your Purpose With Your Business Strategy 221
    Case Study: Super Bowl 50. 222

15. Measuring What Matters 227
    Leading Thought: 231
    Lesa Ukman, Founder of ProSocial Valuation Service

16. Bringing It All Together 234
    Case Study: The Danone Nations Cup 236
    Leading Thought: 238
    Florence Darquie-Bossard, Global Marketing Director at Danone

Closing Thoughts: What Sport Should Do To Become An Essential Service 241

Appendix A: Legacy Sport Podcast Series 246

Appendix B: 17 Sport. 248

References. 250

About the Authors 253

THANK YOU
WE COULD NOT HAVE DONE IT WITHOUT YOU

It is no secret that writing a book is a labor of love. *Legacy Sport* has been no different.

We could not have done it without the support of several amazing people and organizations that share our belief in the power of sport to build a better future for everyone. To you all, we say a HUGE thank you—we could not have done it without you.

To Kevin Martinez and Jennifer Paulett at ESPN, thank you for the fantastic work that you and your team at ESPN do to improve the lives of people through sport. Thank you for believing in our vision for Legacy Sport and for helping to make our dream a reality.

To the Thought Leaders that we interviewed for the book and the companion podcast series, thank you for sharing your wisdom and insights with us. Your contribution will make *Legacy Sport* a more valuable resource for readers. Thank you, Alan Jope, Allen Hershkowitz, Anna Isaacson, Anne-Cecile Turner, Ben Astin, Benita Fitzgerald Mosley, Carol Cone, Claude Atcher, Clementine Painter, Dean Kamen, Edreece Arghandiwal, Florence Darquie-Bossard, Hubert Joly, Joanne Pasternack, John Balkam, John Izzo, Julia Palle, Kevin Anderson, Kevin Martinez, Kely Nascimento-DeLuca, Kirk Souder, Lesa Ukman, Lew Blaustein, Lisa Arie, Lisa Zimouche, Lucien Boyer, Marie Sallois, Matthew Campelli, Mike Geddes, Olga Harvey, Ricardo Fort, Scott Jenkins, Sebastian Buck, Tania Braga, and Tim Shriver.

To Georgina Young, thank you for sharing your great HEC Paris MBA Project Report "Legacy & The Olympic Games" with us and allowing us to use it as the basis for our Chapter on the Olympics.

And to the hundreds of friends and colleagues that pre-ordered one or more copies of *Legacy Sport* on our pre-publication Publishizer crowdfunding campaign, thank you for your trust. A special call out to Jamie Cross, Joanne Pasternack, Kate Beavan, Kevin Foley, Megan Dale, Oladele Sobomehin, Scott Jenkins, Chicke Fitzgerald, and Pat Gallagher for your generosity in pre-purchasing multiple copies of the book.

To Lawrence Knorr and Abigail Henson at Sunbury Press, thank you for believing in us and helping us to tell the story we want to tell. We are excited to be working with you and your team and love the work that you do.

FOREWORD

It is not easy being a Scottish sports fan. Shattered dreams often replace rare euphoria. Nevertheless, sports have been a huge part of my life. Growing up in Glasgow, sports were central to our culture. I had the privilege to experience a childhood of soccer, rugby, and golf, as well as the excitement of a whole host of sporting events on our doorstep. Rugby was my first love, and it set a lot of the values—particularly around respect—that I now carry with me in adulthood.

It is no secret the immense value we can get from sport. Sport can be a powerful resource for individuals to become their best selves. But it goes way beyond that. The collective impact of sport—its social and economic benefit—can be significant. Sport spawns businesses, generates jobs, and can re-birth entire cities. It builds pride and creates a legacy. It removes barriers and brings people together. Sport is one of the world's greatest connectors and one of the world's great levelers.

Many of the standout values of sportsmanship—teamwork, respect, responsibility, integrity, inclusion—are in scarce supply in the world today. I have been privileged to spend over 35 years working for a company that has had these values in plentiful supply. A company where "doing the right thing when nobody is looking" has been baked into its DNA from the very start. Unilever's quest to have a positive social and environmental impact goes back to our founders in the mid-1800s and has followed through ever since. Our belief system is that brands with Purpose grow, companies with Purpose last, and people with Purpose thrive.

I am thrilled that many of our brands, like Dove Men+Care, Rexona, and Clear, have chosen to integrate sport into their plans. Little else speaks to people in a way that sport does.

At the time of writing, we find ourselves in unprecedented and worrying times. The world has been shaken, lives and livelihoods destroyed by the COVID-19 pandemic. We are doubtless facing a global recession. Most of the world is at a standstill, with all sporting games on hold. Without the ability to stage matches and events, most sports organizations are struggling, and we are seeing governments having to offer funding to safeguard the immediate future of sports. At a time when the demands on the public purse are vast, and there are many competing priorities, this may seem a strange decision. Yet, it reflects and acknowledges the profound impact sport can have in unifying communities, including in the most disadvantaged areas. It also acknowledges the power of sport to catalyze collective effort and become a beacon for opportunity and high achievement.

Now more than ever, there is a premium on high standards of corporate conduct. Purpose-led businesses will instinctively find the path to serve their multiple stakeholders properly, and in doing so, will secure more sustainable financial returns for their shareholders. This approach applies equally to the business of sport: the more industries that leverage purposeful, responsible, sustainable business, the better. The sentiment behind this book is all-important as an inspiration for the sporting world to realize its full potential as a force for good.

Meanwhile, "Come on, Scotland!"

—Alan Jope, CEO, Unilever

HOW TO WIN AT THE BUSINESS OF SPORT IN THE AGE OF SOCIAL GOOD

There is a revolution underway across the world of business that is driven by a growing number of people who want to work for, buy from, invest in, and advocate for organizations that stand for something more than just profits. And, it is a world where those organizations that best respond to this expectation are outperforming those that do not and where more people are embracing the idea that it is possible to do good while doing well.

We believe that the business of sport is not immune to all of this and that the brands, properties, athletes, and nonprofits that embrace this new reality will be the winners in the coming decades and that those that do not will become irrelevant.

Legacy Sport will help you to understand and navigate this new world and build and execute strategies to help you and your organization remain relevant and thriving in the age of social good.

We have been fortunate enough to have had the inside track for the last 20 years on how the move to Purpose that is underway across the business sector is positively affecting the business of sport. During this time, we have partnered with some of the most forward-thinking sports properties, sponsor brands, athletes, sports-based nonprofits, and sports agencies in the world—Super Bowl, the America's Cup, Laureus Sport for Good Foundation, streetfootballworld, Serena Williams, Danone, adidas, and ESPN to name a few. In the process, we have learned that it is indeed possible to do good while doing well through sport. It can be achieved by designing and building Purpose-led strategies for sports events, sponsors, athletes, and nonprofits that deliver results on multiple bottom lines—socially, environmentally, and financially.

Thanks to this experience and unique insights, we are now able to provide the tools, the motivation, and the support that busy sports executives and marketers need to embrace this opportunity and be successful in this new world, to remain relevant.

At our company, 17 Sport, we believe that sport is one of the most powerful platforms available to help build a sustainable future. When starting the company, we decided that our Purpose would be to contribute towards building a positive future for the world through sport and that we would do this by inspiring, educating, and enabling all stakeholders across the business of sport to do good while doing well. We had three goals in mind when we decided to write this book. The first goal was to amplify the contribution of sport to a sustainable future by helping fellow professionals working in the business of sport to understand how the world is changing around them. The second goal was to show how the more progressive leaders in sport are responding to these changes. And the last goal was to teach how best they should manage their investment in sport in a way that will help them and their organizations remain relevant and commercially viable.

In Part 1 of *Legacy Sport*, we focus on the evolution of Purpose as a management philosophy across society, culture, and business. We support the claim that people increasingly want to work for, buy from, invest in, and advocate for organizations that stand for something more than just profits, reward those that do, and punish those that do not.

We share real-life examples of successful Purpose-driven companies alongside interviews with recognized Thought Leaders and practitioners that are leading the Purpose revolution.

By the end of this section, you will be well versed in Purpose, its growing role in society, and how it is shaping culture and business at the start of the 21st Century.

In Part 2 of *Legacy Sport*, we provide the inspiration and the permission you require to embrace a more Purposeful approach in your work.

Sport is a mirror on society, reflecting the values of the day and shining a light on what matters most to people. In this section, we reflect on how society's values have shown up across sport and how the business of sport has responded.

We share inspiring examples of sports leagues, teams, sponsorships, athletes, and events that have embedded Purpose within their organization's DNA with positive outcomes and highlight the benefits achieved.

Again, interviews with Thought Leaders and practitioners will provide confidence in the notion that "doing good while doing well" can work in the business of sport and get you thinking about what might be possible in whatever aspect of sports you may be working.

By the end of section two, you will have a good understanding of how Purpose is evolving across the business of sport and what opportunities this represents for you, your organization, and the sports sector as a whole.

In Part 3 of *Legacy Sport*, we provide you with the practical tools that you can use to design, deliver, and measure a Purpose-led strategy for your league, team, athlete, sponsorship, event, or brand using 17 Sport's Purpose Framework.

By the end of this section, you will be able to develop your Purpose strategy or brief an advisor to do the same.

But before you get started, some of you may be interested to learn a bit more about our backgrounds and what led us from the traditional world of sports marketing to the Purpose-led world of Impact on which we now focus our efforts. These are our stories of how the last 20 years have shaped the way we now think and act and will hopefully prove the point that it is possible to do good while doing well in sport.

MY STORY: NEILL DUFFY

Sports, media, and business have been part of my life for as long as I can remember.

My mother would often remind me that the first place I visited after the maternity ward in the hospital where I was born in 1964 in Salisbury, Rhodesia was the local racetrack. Horses have pretty much been a part of my life ever since. My parents were passionate horse people and bred and raced thoroughbreds as their first love. This love meant I had an endless supply of horses to ride as a child until I got too heavy and realized that a career as a jockey was not in my future.

I jumped—no pun intended—at the opportunity to call or commentate on my first horse race at the age of 16, to bid-spot for the auctioneers at the annual thoroughbred yearling auction sales, and spend my summer holidays working at a bloodstock agency writing up pedigrees. Race calling would go on to become a feature of my life for the next 20 years and evolve beyond just racetrack calling into calling races and presenting programming for both national radio and television in Zimbabwe and South Africa. I loved it and thrived on the excitement—the countdown to a live television broadcast is the most exhilarating thing you can imagine.

While horses were my first love, rugby was my second. I captained my high school rugby team and represented my country in two school's rugby tests against England and Scotland. Even though we lost both games, they were a highlight of my sport playing days. My ego was sorely brought down to earth when I realized, in my first year at the University of Cape Town, playing U21 rugby, that I was not as tough as I thought I was. I retired to play social rugby with a broken nose inflicted upon me by an opponent who was closer to 31 than 21.

I studied Business at the University of Cape Town before joining Deloitte in Cape Town as an articled clerk and three years later qualified as a Chartered Accountant. I had already realized by then that I did not want to spend the rest of my life wrestling with numbers and green pens, but I also did not want to waste the tremendous financial training that this period of my life had offered. So, I decided to start my own sports marketing business in Cape Town, figuring that it would be a great way to combine my passion for sport and the media and my financial training.

It was an interesting time to start a sports business in South Africa, an industry that was driven at the time by the 200% tax break afforded to companies sponsoring international sport and the numerous rebel tours that were put on for athletes at the end of their professional careers. Everything changed as the country slowly emerged from its isolation as an apartheid fuelled pariah state. The decision by the government in the early 90s to repeal the tax breaks previously afforded international sport put the industry into a tailspin, and nothing much happened for the next few years. Not a great time to be starting a sports marketing business, but out of adversity comes opportunity.

Things eventually started to normalize along with an appetite once again emerging amongst major corporations to sponsor sports, not as a tax write off or a Chairman's whim, but as a marketing investment. With this view in focus, I started to shape my agency into a full-service strategy-led sports marketing agency to partner with our clients in aligning their investment in sponsorship with their business objectives to maximize their return. It was the right offering at exactly the right time—even a little ahead of its time. As we started to get traction in the market, our efforts were noticed by the international agencies that were then starting to enter the market. I ended up partnering with Stewart Banner, who had set up a partnership in South Africa with Alan Pascoe's API. Stewart would go on to become my mentor and business confidante in the years ahead—meeting and working with Stewart was one of the highlights of my career.

Before Stewart or I, together with our new partners Franco Barocas, John Dixon, Chris Bruwer, and Marc Tudhope, knew it, we had built a significant sports and entertainment communication services business. Our business started winning awards and had become one of the top-performing agencies in the new Octagon Worldwide Group, and we were respected for the great work that we were delivering for our clients. I was highly driven by our bottom line and delivering great solutions to our client partners—the world of Jerry Maguire would have been proud of me.

Frustrated by a lack of literature on the subject of how to leverage sponsorship as a business tool, I decided to write my first book, together with my colleague Jo Ramsay (nee Hooper), called *Passion Branding, How To Harness The Power Of Emotion To Build Strong Brands*. Published by Whiley & Sons, the book went on to do quite well despite not reaching the New York Times bestsellers list. I vowed then that I would never write another book . . . we know how that ended.

Five years into my tenure with Octagon South Africa, I was asked to move to Brussels to run Octagon Europe, Middle East, and Africa with a mandate to export our secret sauce in South Africa and build "One Octagon" from the disparate group of entrepreneurial companies that IPG had acquired in the region. It turned out to be a poorly chosen move. The changing economic environment made it near impossible to match the short-term needs of IPG's income statement and the medium to long term "One Octagon" strategic goals that we held for Octagon at an operational level. To compound matters, I lost my father and was diagnosed with cancer at the back end of 2006, two events that shocked me into re-evaluating my values and what I wanted out of my life. I decided to leave Octagon at the end of the same year.

The break from Octagon presented the perfect time to take a break from work, something I had not done for over 20 years. So, my wife Marion and I bundled our five and seven-year-old sons, Sean and Kyle, and our ancient dog Bert, into the car and toured Europe for several months. I could write a book about that experience, but I will keep that for another time. What I can share with you, though, is that having the time to reflect on what I valued most, and least, up until that point in my life was one of the greatest gifts I have ever received.

As I looked back at Octagon South Africa, I realized that the professional moments that most inspired me and gave me the greatest satisfaction were those where we had used sport as a platform to drive some kind of positive social or environmental outcome. Experiencing this transformative power during the 1995 Rugby World Cup was a highlight. President Nelson Mandela became, and still is, my #1 hero; as was the realization that when we integrated a social or environmental "development" component within a traditional media-driven sponsorship, the results were amplified for everyone—the sponsor, the property, and importantly, the community or the environment.

One of my favorite campaigns, for which we won the Best Large Budget Sponsorship of the Year Award in 2000, was the Green Socks Campaign. In this campaign, many runners participating in the Old Mutual Two Oceans Marathon, one of the largest ultra-marathon races in the world, wore a pair of green socks to raise awareness and funds to support the Save Chapman's Peak Fund. The Fund's mission was to restore Chapman's Peak, which formed an essential part of the race route and had been devastated by fire the previous year. Watching a line of green socks wind its way across the city was quite something, as was the reopening of Chapman's Peak a few years later, thanks in part to the work we had done.

My time at Octagon Worldwide in Brussels had sparked questions in my mind around the sustainability of the Wall Street driven growth-at-all-costs model that the business world had adopted over the previous two decades. This philosophy was leading us down a lousy path as a society. I started thinking about different types of business models, and it inspired me to become a student of the conscious capitalism movement and a committed believer in the power of doing good while doing well. I went on to become a Board Member of the Young Presidents Organization Social Enterprise Network, Chair of YPO at Skoll World Forum, and co-founder of Real Leaders magazine, which still exists today and is a highly respected publication on Purposeful leadership.

Armed with renewed energy and excitement to get back to work after my sabbatical, I decided to start a sustainability-focused sports management business, which I called Tribe Management. Nine months later, the financial crises that led to the Recession struck, and everything ground to a halt as companies and people affected by the Recession went into survival mode. It was not a great time to be starting a new long-term thinking business.

Three years later, and with nothing much to show for my efforts other than having clocked lots of miles traveling the globe in search of business, I moved to London to put down some roots. Nine months on, I was commuting to San Francisco as the sustainability advisor to the 34th America's Cup Event Authority. I helped them figure out how to deliver their commitment to the City of San Francisco to stage a carbon-neutral and zero-waste event. The positive energy in San Francisco was addictive, so much so that my family and I decided to relocate there for the three years leading up to the event.

You can read about what we pulled off with the America's Cup in Part 2, but it was a great success in terms of the results we were able to achieve. From a professional perspective, San Francisco turned out to be just the place to be to try out my newfound interest in what we now call Purpose. I loved the open-minded nature of people, their willing-ness to explore new ideas, and how welcoming they were of this guy with a strange accent from the tip of Africa. We decided to make San Francisco home.

After the America's Cup, I worked on several different Purpose-led initiatives in the United States as a hired gun or advisor, including a role as Chief Catalyst at the One World Play Project. This project was a mission-driven for-profit B Corp that had invented a soccer ball that could survive the harshest conditions in the world and never went flat, thus enabling kids to play anytime, anywhere. Chevrolet became the lead partner in the project and made it possible for us to donate millions of balls to kids all over the world as a Purposeful extension of their partner-ship with Manchester United. It is an excellent example of a Purpose-driven strategy and of doing good while doing well through sport.

During my time at the One World Play Project, I supported the team that put together a bid to host Super Bowl 50 at Levi's Stadium in San Francisco. At the time, as a LEED Gold certified building, it was the most sustainably built football stadium in the world. The Bid team, under the leadership of Tipping Point's Daniel Lurie, really embraced the idea of leading with Purpose and leveraging the event as a platform to improve the lives of young people in the Bay Area. We won the bid, and I became

Co-Chair and Lead Sustainability Advisor to the Host Committee. San Francisco went on to host the most shared, most participatory, most commercially successful, most sustainable, and most giving Super Bowl ever, a record that still stands today.

Armed with the success of Super Bowl 50, I decided to start my next agency, which I called Purpose + Sport and whose Purpose it was to empower the business of sport to do good while doing well. Over the next four years, we worked with some fantastic organizations, including streetfootballworld and Common Goal, the world's leading and largest soccer-for-good initiative, with whom we designed and delivered a groundbreaking partnership with EA Sports. We also worked with the Laureus Foundation USA, with whom we developed a shared mission program called One Team, One Nation, and with The Men's Initiative together with whom we launched the Good Men in Sport initiative. We also dabbled in our first non-sport initiative partnering with the Oakland Zoo, whom we helped to reposition from a zoo to a conservation society around their new $60 million California Trail experience, an incredible Purpose-led property.

And most recently, in January 2020, I merged Purpose + Sport with a Paris based agency started by Fabien Paget called O2 Management to create 17 Sport, the world's first sports impact company with a Purpose to build a positive future for the world through sport. 17 Sport's mission is to inspire, educate, and enable the business of sport to do good while doing well. We do this by providing Purpose-led advisory, commercial, and management solutions to brands, sports properties, athletes, and nonprofits wanting to manage their investment in sport in a more Purposeful way. It is an exciting time for all of us at 17 Sport as we continue to work with our legacy clients and new additions to the family, like adidas, Danone, and ESPN, all committed to doing good while doing well through sport.

As I sit here writing this biographical piece under "stay at home orders," thanks to the rapidly evolving COVID-19 Crisis, I cannot help but think about what has passed over the last 50 odd years of my life and what life will be like for us all post-COVID. Will sports revert to its "profit first" ways post-COVID, or will it embrace the opportunity to reinvent itself and its role in the world by leading with Purpose? I am hopeful that it will adopt the latter and that, through the work I have done, and through this book, I will have contributed to inspire sports to re-imagine its role in a rapidly changing world such that people will relate to sports as the industry that led the reinvention of a post-COVID world where doing good while doing well is the norm.

MY STORY: FABIEN PAGET

I was born in Burgundy, in a city called Dijon, famous for Dijon mustard, which originated in 1856. I was raised, together with a younger brother, in a very traditional and loving family grounded in the values of discipline, honesty, loyalty, and humility. My Dad was passionate about tennis, my Mum with hard work.

I still remember when I started hitting my first tennis balls at three years old with my Dad. Tennis has always been part of my life, and it shaped a big part of the person I am today. I started playing competitively at six years old and, later, played a couple of tournaments on the professional Tour but never intended to make a career in professional tennis. I did not have the talent to make it, nor the mental ability required to succeed at the top level. However, tennis taught me the values of humility, competition, and hard work. I have always been driven to maximize my potential in every aspect of my life, on or off the court.

I pursued business studies, graduated from Bordeaux Business School with majors in Finance and Marketing. I knew early on that I desired to work in the sports industry and combine my passion for sport and business. In 2004, I started my professional career as an intern working at Nike France Headquarters. I am still incredibly grateful for all the things I learned there and for experiencing the "Just Do It" culture that was so integral to the organization. This feeling was special.

In 2007, I joined the Mouratoglou Tennis Academy as Sales & Marketing Director. The eponymous founder was Patrick Mouratoglou, also known as Serena Williams's coach. In 2011, after five years, I needed a new challenge, and I wanted to move into the talent representation business. Despite exciting conversations with the majors in the business—Octagon, Lagardere, IMG—I did not feel aligned with the management philosophy of any of these massive corporations, who put profit first and seemed to treat athletes as products or resources. Rightly or not, I became an entrepreneur and started my own business—O2 Management—which would reflect more accurately the values and the vision I had for the sports business. My motivation was to prove to myself that it is possible to be driven by human values and still succeed. O2 Management was a boutique, more human, more agile, more authentic organization, working with brands and athletes. Growing within this industry showed me that most of the relationships were transactional—you buy, you sell. I wanted to add more meaning to my job.

In February 2014, Patrick Mouratoglou contacted me and asked if I would be interested in meeting with Serena Williams to share my vision. Of course! I met with Serena twice and shared my vision with her, starting with the simple fact that she was well-known as an iconic tennis athlete but less as the inspiring, beautiful woman she is. Instead of chasing the biggest endorsement deals and doing cold calls with tennis-related brands, I focused my work on identifying brands and opportunities that would leverage Serena's story and her commitment to empowering women to achieve their best potential in life. Every single minute I got to spend with Serena and her team was a massive shot of energy and would unlock any single barrier one might have. I had always admired Serena, the champion, but I was more interested in the person she is. One of the partnerships we initiated was the collaboration with Axa Insurance Group. Axa is neither a tennis-related sponsor brand nor a brand used to any sponsorship in sport. In 2018, I read an article in the press containing an interview with Axa's global CEO, Thomas Buberl. I learned about the leadership's commitment to reach a 50/50 gender balance within the entire group by 2023. I thought this was a strong commitment and that this message could be more widespread if a strong advocate for gender equality epitomized it. I went to Axa's executives and the Chief Brand

Officer with my idea, which was well-received, and we ended up signing a meaningful and mission-aligned partnership between Serena and Axa.

Over the past seven years, the pursuit of meaning has occupied a bigger place in my mind and my personality. Of course, I have experienced failures and disappointments along the way, but these moments help you to understand better what you did wrong, what matters most to you, and how to learn from the experience.

Purpose started to grow exponentially in my blood, through working closely with athletes, from the multiple lectures and books I read, and from discussions with like-minded friends and people I met. As a regular practitioner of self-development and meditation, this also helped me to reflect on what my mission in life is and how my job could be an extension of it or, even better, contribute to its achievement. All of this reflection led to the realization that there are multiple facets from my background that I should acknowledge and embrace: high-level excellence in sport, doing good while doing business, and it became evident that Purpose was right here for me. Since that day, I have never felt more aligned.

It is just the beginning.

MY STORY: JO RAMSAY

I was born and grew up in the coastal town of Durban in South Africa. I come from a close family who enjoyed being active and spending time outdoors, making the most of South Africa's warm climate.

I attended a boarding school where I played competitive sports, mainly hockey and tennis, but it was the social aspect of sports that appealed to me more than the competitive element. I loved the camaraderie and friendships I developed through sports, many of which are still strong today. Sports also taught me valuable lessons in perseverance, discipline, teamwork, and resilience.

I have always been a keen sports fan, and, from early on, I knew that I wanted to pursue a career in the world of sport. My initial thoughts were to work with athletes as it was around this time that athletes were gaining in stature as global superstars, signing lucrative endorsement deals to set them up for life. Added to this, South Africa's re-entry into the international world post-apartheid had opened a whole new world of sporting possibilities for local athletes.

I studied Law at the University of Cape Town and then headed to the UK for a gap year of travel and work experience. While there, I sent my CV to every sports marketing company I could find in London, offering even to work for free just to get a foot in the door. My determination eventually paid off, and I ended up working at a few agencies temporarily, gaining my first real exposure to talent management, event management, and sports PR. I was hooked! Even better, this led me to an introduction to Neill Duffy, who was working in Cape Town and whose agency had recently been appointed as part of the Cape Town 2004 Olympic Bid marketing team and was looking to recruit staff to service the business.

I returned to South Africa and began working for Neill, a relationship that has endured until today. I tried my hand at event management for a while before finding my real passion in strategy and ended up developing sponsorship strategies, and measuring their success, for some of the biggest brands in South Africa. Through Neill and the rest of the leadership team at what became Octagon, I was fortunate to work alongside and learn from some of the best people in the business and be a part of Octagon's success in South Africa. These were incredibly happy and fulfilling years.

During this time, Neill roped me in to assist him in writing his first book, *Passion Branding, How to Harness the Power of Emotion to Build Strong Brands*. It proved to be a much more demanding project than I had ever anticipated, and, after that experience, I never thought we would be brave enough to take on something like it again, and yet here we are!

In 2006, the loss of my first child led me to reassess my priorities, and I resigned from Octagon and took some time off. I realized, though, that I needed something external to focus on, and so I slowly began working again, but on a part-time basis. The 2010 FIFA World Cup in South Africa was a couple of years away, which made it an exciting time for the local sponsorship industry, and I got to work on some amazing projects and campaigns and experienced first-hand the transformative power of sport.

Midway through 2010, my family (now fortunately with one healthy child in tow) relocated from Johannesburg to Cape Town, where I began working at a sponsorship agency called Openfield. Openfield's main client was The Gary Player Group, and we managed Mr. Player's global series of charitable golf tournaments that raised millions of dollars for underprivileged children and added a rewarding sense of purpose to what we did.

All good things eventually come to an end, and at the close of 2017, after more than 20 years in the sponsorship business, I was starting to feel jaded and despondent. There did not seem to be any new or innovative thinking happening in the sponsorship space locally, and I began to question the real value of what I was doing. Surely there was more to it than this? So, I called it quits and thought, maybe my time was up.

That was until I reconnected with Neill. Neill and Fabien's passion for Purpose and the potential for sport to be a force for good is infectious, and, before I knew it, I was helping write this book and immersing myself in the world of Purpose. It has been an incredible journey so far, and I see so much potential for sport, and its megastar athletes, to use their platform more effectively to make a positive and lasting impact on the world.

P A R T   1

THE PURPOSE REVOLUTION
AND WHY IT MATTERS

In Part 1 of *Legacy Sport*, we focus on the evolution of Purpose as a management philosophy across society, culture, and business. We support the claim that people increasingly want to work for, buy from, invest in, and advocate for organizations that stand for something more than just profits, reward those that do, and punish those that do not.

We share real-life examples of successful Purpose-driven companies alongside interviews with recognized Thought Leaders and practitioners that are leading the Purpose revolution.

By the end of this section, you will be well versed in Purpose, its growing role in society, and how it is shaping culture and business at the start of the 21st Century.

.

SOCIETY

THE EVER-EVOLVING RELATIONSHIP BETWEEN THEM AND US

We are living in a time of significant societal transformation as people increasingly realize that the way we conduct ourselves, at home, and through our work is putting the sustainability of the planet under stress.

People are yearning for something better for themselves and the world around them. We crave connection and a sense of belonging. Yet, at a time when people can connect on any number of social media platforms, we are feeling more isolated and disconnected than ever before.

We no longer have roots and a strong sense of community grounded in where we live. The old communities of the family, village, and local church have all but disappeared in today's knowledge society where people are far more mobile than any society that has gone before. The world is a global village, and people have greater choice in terms of where we live, what we do, and what our affiliations are. All this has changed the way we interact with one another, what we value in each other's contribution to society, and whom we rely on to take the lead in addressing societal challenges.

Work and the way business is conducted is also in flux, and it is coming full circle, considering that when business was first created, its Purpose was not to generate profits but to serve the community in which it existed and to make the world a better place. Businesses were the enforcers of social good.

Historically, the government was wholly responsible for tackling pressing social issues. However, as populations grew and social problems multiplied, governments struggled to address the issues at hand adequately, so businesses stepped in to help alleviate the burden. Over time, businesses can be credited with helping to improve the quality of life for people in a myriad of ways. This improvement was especially true in the 1950s when, in the aftermath of the two World Wars, tremendous societal pressures saw businesses working alongside the government to rebuild communities and re-ignite economic growth following the social upheaval and large scale destruction born out of the global conflict. The focus was to work together for the collective good of business and society.

New institutions such as the United Nations and the World Bank were established, which sought to rebuild and restore society and infrastructure collectively. The overriding focus was on how to work together for the collective good of all. Programs, such as The Marshall Plan, were implemented and saw more than $15 billion being given by the USA to Western Europe to help finance the reconstruction of cities, infrastructure, and industry; to remove trade barriers between European neighbors; and to foster commerce between Europe and the United States. The world economy, but particularly the American economy, boomed to the extent that the post-war period is often referred to as the Golden Age of Capitalism.

While business growth was fuelled out of a need to rebuild and serve communities and did so very successfully, somewhere along the way, business lost sight of this crucial role. It became more concerned with driving short term profit, often at the expense of the long term sustainability of the planet and the people in it. How did this happen?

Business changes its focus thanks to the Friedman Effect

By the 1970s, big business was thriving, and generating enormous profits and business thinking began to evolve, led by the American economist, Milton Friedman. He challenged the belief that business existed to serve the common good, instead claiming that its primary Purpose was to serve the interests of shareholders. This doctrine had no concern for the common good or ethics at all. Friedman argued that a company executive is an employee of the business owners, i.e., the shareholders, and his or her primary responsibility is to conduct the business as per their desires. The executive is not able to spend company money on social needs because, to do so, they would be spending someone else's money for their purposes. The rationale behind this was that businesspeople were experts at making money and not social policy.

According to Friedman's doctrine: "Insofar as [a business executive's] actions in accord with his 'social responsibility' reduce returns to stockholders, he is spending their money. Insofar as his actions raise the price to customers, he is spending the customers' money. Insofar as his actions lower the wages of some employees, he is spending their money." Friedman argued that the appropriate agents of social causes were individuals, the shareholders, employees, or customers who could separately spend their money on a particular social cause if they wanted to do so.

Friedman's thinking began to take hold and was further amplified by other respected academics and influential business publications. From the 1980s and 1990s, it was the pervasive business theory taught at leading business schools and practiced in businesses across the world. It has had a significant impact on the corporate world, influencing a wide range of factors in business, from performance measurement and executive compensation to shareholder rights, the role of directors, and corporate responsibility.

As one would expect, the universal practice of Friedman's Shareholder Theory fundamentally changed the relationship between business and the communities in which they operated. CEOs were incentivized based on short term goals, usually purely financial in nature, and so did whatever was needed to meet their targets and please their investors. As opposed to being concerned about the impact of their operations on the environment, the people working for them, or the customers who bought their products or used their services. Success was so tightly bound to the achievement of financial milestones that CEOs were comfortable to exploit at any cost so long as it was in pursuit of financial gain. The focus became very much internal as opposed to external to harness greater efficiencies and drive profits regardless of the human or environmental cost. The approach was very short-term and self-serving. In short, business lost touch with its humanity.

C-Suite compensation, usually in the form of company shares, skyrocketed to try and align executive and investor motivations. Resources were reallocated, often resulting in mass lay-offs as manufacturing jobs were diverted to other countries with cheaper labor costs. Business gains were allocated almost exclusively to shareholders as opposed to prior decades when gains had been shared more broadly across the company, and workers were subjected to draconian policies in the relentless pursuit of efficiencies and growth.

The overall result is that we have been left with an ever-widening divide between investors and C-Suite employees on one side and increasingly discouraged workers and the community at large on the other side. While Friedman's theory may have created the top-earning 1%, it has done so at a considerable expense as it has been slowly destroying the balance in the social contract that is so vital for a sustainable future.

The cost of this relentless focus on shareholder value was becoming increasingly apparent in the early 2000s. Once praised as the best way to achieve business success, promoting growth at all costs had resulted in crushing income inequality, a disengaged workforce, unprecedented climate change, and other equally damaging impacts on our environment. People felt exploited and were growing increasingly angry at the corporate world for continuing to operate in such a self-serving manner when the pressures it was putting on the planet and its people were becoming ever more evident. There was a massive disconnect between the way businesses operated and what was happening in the broader social context.

From individual to shared value(s)

The tipping point came at the time of the financial crisis in 2008 when people, at many different levels, began to actively challenge the way businesses were being run and how society was consuming the planet's resources. Business leaders within big corporations began to question and discredit the traditional business model, feeling that there had to be a better way of doing business, a way that was kinder to the planet, and more connected to the people working for them and buying their goods and services. The world was crying out for a reassessment of the Milton Friedman way of thinking towards a more conscious form of capitalism that was softer, more inclusive, and long term in its focus.

One of the first schools of thought to emerge at this time was the concept of Shared Value as espoused by Professors Michael Porter and Mark Kramer. Shared Value called for businesses to adopt new policies and operating procedures that allowed them to maximize revenues while also offering benefits to the wider community. It was different from the philanthropic efforts practiced under the banner of corporate social responsibility in that it still put business opportunities and growth front and center. However, now it needed to be done at the same time as benefiting society and the environment.

According to Porter and Kramer, there were essentially three ways in which company executives could consider embracing Shared Value within their organizations. Firstly, by identifying and successfully addressing industry-related social and environmental challenges while increasing company productivity and boosting revenues. Secondly, by developing profitable products and services that meet the needs of a company's customer base while simultaneously fulfilling social issues and improving the lives of local communities or reducing environmental impact. And, finally, by helping local competitors in the same industry through the sharing of management strategies that have worked for the benefit of the community.

Shared Value has obvious benefits for the community and environment as well as having a positive impact on company profitability. However, there are other advantages for companies that adopt this approach. Defining social Purpose and using this as the company's strategic positioning opens new opportunities for profit and growth while motivating and attracting consumers, employees, business partners, and shareholders. Shared Value calls for a deeper level of commitment to the challenges facing society; it requires an ongoing commitment to effecting positive change, and it was the start of companies putting Purpose firmly on their strategic agenda.

The most credible alternative put forward, and the idea currently being practiced by many businesses around the world centers around Purpose. Purpose beyond just profit, a Purpose that creates value for all stakeholders—customers, employees, suppliers, communities, and shareholders. This view considers people, the planet, and profit in equal measure and understands that to survive, businesses must operate in a way that protects the social and environmental landscapes in which they exist, rather than exploit them.

One of the best examples of a pioneer of this type of thinking is Unilever, starting under the leadership of Paul Polman and continuing with the present CEO, Alan Jope. Unilever boldly developed the Unilever Sustainable Living Plan a decade ago to make sustainable living commonplace. The plan outlines three ambitious goals, namely—to improve the health and wellbeing for more than a billion people, to reduce the company's environmental impact by half, and to enhance the livelihood for millions. The plan has been and continues to be an overwhelming success. It has inspired new ways of doing things across the entire value chain, and there are now 26 sustainable living brands within the Unilever stable that continuously outperform the average growth rate of the company and deliver more than 60% of its growth. By placing sustainability at the heart of its business model, Unilever has proved that a softer approach to business is possible, that doing good is good for business.

Furthermore, it helps the brand stay relevant to consumers while also strengthening relationships with stakeholders. When Alan Jope was appointed global CEO of Unilever in January 2019, he pledged to continue on this journey of a more responsible and purposeful way of doing business. He says, "It is not about putting Purpose ahead of profits, it is Purpose that drives profits." To this end, Jope introduced the Unilever Compass in May 2020—the organization's new, fully integrated corporate strategy—that builds on the past ten years and outlines a new set of commitments around packaging and waste, gender equality, human rights, fair value, climate change, and social inclusion.

Since 2008, many more companies have taken this thinking on board, integrating Purpose as the foundation for strategy, decision-making, and operations. There is increased dialogue, collaboration, and collective action by business to address pressing societal issues. And the best part is that Purposeful companies are consistently outperforming companies that still focus primarily on growth, thus giving hard proof of the success that can be achieved this way. As we sit now, in 2020, it is fair to say that Purpose has finally entered the mainstream of business philosophy and practice.

People want to work for and buy from Purposeful organizations

The Purpose revolution in business has not been driven wholly by altruistic motives and a desire to protect the planet from further harm, but equally because companies have realized that a failure to do so will drive customers and employees away and lead to inevitable demise. Companies know that in today's economy, to remain relevant, attract quality staff, and retain customer loyalty and trust, they must be Purposeful.

In the knowledge society in which we now live, people are increasingly finding status, function, and a sense of community at the places where they work and are looking to these organizations and businesses to address the issues facing them in their lives. According to a 2018 study of nearly 30,000 people, undertaken by Accenture Strategy, 62% of customers want companies to take a stand on the issues of the day, and more than 53% will be vocal if they are disappointed with a brand's words or actions regarding a social issue. In addition, a study conducted by BetterUp in 2018 revealed that 9 out of 10 employees are prepared to trade a percentage of their earnings for greater meaning at work. Without a doubt, the closer a company's Purpose and values align with a person's beliefs, the better it is for their bottom line and staff loyalty and engagement.

On a personal level, societal transformations have left many people feeling challenged, insecure, and disconnected. Not only concerning the sustainability of the planet but also job security and wellbeing. Artificial intelligence, biotechnology, and other advances are having a far-reaching impact, from transforming the job market to extending life expectancy, such that people are outliving their retirement savings, and people are wondering what their future holds.

Despite the ever-present promise of connection through social media, people are also feeling less connected than they have ever felt before, and there are high levels of loneliness, suicide, and mental health problems emerging globally, particularly amongst millennials. According to the 2016 VICELAND UK Census, loneliness is the number one fear among young people today, ranking ahead of losing a home or a job, and 48% of 18 to 24-year-olds said they often feel lonely compared to the overall average of 34%. This statistic is mirrored in the US, where 46% of Americans say that they sometimes or always feel alone.

All these factors are causing people to re-evaluate how they behave with one another and the world around them. They want a more mindful way of living that gives them a more profound meaning and protects their wellbeing and that of the planet.

They have also realized that they have the power to influence corporate decision making by making their views heard and by exercising their purchase power effectively. People are reflecting their value system through their purchase behavior and are actively seeking out and supporting companies who share their beliefs. In the words of business visionary, Simon Sinek, people are not buying what you do; they are buying *why* you do it. People now have high expectations of business and want companies to be more conscious about their impact on the planet and its people in the way they conduct themselves. They expect companies to do more than just talk about responsible business practices but to demonstrate it in their actions, and they are holding businesses accountable.

People want brands to stand for something more than just profits. They want to work for, buy products from, and invest in purposeful companies. They will advocate for them and have multiple, far-reaching platforms from which to do this. Through social media, people can spread the word and take a stand against companies or brands that are not acting in the best interests of all stakeholders and, within minutes, this can go viral, causing significant damage to a company's goodwill and bottom line.

Business and society depend on one another. Businesses need people to buy their products or use their services, and people need businesses to provide them with jobs and with the goods and services they need. Corporates cannot and should not expand and grow at the expense of the people who support them and the world in which they operate.

As we enter the 21st Century and start to recognize the pressures that our traditional approaches have placed on the sustainability of our planet and society at large, a new form of capitalism is taking hold. One that considers all stakeholders and creates value in ways that benefit all of society. In short, it places stakeholder value over shareholder value.

Business is returning to its original roots, the purpose for which it was initially created—to serve the community in which it operates. This shift in business practice is creating the context for an inclusive and just economy where the productive power of capitalism can be harnessed to unlock better ideas and outcomes for everyone in the long term. We owe it to future generations to embrace Purpose.

KEY INSIGHTS: THE MACRO VIEW

➤ Societal structure, and the values upon which it is based, has transformed significantly over the last two centuries.

➤ Over this period, how we behave and interact with each other and what we value in each other's contribution to society at large has dramatically changed.

➤ As we enter the 21st Century, we are now questioning whether we would not be better served as a society and as individuals by a structure and set of values that are a hybrid of everything we have tried over the last 200 years.

➤ This societal transformation is altering the way we operate as a global society, the way we relate to and support each other, and the way we do business.

➤ A new form of capitalism is taking hold, one that places stakeholder value over shareholder value. Business is returning to its original roots, the purpose for which it was initially created—to serve the community within which it operates.

HOW BUSINESS IS RESPONDING TO THE SHIFTING MORAL LANDSCAPE

In response to the rapidly evolving social structures in which businesses find themselves today, there are significant changes in the way they operate, some of which have been highlighted already but which we will delve deeper into now.

According to the latest Edelman Trust Barometer, an annual trust and credibility survey, 56% of people believe that capitalism, in its current form, is doing more harm than good in the world. Trust in institutions has eroded over time to the extent that people now feel neither the government, media, NGOs, nor business are sufficiently trustworthy or competent to change society and our planet. People have suffered job losses, a global recession, dwindling resources, and the devastating effects of climate change. In contrast, the fat cats in business and the politicians have flourished or primarily ignored their plight. Governments have failed to safeguard our future on many levels, and, as a result, people are increasingly demanding that the corporate world steps in to respond to these challenges.

Of the four institutions (i.e., government, business, the media, NGOs), business is seen as the most trusted and competent, albeit at only 58%, which suggests that business must forge ahead to bring about change. More telling is that 92% of employees say CEOs should speak out on the issues of the day, and 75% of the general population think

CEOs should take the lead on change instead of waiting for the government to impose it. Public expectations of companies have never been higher than they are today. People are impatient for change, and they are looking to the corporate world to lead the way, even if they are still somewhat circumspect as to the motivations of some corporations. It is up to the business world to drive collaborations with government institutions and NGOs to bring about necessary and positive changes to the world around us and how we conduct ourselves in it.

Corporations spearheaded by more enlightened leaders are taking this on and are embracing a more purposeful approach to business, focusing on stakeholder benefit as opposed to shareholder benefit. And it is paying off, which is evidenced in various studies around the world. One study being The Kantar Purpose 2020 study, which found that brands with a higher sense of Purpose have seen their brand valuation increase by 175% over the past 12 years relative to a median growth rate of 86% and a growth rate of 70% for brands with a low sense of Purpose. Likewise, a Havas Meaningful Brands study in 2017 reported that brands with meaning had outperformed the stock market by a staggering 206% over ten years between 2006 and 2016. The evidence is quite telling that Purpose can and does drive business growth.

Purpose is now being embraced by business to the extent that, in August 2019, the Business Roundtable, America's most influential business lobby group, released a new Statement of Purpose of a Corporation. It was signed by 181 CEOs who committed to lead their companies for the benefit of all stakeholders—customers, employees, suppliers, communities, and shareholders. Signatories included the likes of BlackRock Inc.'s Larry Fink, Amazon.com Inc. founder Jeff Bezos, and CEOs of several Wall Street banks, such as Goldman Sachs Group Inc., Morgan Stanley, and Moelis & Co. among others.

Even Jamie Dimon, the high profile arch capitalist and JP Morgan Chase CEO, has re-evaluated his pro-shareholder stance to the extent that he has publicly endorsed the role of companies to "aggressively work to improve society." In April 2019, in a letter to JP Morgan Chase shareholders, he wrote, "If companies and CEOs do not get involved in public-policy issues, making progress on all these problems may be more difficult."

The Business Roundtable Statement does not offer much detail on how this signed commitment is to be translated into action and relies on each company's CEO and leadership team to drive the change in bold, meaningful, and sustainable ways. For example, Larry Fink, Chairman and CEO of Black Rock Inc., the largest money management firm in the world, with more than $6.5 trillion assets under management. In 2018, he wrote to CEOs saying that sustainability would become one of Black Rock's investment criteria going forward and that they would not invest in any business that does not adopt a more purposeful approach to how it conducts itself. Fink's statement is no idle threat considering the size and influence of Black Rock. Since then, impact investing has become the fastest-growing investment strategy in Europe with dedicated conferences, such as the 2020 Impact Summit at The Hague in Europe, focusing on ways to "catalyze private institutional capital to support the financing of SDGs."

Marc Benioff, the Founder and CEO of Salesforce, wrote to the New York Times in October 2018 that "business must have a Purpose beyond profits and that such Purpose can, over time, benefit both stockholders and stakeholders." He used this as the rationale for his support of the proposal that San Francisco's wealthiest businesses (his own Salesforce among them) be subjected to a small tax to help raise funds to solve the homelessness crisis in the city.

Former Unilever head, Paul Polman, is another leader who can be credited with leading the change towards a fairer, more ethical way of doing business. In 2018, the Financial Times wrote that he had been one of the most influential CEOs of his era, and "his approach to business and its role in society has been both valuable and path-breaking." As far back as 2010, Polman boldly declared his business philosophy—a "long-term value-creation model which is equitable, which is shared, which is sustainable." He even went on to address shareholders directly, saying if they did not buy into this model, then they should not invest in the company. Polman's bold approach has paid off as Unilever's Sustainable

Living Plan continues to deliver value for all stakeholders under the charge of the company's current CEO, Alan Jope.

Added to this growing chorus of influential business leaders calling for a more sustainable and inclusive form of capitalism was the release of a new Davos Manifesto in January 2020 by the Founder and Executive Chairman of the World Economic Forum, Klaus Schwab. The newly updated Davos Manifesto is a set of ethical principles to guide companies in today's operating environment. It is intended to drive the agenda of a more Purposeful, sustainable, and inclusive approach to business and advocates strongly for stakeholder capitalism. It states that companies should pay their fair share of taxes, show zero tolerance for corruption, uphold human rights throughout their global supply chains, and advocate for a competitive level playing field. It also highlights that, to uphold the principles of stakeholder capitalism, companies will need new metrics. i.e., measures that include environmental, social, and governance goals as well as the traditional financial ones. Executive remuneration also needs to be relooked to reflect stakeholder responsibility.

The theme of the 2020 Davos gathering summed it up— "Stakeholders for a Cohesive and Sustainable World" and the six themes that dominated the 50th anniversary of the Forum brought the key issues front and center for the business community. There was a palpable sense of urgency evident at the event with the world's leaders acknowledging that swift action is required now if we are to turn the tide on issues such as climate change. The debate is no longer around what individual companies can do but what can be done as a collective through a complete shift in mindset in the business world and a far more collaborative approach both within the corporate sector and with government, NGOs, and other relevant stakeholders.

Identifying as a company what is best for the world

Purpose as the mainstream business philosophy is also being acknowledged and encouraged through growing organizations like the B Corp movement. In 2006, friends and business partners Coen Gilbert and Bart Houlihan were looking at ways to harness the power of business to address social and environmental concerns. Together with Andrew Kassoy, they co-founded B Lab, a nonprofit organization dedicated to making it easier for Purpose-led companies to protect and improve their positive impact over time. The idea was to build a global movement that would lead the way in redefining success in business so that businesses compete with one another, not just to be the best *in* the world, but also to be the best *for* the world. The founders wanted a B Corp certification to create a community whose members could learn from one another and collaborate on common societal issues while also helping to attract new employees, customers, and investors.

B Lab collaborated with leading businesses, investors, and lawyers to create a comprehensive set of performance and legal requirements across five areas. Companies needed to meet these requirements to be awarded the B Corp certification that would publicly hold them accountable for how they benefited employees, customers, communities, and the environment through their business operations. The first companies who met these criteria were granted a B Corp Certification in 2007, and, as of April 2020, B Corp's global community consists of 3,285 companies, both large and small, across 150 industries in 71 countries. It truly is a global community of leaders being recognized for successfully using business as a force for good. To be granted and to maintain certification, businesses must receive a minimum score from an online assessment and pay an annual fee ranging from $500–$50,000 depending on annual sales. Assessments must take place every three years to retain the B Corp designation.

The success of the B Corp movement is evidence of the ever-growing number of businesses that are actively pursuing Purposeful goals alongside financial ones, not only because they believe it is the right thing to do, but because they believe there is a robust commercial upside as well. Research conducted by the UK arm of B Corp further emphasizes this upside. It reveals that companies who have been certified for at least two years are growing at an average rate of 14% per annum, and roughly a third of these companies said they had reached new customers since certification. Nearly 50% said their B Corp status had helped to attract new employees. This last point is particularly relevant considering that millennials will soon dominate the workforce, and over three-quarters of them choose their place of work based on a company's Purposeful approach to business.

Doing good proves good for business

The growing evidence proving the positive impact of Purpose on bottom-line profit is forcing even the most resolute objectors to this approach to take notice. Nike's 2018 campaign against racism using American Football quarterback Colin Kaepernick saw online sales grow by 31%, and Unilever's sales of Dove brand products increased from $2.5 billion to $4 billion in the last decade. These and other examples highlight a marked change from the past where brands and businesses used to avoid taking a stand on issues. Today, the risk is *not* being sufficiently committed to the issues of the day.

Adherence to the profit-focused model of business management is not sustainable and is a betrayal to future generations. It is no longer a question of whether to change to a more Purposeful approach to business, but rather how to do it. A company must have a clear and actioned Purpose to ensure longevity—what problems it is solving, for whom, when, and why they are the company best suited to do so. The Purpose could be related to the environment, social justice, or any societal need so long as it is about giving something back and making the world a better place. A credible statement of Purpose that is consistently actioned by a company and demonstrates a real commitment to doing good while also making profits will build trust and loyalty from all stakeholder groups, from customers to employees to shareholders.

Going forward, the Purpose-led approach to business must and will continue to flourish. Without it, no company can achieve its full potential. It will ultimately lose the license to operate from key stakeholders. It will fail to attract loyal and productive employees, it will risk being the target for activist campaigns, and ultimately it will deliver sub-par returns to shareholders. Companies must, therefore, adopt a long-term view to activate Purpose deliberately. They must continue to create a new business model that harnesses their core competencies, skills, and resources in collaborative partnerships with diverse stakeholders to improve the state in which the world and its people find themselves. Purpose-led companies can make a tremendous difference in the world. Businesses have the size, reach, clout, and trust it takes, and increasingly people expect companies to use this power for a good Purpose.

KEY INSIGHTS: THE MICRO VIEW

➤ In response to the rapidly evolving social structures in which they find themselves operating today, those corporations led by more enlightened leaders are embracing a more Purposeful approach to how they do business with a focus on stakeholder vs. shareholder benefit.

➤ Those corporations that have authentically embraced Purpose as a management philosophy are demonstrating that doing good is good for business and that it is possible to do good while doing well.

➤ We have entered a phase where businesses will exponentially embrace Purpose as the new normal and where those that do not will become irrelevant in the next decade.

LEADING THOUGHTS
BUSINESS AND PURPOSE

ALAN JOPE   CEO at Unilever PLC

UNILEVER IS ONE OF THE WORLD'S LEADING EXAMPLES OF HOW TO
EMBRACE PURPOSE AT AN ORGANIZATIONAL LEVEL.

On the importance of Purpose:

I think the more sectors of the economy that are trying to land the message
of Purposeful business, the better it will be for society. It is a path to a more
durable company and better financial returns. And there is no better time to be
appreciating that than in the crazy circumstances we are in right now.

**On Unilever's plan around Purpose going forward and building
on the legacy left by Paul Polman:**

Paul did an unbelievably good job of bringing his passion around sustainability,
initially, and then Purpose to the business and, in that regard, he built on an old
legacy. Unilever has been a Purposeful business for well over 100 years. When
William Lever founded Lever Brothers, the firm's mission was to make cleanliness
commonplace and to lessen the load for women. By cleanliness, he meant
eradicating diseases like cholera and typhus in Victorian Britain. He often talked
about work with meaning and treating his employees as essential members of his
team and not just units of labor. So, there is a long thread of DNA, and Paul did a
sensational job of bringing that back into the foreground of the company.

The business case for sustainability is very well-proven. Purposeful brands
are growing faster year after year, and it takes costs out of the company. If
sustainability is about using fewer resources, it is logical that it takes cost out, and
we can trace about €800 million of avoided cost through sustainable sourcing and
using green electricity. Purpose is also a trigger for innovation. We have seen many
product innovations come out of this commitment to sustainability. Finally, it is a huge

magnet for talent. Our employer brand has never been more appealing. There is a whole generation of people who join Unilever precisely because of our Purposeful approach to business.

When I took the job, the leadership team and I said we wanted the company to become even more famous for three things. First, for shaping an enviable stable of purposeful brands; second, to have sealed the business case on how Purposeful business leads to better financial performance; and third, to be a beacon for diversity and inclusion in business. That is what my leadership team and I would love to do over the coming years.

On the extent to which Unilever's commitment to Purpose drives pride and loyalty amongst employees:

We have unequivocal data around the fact that our commitment to Purpose drives employee loyalty. The first is the extraordinary development of our employer brand on campus. We have a graduate recruitment program in 54 countries around the world and, in our sector, we are the number one employer of choice for university graduates in 52 of those 54 countries. A few years ago, that number was in the teens. The more we put sustainability and Purposeful business at the forefront of what we stand for, the stronger our reputation amongst prospective employees is.

We have also run 40,000 people through a Purpose workshop that helps people figure out what their Purpose might be. What we have discovered is that employees who have been through that workshop and can align their personal mission with the work that they do, show an incredible step up in the probability of recommending Unilever as an employer and have lower attrition. The aggregate picture of all of it is that around 90% of our employees are proud to work for Unilever. I think it is reflective of what we see with consumers, particularly millennials and GenZennials, who are increasingly making brand choices based on the Purposefulness of a brand. They articulate their choices by looking at the actions a brand is taking that are good for the planet. We should not forget that our employees and the consumers we are proud to sell our products to are the same people. There is a strong business case linking trying to do business in the right way to creating a valuable proposition for our team members.

HUBERT JOLY
Executive Chairman and former CEO at Best Buy

JOLY TRANSFORMED BEST BUY AND QUADRUPLED THE COMPANY'S STOCK WHEN HE SERVED AS CEO, BY EMBEDDING PURPOSE AT THE HEART OF THE COMPANY'S ORGANIZATIONAL PHILOSOPHY AND PRIORITIZING HIS EMPLOYEES.

On how he introduced Purpose as one of the fundamental operating principles at Best Buy:

When I became CEO, it was during a difficult time for the company, and everybody was telling me to cut costs and close stores, but we did the opposite. We did not consider the people of Best Buy as the problem. Instead, we saw them as the solution. I spent my first week on the job in stores listening to frontline workers, and I spent time building the team at the top to improve the performance of the company. We focused on how to increase revenue, then looked where we could cut non-salary expenses, then we looked at the management of compensation and benefits, and only after that did we look at headcount. So the turnaround of Best Buy was a very human undertaking. When it was complete, we started working on the growth strategy, the anchor of which was the Purpose of Best Buy, which was not to sell TV's and computers but to enrich lives through technology by addressing critical human needs. This strategy was an ideal way to expand the addressable market and meet the human needs of customers. It was the reinvention of business with Purpose as the North Star and people as the engine to make it happen.

On whether they experienced any difficulties along the way in embedding Purpose within Best Buy:

We did it over a three to four year period with much hard work. We knew it was not sufficient just to state our Purpose. We had to make it part of the fabric of the company and work to ensure that staff could connect their Purpose with the Purpose of the company. It was several years of profound transformation at the company, both from a strategic level and, more importantly, from a people level, including how we lead.

On how collaborations and partnerships were established at Best Buy and how these partners were persuaded to come on board:

It was not very difficult because, if you are a tech company like Samsung, HP, or Sony, you invest billions of dollars into R&D, and you need to showcase your products, which cannot be done online or on the shelf in-store. In North America, Best Buy is the best place for this—we have the store network, the foot traffic, and all the salespeople that customers may need. So, Apple, Microsoft, Sony, Samsung, LG, Canon, Nikon, as well as Amazon and Google now have a corner in a Best Buy store where they can demonstrate their various products. In life, if you have a good idea and you give it to me, you still have it. We do not need to be afraid of competitors. We need to look at possibilities. So we approached our partnerships in this manner, and it has paid off.

On connecting the personal Purpose of employees and the company's Purpose:

It starts with a basic idea, which is that a company is a human organization made up of individuals working together in pursuit of a particular goal. Size does not matter; it is about how you interact with everyone around you, one employee at a time. Whether you are the CEO or a store general manager, it is the same. There are several ingredients to create human magic, and the first one is making people feel seen, valued, and respected, and then to help them connect their Purpose to the Purpose of the company. As a leader, your role is to create this environment where others in your organization in positions of leadership know that their role is to connect with every employee at a very personal level. People have been talking for ages about bringing your whole self to work, and now, in this COVID crisis, when we are working from home, it has become that much more apparent. The implication for the leaders of organizations is that we need to deal with our employees as the whole person, considering all their needs—for connection, love, respect, meaning, mental health, and anything else they may need. We need to get to know our staff at a much deeper level.

On whether the world is ready to embrace Purpose:

Yes, because it is a universal human need. When I see how CEOs in the US are leading their companies, especially during the COVID crisis, it is extremely inspiring. There are many role models for Purpose in business. Jeff Bezos recently told shareholders and investors to take a step back as he would be spending $4 billion on the safety of his employees and customers. Sebastian Bazin in France, the CEO of Accor Hotels, has reinvested a good chunk of the company's dividends into the wellbeing of employees. Other role models include Arne Sorenson at Marriott, John

Donahoe at Nike, Marc Benioff at Salesforce, and Larry Fink at Blackrock, so it is very pervasive at the moment. The idea that shareholders do not want you to do the right thing is incorrect. Any CEO who uses the shareholders as an excuse not to embrace Purpose is confused. We can assume that a sense of meaning drives most people because they are human beings, and they do not want to be a jerk. The question then becomes how to do it.

On the characteristics of a Purposeful leader today:
At Best Buy, we have something called The Five Be's of Leadership. The first is to be a Purposeful leader. You must be clear about your own Purpose. Understand the Purpose of the people around you and connect all of this to the Purpose of the organization. The second is to be clear about your role as a leader. It is not about being the smartest person in the room; rather, it is about creating an environment in which others can flourish. Third, be clear about whom you serve. If you believe you are serving yourself or your boss, that is OK, but then you should not work at Best Buy. If you are serving the people around you, then that is good. The fourth is about being a values-driven leader. Things like integrity are essential. Finally, you have to be an authentic leader. Do not be afraid to be vulnerable, to show empathy, to show all parts of yourself, and be open to those around you doing the same.

SEBASTIAN BUCK   Co-founder and Strategic Lead at enso

WITH CLIENTS LIKE GOOGLE, MATTEL, AND THE KHAN ACADEMY, ENSO IS ONE OF THE MOST RESPECTED SOCIAL IMPACT AGENCIES IN THE WORLD.

On where the drive for change was coming from within business:
I think there were a couple of motivations. The predominant motivation of the organizations that I admired was an innate motivation from the leaders of those organizations. If you look at Sal Khan, for instance, he was a hedge fund analyst who started helping his niece learn, and he made YouTube videos so that she could replay the lesson he was teaching her. He found that there was real utility in those videos, and other people began watching them, including Bill Gates, and out of that came Khan Academy. So, in this case, it was coming from an innate motivation from Khan, and I think the same is true of many other Founder-driven

organizations. However, around 2000, there was the Battle of Seattle and the WTO protests, which led more prominent companies to look at how best to react to this hacktivist impulse. They did so with a lot of corporate social responsibility teams and corporate foundations, which, in some cases, did good work, but were often at arm's length to a company's core business.

From about 2000–2008, companies approached doing good in this way. After Obama was elected, a surge of energy, that was partly inspired by the depths of the recession, caused many people to reflect on the way we lived and how companies operated. Big brands began getting involved in social impact initiatives, and it was primarily coming from consumer pressure. It had become a marketing priority, and CMOs were paying attention to Purpose.

The third phase, which I think we have entered into in the last couple of years, from 2017 onwards, is even more exciting. This phase sees companies having to react to their employees who are demanding more Purposeful business. The pressure has shifted from activist pressure in the early 2000s, which was extrinsic pressure, to consumer pressure from 2008 onwards, which was also extrinsic, to the third wave, which is now an intrinsic pressure from employees demanding that their companies live up to higher ideals. And so, you are seeing things like employee activism at Google, and a lot of the best talent is quite discriminating about where they work and compelling their managers to listen.

On the authenticity of Purpose in the business world currently:
I think, sadly, there are some companies whose motivation is not credible. Purpose marketing has become a buzz term, and some companies approach it quite cynically. It is still just skin deep, a veneer around the same old business. I think the real leaders who are advancing the state of the art of business are putting Purpose at the center of their intention, like Paul Polman, who modernized Unilever during his time as CEO. They thought about Purpose genuinely, looking at how to make it fundamental to their supply chains, their product formulations, packaging, distribution, and marketing. I think that is the way people need to think about this transition, not only because consumers can see through the skin-deep stuff but also that employees know the realities of how committed a company is. Increasingly, the motivation to work for a firm is based on their commitment to Purpose, and

companies are struggling to hire and retain the best people, so it is becoming an intrinsic motivation for companies to be more Purposeful.

On the direction and pace of the evolution towards Purpose:
In terms of business progression, I am heartened that things are changing relatively fast. When we started, Michael Porter had just published his shared value article in the Harvard Business Review, which got many people talking about the idea of aligning business success with social impact. It was striking, particularly coming from him, because as the author of Porter's Five Forces, he had championed a concept of business that was antagonistic. You had to fight your suppliers and get one over on your customers and your employees. For him to write about shared value was striking. When that came out in 2009, I thought the mainstream would shift fast, but sadly, it did not, and it has taken a while.

On the impact of the coronavirus experience on the shift towards Purpose:
As we sit here now in the cycle of the pandemic, it's hard to say exactly how radically things are going to change, but I do think that any time of real stress causes people to reflect on what they are doing, how they are spending their time and how they want to spend their time. The optimist in me would like to believe that collective reflection can be healthy. I would hope that, as we come through this, the urgency around playing a meaningful role in the world is heightened, and that impacts people in their careers and how they work, and that will ripple out to the companies where they work.

On where things are going and what is next in society:
I am still fundamentally optimistic that business can be a force for good. The awakening that is currently happening in business is exciting, and I think the current generation of leaders who are committing themselves and their organizations to something more than just driving shareholder returns gives me real optimism. When you have more and more people creating incredibly valuable businesses based on a core motivation within themselves that they then infuse a team with who then animate the customers around them that builds meaningful brands, it is how we can scale social impact very fast. I think we are close to a tipping point where that will become business as usual.

DR. JOHN IZZO   Leading Author, Speaker, and Executive Coach

JOHN IS ONE OF THE MOST RESPECTED NAMES IN LEADERSHIP, PURPOSE, AND THE BELIEF THAT DOING GOOD IN BUSINESS CAN ALSO MEAN DOING WELL.

On the idea that social good has entered the mainstream of business:

Purpose has gone mainstream in a variety of ways. Every year the percentage of customers and employees who say this is an integral part of their decision making has gone up. The number of people who punish a company if they do not agree with how it does things and reward those who align with their values has gone up. The percentage of talent for whom this is a major part of why they continue with a company, having meaning or alignment of values in your work, its effect on employee engagement, commitment, and performance—have all gone up. All these trends have accelerated in the last ten years and, I believe, will continue to accelerate.

It may even grow more deeply post COVID, just as it did from the financial crisis in 2008 when people questioned what was going to happen to Purpose and social good. And it grew because people saw the impact of corporate malfeasance on everyday lives, and they saw companies that were not loyal to them, which led to an acceleration of the desire for meaning and alignment with companies that support our deepest values.

On people's need for connection and togetherness, especially in times of crisis:

A fascinating thing about a crisis is that you gain more market share during downturns than you do during upturns. That does not mean your business grows during a downturn, but your market share grows. The obvious reason is that some of your competitors go out of business. However, the lion's share of that growth in market share comes from what you do during that downturn that makes you even more valuable to your customers and team members than you were before. I think many companies right now need to be mindful of that. People are watching them during this crisis and noticing how companies are stepping up for their people, for their communities, for the world, and if you take your eye off the ball, you will fall even further behind.

On the importance of leadership in driving a Purpose agenda:

There is no doubt that the top leaders are critical. If I think about every company that I have worked with or research that has made tremendous strides in this area, they had a CEO and a senior team that was on fire for Purpose and social good. So, hands down, it matters. But, does that mean nothing good can happen without that? Of course, some good can happen, but nothing profound will happen.

My experience has been that those leaders who connect Purpose to their legacy, who get a taste of how they and their company can make a difference in things that matter to people, do a lot better than those who only do it for business reasons. There is nothing wrong with doing it for business reasons, but it is also crucial that leaders also get connected to the part of this that is about their legacy.

On the impact of Purpose on employee retention and engagement:

Research from Yale University looks at three ways people see their role at work. It can be seen as a job, meaning that they're trading their life for money as a career. Or they see themselves as being in a role to learn and grow. Basically, selfish reasons so that one day they can go and do something else they want to do. The third group view work as a calling that they are serving some value and care about their role. These three are not mutually exclusive, but people who see their job as a calling perform better on every metric that we care about as leaders—they are more productive, more committed, more engaged, and they provide better service.

If you compare people's engagement and commitment on two separate variables, namely how aligned their values are with the Purpose of the company they serve, and how much they feel like they get to live their Purpose at work, people's experience of living their Purpose is a much more significant predictor of engagement and commitment than alignment with the company's Purpose. It does not mean that company Purpose is not valuable, but what is more important is how you help the individual employee connect the dots between their job and how what they are doing every day is impacting the community and the world. If they do not make that connection, it is not enough for people just to be aware of all the things the company is doing. One of the things leaders have to do to get a powerful impact is to continue to drive down to a very personal level for people in their organization how their job is making an impact on something. What the company is doing matters, but it turns out it does not matter as much as people's own experience of feeling they are doing good and making a difference in their day-to-day role.

On the role of the customer in a company's Purpose conversation:
About 34% of consumers globally fall into the category of Purpose-driven consumers, meaning that Purpose is a regular part of their decision-making. Then, about 80-85%, depending on the country and the generation, say it matters to them, but it is not necessarily a big driver of their everyday decision making. If about a third of your customers or potential customers care about Purpose a lot, then think about what impact this could have on your market share? Where it gets interesting is the level of loyalty these people have. Ben & Jerry's have studied the behavior of the customers who buy from them mostly because they like the ice cream and those who buy from them mostly because they feel aligned with the values of the company. And the interesting thing is, the people who buy because they like the ice cream often switch when another premium ice cream goes on sale. They will come back often, but they are very price sensitive. However, the one-third who buys from them mostly because they are aligned with the brand's values and, like the ice cream, rarely switch brands. The most intriguing thing about the values-driven customer is that it is difficult to win them over, but, once you do, their level of loyalty and their commitment to getting others to buy from you is unparalleled.

That says to me that you do not want to be in the middle of the bell curve when it comes to Purpose. There probably are other ice cream companies in the middle of the bell curve who are good, but not great, corporate citizens, and they have not thought through who the exact Purpose-focused customer is like Ben & Jerry's have. They will never get that 34% because they are just good enough that the 80% group might take notice, but the 34%, the group of Purpose-driven consumers, will not be any more loyal. The biggest winners in the Purpose game are, ironically, the people who take it most seriously because that 34%, which is growing every year, by the way, is the group that makes the biggest difference, not the 80% who kind of care about your brand.

CAROL CONE   CEO at Carol Cone ON PURPOSE

CAROL IS KNOWN AND RESPECTED GLOBALLY FOR HELPING MANY
LEADING COMPANIES ACTIVATE THEIR PURPOSE BEYOND PROFIT,
SOMETHING SHE HAS DONE FOR DECADES.

**On using business as a force for good when it was not common
practice yet:**

It was not standard practice when I first started. I joke that it was just American
Express and me at the time linking a company to a social Purpose to drive company
growth. It was always a win-win. It was to grow the company, but also have a
different, real, and authentic story that would be engaging. I love brands, I love
positioning, and I love marketing, and my intuition was to give them a real story to
tell, give them a way to engage that is meaningful. I did it because it felt right, and
I loved doing it, and we just kept doing more and more. We were the only ones out
there doing it.

On the defining difference between Purpose and what has come before it:

Purpose is more about why an organization exists. When it is practiced
authentically and deeply as a strategy, it will create alignment internally, provide
many vital reasons for employees and stakeholders to engage, and it will be a lens
that drives innovation, culture, and social engagement. I call it the golden thread
that ties a company or brand when there is an understanding of why they exist
beyond just selling stuff. It is a business and organizational strategy. It is not siloed
and tactical. It also expands the aperture of what a company or brand can do.
When you open the aperture, and you drive it into behaviors and KPIs and such, it
creates much more opportunity for an organization.

On the top three things being preached to companies in 2020:

I would say that companies need to grow, so develop a growth strategy. Purpose
is a powerful growth strategy. Secondly, the strategy must be authentic. It is hard
work to discover, but it is worth the journey. And then the third thing is to engage
your stakeholders and employees. They are the engine of a company. The more you
engage your employees in discovering your Purpose, the more they will buy into it.

Then you need perfect execution. You cannot just make it up in a room, put it on a wall, and then move on to the next thing.

On what is currently happening in the Purpose space, with the Business Roundtable, Davos, and other platforms and if these are authentic commitments or just driven by opportunism and trends:
It is about the shift in capitalism and that the top 1% owns over 50% of the world's wealth. Capitalism is not working, and people are striking, whether it is employees or people in the streets refusing to buy certain products. The internet is driving changes. Everybody is a broadcaster, so companies can run, but they cannot hide. Declaring your Purpose is not enough. You must act on it, and that is what makes the difference. So, the question for the Business Roundtable is, what are those companies going to do? And how are they going to be held accountable?

RICARDO FORT   Head of Global Sponsorships at The Coca-Cola Company

COCA-COLA IS AT THE FOREFRONT OF THE PURPOSE MOVEMENT AND SUCCESSFULLY INTEGRATES ITS PURPOSE VISION ACROSS ALL FACETS OF ITS BUSINESS, INCLUDING ITS SPORTS INVESTMENTS.

On Coca-Cola's organizational Purpose and making the world a better place:
The Purpose statement of the company is "Refresh the world. Make a difference." We undertook to rethink our Purpose, which involved going back to our roots and looking at what Coca-Cola has always stood for. Regardless of how we express our Purpose, The Coca-Cola Company is deeply connected with the communities where we work. We have the benefit of having hundreds of thousands of people every day selling, delivering, or enjoying our products, and we employ many people, so we have a broad footprint that is very deep in every country. It is normal for us to have deep connections in other countries, and this idea of making a difference is not something new for us.

On the two strands of Coca-Cola's sustainability mission, one is operational, and the other focuses on creating a better future:
From a sustainability standpoint, we have a lot of projects and investments, one of which focuses on water. Water is critical to the world but is also the core product

for all our beverages. Back in 2009, we came up with the idea of returning to the environment every drop of water that we took from it, which was unheard of at the time. That was a long-term goal, which we achieved in 2017, three years ahead of target. And, today, Coca-Cola is not only water neutral; we are now water positive.

Another big focus area for us is the recycling of plastic, aluminum, and glass, but primarily plastic. We have several projects to redesign or think differently about how we use and reuse plastic; these range from investing in bottle recycling facilities, to cleaning up projects on beaches and riverbanks around the world, and to investing in science. A few years ago, we came up with a fully recyclable plastic called PlantBottle, and we have licensed it to other industries. Today, there are countries like Sweden, where 100% of our plastic is PlantBottle based, and part of our role is to push the industry to use these bottles. The whole idea of the circular economy in plastic is genuine to us.

We also focus on women's empowerment. In 2010 we started a global initiative called 5by20, which aims to empower five million women entrepreneurs across the company's value chain by 2020. It is a very comprehensive program whereby we train women and prepare them for the workforce in several countries. It is a beautiful project.

On the rationale for Coca-Cola's Purposeful approach:
Our Purposeful approach is not charity work for us. It is the intersection of what is important for the world but also what is important for our business—issues like water supply, recycling, and female empowerment, so it just reinforces the need to invest in each of them.

CLEMENTINE PAINTER   Senior Manager of Strategic Planning at adidas

PURPOSE SITS AT THE HEART OF THE ADIDAS BUSINESS, PARTICULARLY AROUND THE ISSUES OF PLASTIC WASTE, BREAKING BARRIERS FOR GIRLS, AND INCLUSION.

On what sustainability means for adidas:
Sustainability is at the heart of everything we do. Our mission is to be the best sports company in the world, and by that, we mean that we design, build, and sell the best sports products in the world with the best service and experience for our

consumers and, more importantly, in a sustainable way. It is nothing new. We have been working like this for more than 20 years, looking at all parts of our supply chain, from the material we use to what we deliver to our consumers.

On the reasons for adidas embracing sustainability to such a large extent:
There are many reasons. Consumers expect brands, corporations, and governments to be more sustainable. It is important to us that we do things in the right way through the manufacture of our products, using more sustainable material, and also looking at what happens to our products when the consumer does not want them anymore. In October last year, in the UK, we launched a service for our consumers called Infinite Play, which allowed them to return their old shoes and clothes to us in exchange for a voucher that could be used to purchase something new. We adopt a circular approach where we track our footprint through the entire supply chain loop, which helps us identify the places where we need to have a sharper focus.

On how adidas has created a Purpose division that ensures the company walks the talk and carries out its Purpose agenda:
In December 2018, adidas created a global Purpose team to prioritize and focus the company's Purpose-led efforts. The team identified three pillars on which to focus—plastic waste, breaking barriers for girls through sport, and giving everyone equal opportunity—and all of these are embedded into our strategy and everything we do.

On the strategy around ending plastic waste and how this plays out:
From as far back as 2015, we have looked at how to reduce our plastic waste. We produced a shoe made entirely of recycled polyester. And now, in 2020, we will produce 15–20 million pairs of these shoes compared to 11 million pairs in 2019, so it is growing every year. From a product perspective, this was the start. Our first fully recyclable running shoe, Futurecraft Loop, has been tested internally and will be launched in 2021. We are looking at clothing as well, and the desire is to ultimately have a regenerative loop, where we create products made from biodegradable material.

It is not only about the product, but we also carry our message of sustainability through our communication strategy. For example, we created an initiative called

Run for the Oceans that addresses marine pollution. It is a collaboration with Parley, an environmental organization focused on raising awareness of the problem and inspiring action to address it. The success of the campaign has shown us that many people are interested in sustainability but do not know what to do, and this allows them to do something positive.

THE GLOBAL GOALS
A SHARED VISION FOR SUCCESS

As far back as 2000, the United Nations recognized the need for a change in mindset and behavior and initiated the Millennium Development Goals. This declaration laid out eight goals that addressed issues such as poverty, hunger, disease, illiteracy, environmental degradation, and discrimination against women. All 191 UN member states signed it and at least 22 international organizations, committing world leaders to meet specific targets relating to all eight goals by 2015.

While the Millennium Development Goals were regarded as an influential and effective framework to galvanize commitment, and drive the allocation of resources towards key global development priorities, progress towards the achievement of the Goals was unconvincing. As the 2015 deadline approached, the improvement was uneven, with some countries achieving many of the targets set while others had struggled to meet any of them. There was also criticism that some of the Goals had not been adequately thought through and were impossible to achieve.

As a result of the unconvincing progress, the 2030 Agenda for Sustainable Development was created. It is a shared blueprint for peace and prosperity for people and the planet. At its heart are 17 Sustainable Development Goals (SDGs), which are an urgent call to action by all countries, both developed and developing, to work together in a global partnership to make our world a better place for all. It was signed in September 2015 by all 195 UN member states and calls on the collaboration of government, business, media, institutions of higher education, and local NGOs to work together to build a better future for everyone by 2030.

The Goals are much more comprehensive and far-reaching than the Millennium Development Goals, focusing on three main areas, namely—to end extreme poverty, to fight inequality and injustice, and to tackle climate change. They recognize that ending poverty and other deprivations must go together with strategies that improve health and education, reduce inequality, and spur economic growth—all while tackling climate change and working to preserve our oceans and forests. They are the most ambitious agreement for sustainable development that has ever been signed by world leaders, and everyone everywhere is called on to play their part in achieving them.

A summary of the 17 Sustainable Development Goals is as follows:

GOAL 1: NO POVERTY
End poverty in all its forms everywhere.

GOAL 2: ZERO HUNGER
End hunger, achieve food security, improve nutrition, and promote sustainable agriculture.

GOAL 3: GOOD HEALTH & WELLBEING
Ensure healthy lives and promote wellbeing for all at all ages.

GOAL 4: QUALITY EDUCATION
Ensure inclusive and equitable education and promote lifelong learning opportunities for all.

GOAL 5: GENDER EQUALITY
Achieve gender equality and empower all women and girls.

GOAL 6: CLEAN WATER & SANITATION

Ensure availability and sustainable management of water and sanitation for all.

GOAL 7: AFFORDABLE & CLEAN ENERGY

Ensure affordable, reliable, sustainable, and modern energy for all.

GOAL 8: DECENT WORK & ECONOMIC GROWTH

Promote sustained, inclusive, and sustainable economic growth, full and productive employment, and decent work for all.

GOAL 9: INDUSTRY, INNOVATION, & INFRASTRUCTURE

Build resilient infrastructure, promote inclusive and sustainable industrialization, and foster innovation.

GOAL 10: REDUCED INEQUALITIES

Reduce inequalities within and among countries.

GOAL 11: SUSTAINABLE CITIES & COMMUNITIES

Make cities and human settlements inclusive, safe, resilient, and sustainable.

GOAL 12: RESPONSIBLE CONSUMPTION AND PRODUCTION

Ensure sustainable consumption and production patterns.

GOAL 13: CLIMATE ACTION

Take urgent action to combat climate change and its impacts.

GOAL 14: LIFE BELOW WATER

Conserve and sustainably use the oceans, seas, and marine resources for sustainable development.

GOAL 15: LIFE ON LAND

Protect, restore, and promote sustainable use of terrestrial ecosystems, sustainably manage forests, combat desertification, halt and reverse land degradation, and halt biodiversity loss.

GOAL 16: PEACE, JUSTICE, & STRONG INSTITUTIONS
Promote peaceful and inclusive societies for sustainable development, provide access to justice for all, and build effective, accountable, and inclusive institutions at all levels.

GOAL 17: PARTNERSHIPS FOR THE GOALS
Strengthen the means of implementation and revitalize the global partnership for sustainable development.

Each of the 17 Goals has several sub-goals and targets beneath them—169 in total. Despite this, having the world's biggest challenges laid out, with clear objectives and metrics associated with them, has been welcomed as it offers a much-needed roadmap in these uncertain times.

Furthermore, at the United Nations, within the Department of Economic and Social Affairs, there is a dedicated division, the Division of the Sustainable Development Goals (DSDG), that provides comprehensive support and capacity-building for the SDGs. It evaluates the systemwide implementation of the 2030 Agenda and assists with outreach activities that relate to the SDGs. These Goals must translate into a strong commitment and action by all stakeholders to implement them, and the DSDG plays an important role in facilitating engagement between parties and the steps that follow.

It is believed that the SDGs have a greater chance of success than the Millennium Development Goals because, instead of focusing narrowly on donors and recipients, they are owned by all countries. They are universally applicable and require a collective response. They are far more inclusive. And are built on the idea of leaving no one behind, calling on leaders to be accountable to *all* their citizens, even the most vulnerable. They acknowledge that new approaches are required to redistribute wealth and resources better to reduce inequality and that these approaches need to integrate and balance the social, economic, and environmental elements of the SDGs.

Businesses, in particular, are embracing the goals, using them as a means by which to understand better the challenges facing the planet, to establish their responsibility in addressing these challenges, and then to ensure that their social responsibility efforts are aligned to them. Companies can look at the full spectrum of SDGs and decide which is the most relevant to their business and where they can make the most meaningful contribution so that they can be part of this enormous collective effort to make the world a better place.

Private equity funds are also helping to lead the way with SDG impact by launching investment products aligned to the SDGs, e.g., UBS has committed to directing 5 billion US dollars of client money over five years, from 2018, to impact investments related to the SDGs. Impact investing is now the fastest-growing investment strategy in Europe.

One of the downfalls of the Millennium Development Goals was that few people were aware of them. They were never successful in inspiring action. As a result, their impact was minimal. If the SDGs were going to serve as a compelling call to action and achieve their targets, a different approach was required. Far more effort has gone into generating awareness about the SDGs and the role that every single one of us can play in working together to effect change.

Making the goals famous

There are several different initiatives in place to drive awareness and accelerate the progress of the SDGs. One that has been particularly successful is Project Everyone. Started by Richard Curtis, filmmaker and founder of Comic Relief in the UK, Project Everyone creates communications campaigns with partners around the world to bring the SDGs to life in ways that are relevant to specific markets. It comprises a not-for-profit team of communications and campaign specialists that creates campaigns, short films, multi-platform content, convenes partners, works with influencers, and stages unique events that drive awareness of the SDGs and urge business, governments, NGOs, and individuals to take action. Curtis and the Project Everyone team have done a brilliant job of connecting people on an emotional level with the SDGs. He has made the SDGs something that people can relate to and rally around and, more importantly, want to support in both big ways and small.

The starting point for Project Everyone was to create a logo and a series of icons to represent each of the 17 Goals, thereby giving the SDGs a visual identity and a brand around which people could pin their support. Thanks to the support of founding partners such as the Bill & Melinda Gates Foundation, Unicef, Hasbro, and Evian, Project Everyone has also created global campaigns and events to drive the message home. The World's Largest Lesson is a worldwide campaign created in collaboration with Unicef that raises awareness of the SDGs among young people and encourages them to become actively involved. Another example is Goalkeepers, a multi-year campaign, in partnership with the Bill & Melinda Gates Foundation. These events bring together leaders from across the world to focus on specific themes contained in the SDGs, and, through pooled expertise and innovation, accelerate progress towards their achievement.

As we enter the final decade for the achievement of the Sustainable Development Goals, various stakeholders across society are adopting the Goals more collaboratively. Leading businesses understand the challenge and that achieving the SDGs will lead to a more prosperous, inclusive, and peaceful world. However, unless the speed of progress is stepped up, the 2030 deadline to achieve the SDGs will be missed.

On September 25, 2019, the anniversary of the signing of the Global Goals agreement, the World Business Council for Sustainable Development, the B Team, and the World Benchmarking Alliance launched the "Business Avengers." This campaign focuses on accelerating private sector awareness, collaboration, and action in support of the SDGs and brings together 17 global companies, each chosen, to represent one of the 17 SDGs. Each participating company is responsible for communicating the overall importance of the Goals, the opportunities the Goals represent, and what they are doing to help achieve them in the hope that this will inspire others to follow their lead. The Business Avengers include global giants such as Arm, Avanti, The Coca-Cola Company, Commvault, Diageo, Google.org, Mars, MasterCard, Microsoft, Nike, RB, SAP, Salesforce, and Unilever. Together, they represent over $500 billion in revenue and 900,000 employees.

2020 is a critical year in terms of taking decisive action. It is the start of the 'decade of delivery' so that the 17 SDGs gain impetus and have a realistic chance of being achieved by 2030. There is a higher awareness around the Goals now, at both corporate and consumer levels, and companies are taking the lead in creating and driving change. However, we need to see an increase in public-private cooperation to meet the 2030 deadline.

KEY INSIGHTS: A FRAMEWORK FOR A GLOBAL SHARED MISSION

➤ The 2030 Agenda for Sustainable Development, adopted by all United Nations Member States in 2015, provides a shared blueprint for peace and prosperity for people and the planet, now and into the future.

➤ At its heart are the 17 Sustainable Development Goals (SDGs), which recognize that ending poverty and other deprivations must go hand-in-hand with strategies that improve health and education, reduce inequality, and spur economic growth—all while tackling climate change and working to preserve our oceans and forests.

➤ The Sustainable Development Goals are a call to action for governments, businesses, civil society, and the general public to work together to build a better future for everyone.

➤ The goals address the needs of people in both developed and developing countries, emphasizing that no one should be left behind. They address three dimensions of sustainable development: social, economic, and environmental, as well as important aspects related to peace, justice, and effective institutions.

➤ Various stakeholders across society are starting to accelerate progress and deliver on the promises made by all nations in 2015.

➤ On September 25, 2019—the anniversary of the Global Goals agreement—17 global giants representing over $500 billion in revenue and 900,000 employees joined forces under a coalition called the "Business Avengers."

CHAPTER 4

PERSONAL PURPOSE
YOU ARE MORE THAN WHAT YOU MAY HAVE BECOME

Just as organizations are embracing Purpose as a business philosophy, so too are individuals realizing the value in defining their Purpose to serve as a beacon for the way they conduct themselves in their daily lives. According to enso's World Value Index, there has been a rise in people's expressed importance to live life with a sense of Purpose, from 80% in 2016 to 91% in 2018. This desire for Purpose is mostly born out of a yearning for something more and a concern for the current state of the world. Political turbulence, an ailing planet, food and water security, poverty, unemployment, and huge income inequality are all contributing to increased levels of anxiety and disenchantment. People want something better from the world and for themselves.

At the same time, people are also re-evaluating the definition of success. The success of the 1980s and 1990s, which was so closely tied to wealth and earnings, is being overturned. Remember the movie Jerry Maguire where Tom Cruise plays a sports agent who has a crisis of conscience in the money-fuelled world of win-at-all-costs professional sports? Who can forget the catchy mantra "Show me the money" that his client, played by Cuba Gooding Jr., demanded of him? Feeling disillusioned with the relentless pursuit of money in the sports industry, Maguire wrote and distributed a manifesto to his colleagues, urging them to "bring soul and character" back to their work and to search for a higher Purpose in what they did. He was fired for his outburst, and only one staff member identified with his words and chose to go with him, which typifies the thinking of the time. Success in the business of sports was most certainly all about the money and agents' commissions.

Jerry's manifesto was released in full by screenwriter Cameron Crowe a few years ago. Now, nearly 25 years since the film's release, the words of the manifesto are reverberating in the corridors of business—"we must crack open the tightly clenched fist of commerce and give a little back for the greater good. Eventually, revenues will be the same, and that goodness will be infectious." What is more, if Jerry Maguire were to make this declaration to his colleagues today, chances are he would have more than one person join him.

A sense of Purpose exists in everyone, whether we are conscious of it or not. And it is important because, once you can articulate what drives your behavior and makes you feel fulfilled, you will have a point of reference that can serve as the basis for more intentional decision making with regards to all facets of your life. Individuals with a clearly defined Purpose are happier and more successful in life.

But the issue is, how does one go about finding and articulating one's Purpose so that it can channel the best use of one's talents and treasures to improve the lives of other people and, in doing so, enrich one's life? There are various ways it can be done. A good starting point is to ask people close to you (family members, friends, work colleagues) what it is that they value most about you. The good that you do for others is often a reflection of your Purpose as it is what you feel inclined to do naturally. It also helps to read about how others have applied Purpose in their own lives as this can stimulate ideas regarding what moves you or concerns you in your life. People can be motivated to make an impact in an area of benefit in their personal life, something they appreciate but that others do not easily have access to to the same extent. Purpose can also stem from our connections with others. Experiencing or empathizing with the pain and hardships of others can often lead us to act and help change or alleviate that pain. No matter how you go about finding what matters to you, what drives you, what is core to your happiness and fulfillment, i.e., your Purpose, once you find it, chances are you will want to seek out a community and a place of work that mirrors it.

It is a natural inclination for people to want to spend their time doing something they are passionate about and, it is even better if, at the same time, they can be doing good for the world around them. People want to work for something more than a paycheck, and they are using their Purpose to direct them to jobs that matter to them. Doing good while doing well is now an accepted life philosophy. Kin&Co's research has shown that for younger employees, particularly millennials, working for a company whose values and Purpose they believe in is critical. More than 75% of 18-24-year olds would be more motivated and committed at work if they felt their employer made a positive impact on society, compared to only 46% of those 65 years and older.

The good news is that not only are those who live a Purpose-driven life known to be happier and more successful, but the companies they work for are doing better. You get to live your truth through your work, and the outcomes can be brilliant. Staff are more energized and productive, there is less absenteeism, and there is a positive impact on the bottom line. A Frontline Leadership report in 2018 claimed that highly engaged employees contribute towards 44% higher profitability, 70% higher productivity, 86% higher customer service ratings, 70% more success in retention, and 37% lower absenteeism. These days people actively seek out companies that stand for something meaningful to them and will accept a lower salary if it means working there.

In a time when talent acquisition and retention is so important, having a clear Purpose becomes a way of attracting the right staff and keeping them happy. Businesses, therefore, need to be aware not only of what their customers care about but, perhaps more importantly, the cares of their employees. An engaged workforce, united behind a common goal, inspires innovations and improvements and will deliver sustained economic and social benefits. A Deloitte survey regarding millennials in the workplace stated that 63% of millennials chose "improve society" over "generate profit" as what businesses should try to achieve, which shows how important it is to the growing millennial workforce that businesses have a Purpose that they can identify with personally. Having a Purpose will attract engaged employees, it will unite employees behind a common goal, it will inspire innovation and improvements to the business, and it will deliver sustained economic and social benefit.

British business magnate and founder of the Virgin Group, Richard Branson, has always maintained that at Virgin, employees (not shareholders or customers) come first, and this is played out in several ways. His thinking is that if you take care of your employees, they will take care of the clients, which will, in turn, positively impact shareholder value. If you can ignite your employees through this lens of Purpose, there is little they would not do to ensure the success of the business. It becomes a circular argument, with a central organizing idea (i.e., a clear Purpose) at the core. Employees embody and live that Purpose, which makes customers enjoy their interaction with that business and support it in their purchase behavior, which then adds to the bottom line and ultimately makes shareholders happy.

Just as personal Purpose is important to create a sense of fulfillment within an individual, it has also been shown to have an impact in positions of corporate leadership. Through his work with business leaders globally, leadership coach, Kirk Souder, has found that when an organization's leadership team sees an intersection between its Purpose and the broader mission of the company, it fuels business success in three ways—greater engagement between the leadership team and their employees, greater innovation and creativity, and the development of new products and services that align business growth and positive social impact. Many leaders are only now starting to see that the company they lead can be used with Purpose to achieve results in areas that are true to their personal Purpose. It is the authenticity of this alignment between the leadership's Purpose and that of the company they lead that is an attractive hook for prospective employees. Great leaders of the future will inspire and connect people through their values and, in this way, will harness the power of motivated people.

Ben & Jerry's may be a manufacturer of premium ice cream. However, the company's Purpose, which was deeply ingrained from the start by its founders Ben Cohen and Jerry Greenfield, is what drives the business and entices people to work there. It is this overlap of the company's Purpose with that of its founders and the people who choose to work there that creates something special in terms of the brand's social impact. Ben & Jerry's has three missions—each treated with equal importance. The product mission is about making the best premium ice cream, the economic mission makes sure that all stakeholders in the value chain benefit from the prosperity of the business, and the social mission is about being a force for good both internally and externally. Ice cream is merely how the brand interacts with customers and engages staff, opening their eyes to the social injustices that the brand is fighting and creating a work environment that is inclusive and energizing. People love working at Ben & Jerry's—not only are they actively contributing to creating positive change in the world, but they genuinely feel heard, valued, and looked after (staff benefits include free online skills-based courses and a wellness center, among others). As a result, job applications are always heavily oversubscribed, and staff turnover is significantly lower than the average across US businesses. And when Unilever bought Ben & Jerry's in 2001, a critical element of the negotiations was for the establishment of an independent board of directors to oversee the company's social mission and to ensure it remained intact.

Having an evangelical founder whose personal Purpose is boldly reflected in the company's Purpose is not critical. There are many examples of businesses that have been just as successful in acting on their Purpose and cultivating a workforce of engaged and fulfilled employees without a high-profile social evangelist at the helm.

Purpose can be driven from the bottom up. Because of social media and technology, we are all connected now like we never were before, which amplifies the rate at which change can happen. People have the confidence to speak up these days because their message can be spread quickly, and others can join in. If many people unite in expressing similar views regarding a pressing issue facing the planet or how an organization is compromising its stated Purpose, then everybody is going to know about it. Personal Purpose has attained greater influence. Without social media, Greta Thunberg would not have had nearly the impact that she has had in fulfilling her Purpose and drawing the world's attention to the climate crisis.

Purpose has moved beyond good intentions. Developing one's Purpose is not only about clearly articulating what it is. It is about *living* that Purpose as well. Society is wanting to see action, and they are more than happy to be part of the effort through a shared Purpose. But behavior does not change overnight. It is a work in progress, a journey towards a better planet.

KEY INSIGHTS: PURPOSE IS ALSO PERSONAL

➤ Just as important as it is for organizations to define their Purpose is the opportunity for the individuals working in those organizations to define their Purpose.

➤ Individuals with a clearly defined sense of Purpose are happier and more successful in life. Doing good while doing well is now accepted as a life philosophy.

➤ Spend time thinking about and defining your Purpose and how you are going to use your talents and treasures to improve the lives of other people.

➤ When personal and organizational Purpose overlap, magic happens for the individual and the organization and, by extension, society.

LEADING THOUGHTS:
PERSONAL PURPOSE

KIRK SOUDER   Co-Founder at enso and Soul Purpose

WITH CLIENTS LIKE GOOGLE, MATTEL, AND KHAN ACADEMY, ENSO IS ONE
OF THE MOST RESPECTED SOCIAL IMPACT AGENCIES IN THE WORLD.

On the connection between personal Purpose and organizational Purpose:
I think it is really important for people, leaders, or anyone in an organization,
to understand what brings them alive, to know their calling, and then find the
intersection of that and the broader mission of the company. And to create,
innovate, and lead because, if that is not understood, then we are unable to be our
best selves or give our best selves to the company and its mission.

If you look at the latest Gallup polls, only 14% of the world's workforce is
engaged in the job they are doing, because they do not see the connection between
that and why they are here. So, it is important to establish that connection, and that
fuels much greater engagement, innovation, creativity, and collaboration in the
workplace. It amplifies, in an exponential degree, the productivity and innovation
within every person. They benefit because the company becomes a platform for
them to actualize their Purpose, and the company benefits by getting a leader or
employee who is wholly engaged at work.

**On the fact that sometimes work changes need to happen to align personal
Purpose with organizational Purpose:**
Sometimes it does happen, but I think of it less that there was not an intersection
and rather that you are simply meant to be somewhere else to actualize what is in
your heart. However, there is a wide berth between how we find our calling and its
intersection with our work.

On breaking the cycle of dependence on a role if it is not fulfilling and not aligned with one's Purpose:
I would say there are three different ways to go there. The first one would be to see it as an opportunity to create something new that will sustain me, bring me alive, and have a positive impact on the world. Secondly, start to explore and lean into opportunities in other companies and see if something aligns. And the third way would be to take a deeper look at oneself and what one is instinctively called to do. It comes down to where we are, what we are being called to do, and sometimes we are being urged to go out and create something entirely new.

LISA ARIE
Founder at The Visa Caballo

LISA RUNS THE SUCCESSFUL EXPERIENTIAL LEARNING CENTER, THE VISTA CABALLO, WHERE SHE USES HORSES AS THE TEACHERS TO HELP PEOPLE MOVE PAST FEAR TO PURSUE MEANING IN THEIR LIVES. FAST COMPANY MAGAZINE DESCRIBED LISA AS "THE CEO WHISPERER."

On what makes a business responsible and why people should be paying attention to the shift in how business is done:
I use the word "responsible," meaning the ability to respond and, with things changing as quickly as they are, those of us who want to have a positive influence on the world need to understand that we must be the change that we need in the world. Businesses that conduct themselves from the place that all living things matter, and know that we are dependent on each other and have a responsibility to future generations are the ones that will lead and succeed. Consumers are now aware of the impact that businesses have on our planet and are taking a stand on the choices they make. Businesses that are not leading from a conscientious core will ultimately have to transform themselves if they want to stay alive, and that starts with conscious and conscientious leadership as part of their natural operating system. It is a whole new level of leadership.

On the overlap between personal Purpose and corporate Purpose:
Businesses cannot live their Purpose without their people because companies are a collective of people, and whole-person development leads to high performing teams, transformation, and advancement that our world is requiring of us now. People are

no longer willing to sacrifice their lives for a paycheck. They want something more. They want meaning and Purpose. They want to live life fully, and they look for businesses that create those environments where they can fulfill themselves while they are helping businesses to live their Purpose, so the two are tied.

On the connection with horses and how they feature in Lisa's work at Vista Caballo:

Horses are prey animals. So, they wake up every day wondering what will eat them. They do not take anything for granted. They stay present in the here and now and are a hundred percent honest. They have no agenda. It is what keeps them safe. We create simulators at Vista Caballo so that people can have that experience for themselves, feeling safe so that their best selves can show up. People then see how they behave outside of their normal comfort zone, which is critical for leaders who are going to lead us forward. If they understand where that edge is and how they respond or react at the edge, they can expand that zone and take us all forward. The last thing you want to do when you are out of your comfort zone is to react and try to scramble back to your comfort zone because there is no progress there. True leaders learn how to lead outside of that zone, and the benefit is that you get the information from that moment for that moment. So, everything is a hundred percent relevant.

A message of hope to inspire people to become their best selves and make the world a better place in the process:

I would say never give up hope. You must know that you can make a difference, but that is a mindset and a decision. History is full of people who have shown us this. You are more equipped than you know, and you must get up every day and challenge yourself. When we feel happy, that is an indicator that we are being directed towards hope, which is why finding and living your Purpose is so critical. Finding and living your Purpose is not selfish. Our survival and our evolution as a species depend on it.

PART 2

DOING GOOD WHILE DOING WELL IN SPORT

Sport is essentially a mirror on society, reflecting the values of the day and shining a light on what matters most to people at a given point in time. In this section, we reflect on how society's values have shown up across sport and how the business of sport has responded.

We share inspiring examples of sports leagues, federations, teams, sponsorships, athletes, and events that have embedded Purpose within their organizational or personal DNA, usually with positive outcomes and lasting benefits.

We include more interviews with Thought Leaders and practitioners to provide confidence in the notion that "doing good while doing well" can work in the business of sport and get you thinking about what might be possible in whatever aspect of sports you may be involved.

By the end of this section, you should have a good understanding of how Purpose is evolving across the business of sport and what opportunities this represents for you or your organization and the entire sports sector.

ATHLETES
A MIRROR ON SOCIETY

It is no wonder that, over time, athletes have often been moved to speak out or make a show of protest on an issue, whether it be about race, gender, earnings, or climate change. Athletes have influence. Sport has the unique ability to inspire and unite people in a way that little else does, and athletes are at the center of that. They command attention, not only because of their athletic prowess but also because they are role models to a global community of fans.

A clear, intentional statement or act of protest by an athlete can be a powerful way to raise awareness, stimulate conversation, and fast track change. Thanks to a loyal fan base and the global reach of social media, athletes have the power to reach more people with an intentional message than just about anyone. And, once people start talking, the momentum can build and ultimately lead to positive change.

Like anyone else, athletes are citizens of the world we live in, and they share the same concerns for the state of the planet and society's behavior within it. It is no wonder then that the views expressed by athletes are often just a mirror of what is being felt by members of society.

However, having a conscience and putting oneself out there as a spokesperson on an issue can land an athlete in hot water. With the polarization that exists in society today, standing up for what you believe in on a global stage can have detrimental consequences for an athlete. It can be a difficult path to walk, and not all can navigate this road successfully.

Athlete activism can broadly be divided into three eras. Although athlete activism goes back a long way, it was the 1960s and 1970s that saw the first surge in the number of athletes using their position of influence to draw attention to the issues of the day, often with harsh and lasting consequences. By the 1980s and 1990s, athletes had become much more commercially focused, and the emphasis shifted to being more about building their brand and maximizing their earning potential through product endorsements, branded merchandise, and the like. But, the 2000s have seen a re-emergence of athletes using their influence to highlight social and environmental issues. While today it seems to be more accepted that athletes stand for something and fight for change, it still carries risk and can have negative repercussions.

It is worth taking a closer look at the evolution of athlete activism over the past few decades to understand better where we have come from and how athletes use their influence to draw attention to and bring about change in areas where it is needed.

When standing up for what you believed in killed careers

In the past, there were several athletes who, by standing up for what they believed in, were shunned by the public and the sporting community. One of the most high-profile examples highlighting the power of athlete protest is that of Tommy Smith and John Carlos, the 200m stars of the US Olympic team at the 1968 Summer Olympic Games in Mexico. The image of these two African American athletes, with their raised-fist salute and black socks instead of shoes, is one of the most iconic images in sport.

At the time, the US was deeply divided over the Vietnam War, and the civil rights movement was underway with protests and violence escalating across many cities in America. The assassinations of Martin Luther King Jr. and Robert F. Kennedy, as well as various acts of police violence towards peaceful protesters, had provoked deep-seated anger. African Americans, in particular, were outraged at the escalating racial tensions and frustrated at the passive nature of much of the civil rights campaigning at the time. There was talk amongst the African American members of the US Track & Field team of boycotting the upcoming Olympic Games in protest of the racial injustices in the United States, but this never materialized.

Smith and Carlos used the medal ceremony after the 200m final at the Olympics as the stage for a silent protest. Finishing first and third, respectively, they were the gold and bronze medalists and used this opportunity to highlight the segregation and racism taking place in their home country. While on the medals podium, they each bowed their heads and raised a black-gloved fist into the air in salute, a powerful symbol of black power and protest through which Smith and Carlos were calling for better treatment of black people in America and around the world. This defiant act was witnessed by millions around the world and led to angry jibes and sneers inside the stadium and harsh treatment outside of it. The prevailing view was that they had scandalized the Olympic Games, and they were vilified for it. Their medals were taken away from them; they were kicked out of the Olympic Village and, under pressure from the International Olympic Committee, US Olympic officials suspended the athletes, banning them from the Olympics for life. They arrived home in disgrace and endured death threats and taunts in public.

Conversely, amongst the black community, they were lauded for sacrificing their glory for the good of humankind. Either way, their days of competitive track & field were done. Over time, tensions did ease somewhat, and Smith and Carlos were gradually accepted back into the Olympic family. However, the statement had been made, and its impact felt with neither athlete ever competing successfully again.

The second-placed athlete on the day, Australian Peter Norman, also endured harsh consequences. He had joined the Americans in protest, albeit less overtly, by wearing a small badge on his left breast that said, "Olympic Project for Human Rights"—an organization that opposed racism in sport. He supported the protest because he sympathized with the Americans and because of racial injustices taking place in his own country. The Australian sporting community also punished Norman for the rest of his life. He never ran in the Olympic Games again, despite recording qualifying times in subsequent years, and he died without ever being acknowledged for his contribution to athletics in Australia. His outburst well and truly cost him his career. He was one of the best sprinters ever to have come out of Australia, and yet because he chose to use his influence as an athlete to draw attention to racial injustice, he was rejected. It was only in 2012, six years after Norman's death, that the Australian government chose to apologize for the appalling treatment he had received in his home country.

The protest action taken in 1968 has been brought to focus again recently in light of the IOC's new guidelines that reiterate and clarify its ban on athletes making any kind of political, religious, or racial protests at the next Summer Olympic Games in Tokyo. It remains to be seen whether this will be enforceable given the multitude of platforms available to athletes today to make their voices heard. The 400m hurdles legend, Edwin Moses, one of the most respected people in sports today and good friend of Carlos and Smith, believes the IOC's attempt to clamp down on athletes will be futile, and he is probably right. He believes protests are going to happen and will be impossible to stop. Looking back on the actions of his friends Carlos and Smith in 1968, Moses is fully supportive of what they did, saying it was "absolutely the right thing to do." Despite the IOC's ruling, he encourages athletes to continue protesting at the Olympics if they feel the need to do so. "I think it's a very personal individual choice to have to make." It remains to be seen what will unfold at the Tokyo Games and how the IOC responds.

But, let us turn our attention back to the athlete activists of the 70s. They can be credited with establishing a path for today's athletes in standing up for what they believe in and using their influence to bring about positive transformation.

One of the most outspoken athletes of the era was Muhammad Ali. He was one of the first global sports stars who was prepared to challenge the status quo and boldly speak out on social issues regardless of the consequences, but his career also suffered as a result. In 1966, Ali refused to be drafted into the US Army because of his religious beliefs and opposition to the Vietnam War. He was arrested and found guilty of draft evasion. Also, he was stripped of his boxing titles and denied a boxing license in every state across America. His flourishing boxing career was over.

However, he was not deterred, and he took to spending his time traveling the country, speaking out at college and university campuses where he criticized the Vietnam War and advocated for African-American pride and racial justice. This itinerary and influence were previously unheard of for an athlete. It was only in 1971 that his conviction was overturned. Meanwhile, Ali lost out on four years of competition in the prime of his boxing career, thus denying him the opportunity of maximizing his earning potential from the sport.

Mohammed Ali's example, as a conscientious objector, had a far-reaching impact and inspired many people. He pioneered a shift in the way people saw athletes and the power they possessed to bring about change. New York Times columnist William Rhoden spoke for many when he wrote, "Ali's actions changed my standard of what constituted an athlete's greatness. Possessing a killer jump shot or the ability to stop on a dime was no longer enough. What were you doing for the liberation of your people? What were you doing to help your country live up to the covenant of its founding principles?"

Ali continued to speak out and drive social change on a variety of issues, from hunger and poverty to the plight of the world's refugees. Such was his influence that he is even credited with talking a suicidal man down from jumping off a ninth-floor ledge in Los Angeles in 1981. Ali went on to become one of the most outspoken and active athlete activists the world has ever seen.

Both sides of the activism spectrum on the tennis tour— respectful dialogue vs. loud and proud

Not all athletes were as confrontational or vocal in their activism, but even with a milder approach, they still put their career at risk. American tennis icon Arthur Ashe also considered one of the greatest activists in the history of sports, used a more softly spoken approach of respectful dialogue. Nevertheless, he was just as effective in highlighting issues and advocating for change.

Ashe catapulted to prominence in 1968 when, at the age of twenty-five, he became the first African American to win the US Open tennis championships. Ashe was the highest-ranked amateur at the event but was never expected to beat the best professional tennis players in the world ranked above him. Yet, that is what he did. The significance of his win was not so much felt on the court but in what came out of it. Ashe was an introvert at heart, but this victory gave him the confidence and the public profile to find his voice on a wide array of social justice issues, including civil rights, economic empowerment, refugees, and HIV/AIDS.

Having experienced the humiliation of racial discrimination first-hand, Ashe became a leader in the fight against apartheid in South Africa. The international sports community boycotted South Africa because of its apartheid policies. However, Ashe took a different approach to the resistance and wanted to visit the country and play tennis there, but the South African government repeatedly denied him a visa. Eventually, on his third attempt, Ashe was granted a visa and went to play in the South African Open tennis tournament. Upon arriving in Johannesburg, he successfully negotiated with the apartheid government to integrate seating at Ellis Park, the venue where he was to play. The Black tennis fans who saw him play, and win the doubles title there, called him "Sipho," which means "gift from God " in Xhosa, one of the African languages in South Africa. Ashe continued to speak out against apartheid for the next 20 years, even getting arrested once when part of an anti-apartheid march in Washington. He was one of the founders of Artists and Athletes Against Apartheid. He also joined a delegation of 31 prominent African Americans who visited South Africa to observe the political change there as it approached racial integration.

In the 1980s, Ashe contracted HIV from a tainted blood transfusion he received during heart bypass surgery. He went public with his illness in 1992 and dedicated the rest of his life to fighting the disease. He established the Arthur Ashe Foundation for the Defeat of AIDS and used this platform to raise awareness and advocate for new treatments. He was also a vocal proponent for the steering of government resources to AIDS-related research and public education about the disease.

Arthur Ashe was almost a reluctant activist. Having such a public profile did not come naturally to him. He was soft-spoken and shy but somehow felt compelled to use his celebrity status for social good, becoming a forceful civil rights activist, a humanitarian, philanthropist, and an unrivaled ambassador of sportsmanship and fair play. He once said, "From what we get, we can make a living. What we give, however, makes a life." In the 25 years that followed his first win at the US Open, Ashe worked tirelessly as an advocate for civil and human rights and more than cultivated a meaningful life for himself. His views sometimes cost him, like when he was removed as Davis Cup captain because of his arrest during an anti-apartheid demonstration, but he stood firm on his beliefs.

Ashe offered a unique model for activism, one based on patient consideration and intelligent, intentional, and respectful dialogue. He may well have been quiet, but the impact of his activism is still felt today. He is an inspiration and positive role model for athletes who desire a Purpose beyond fame and fortune, and for anyone who shares his shy, quiet nature and doubts their ability to take a stand and be heard.

Another influential tennis player from this era who deserves mention is Billie Jean King, the former world number one and long-time advocate for gender equality and social justice. King was the driving force behind the establishment of the first women's professional tour, which led to the creation of the Women's Tennis Association, where she served as President for many years and which still governs the sport today. She was a firm believer in gender equality and equal prize money and campaigned relentlessly for this. In 1973, she even threatened to lead a boycott of the US Open if the prize money for the winning male and female was not equal. Her demands were met, and the US Open became the first major tennis tournament to offer equal prize money to the male and female singles winners, which is now the case at all four Grand Slam events.

That same year King responded to former champion Bobby Rigg's claims that the women's game was so inferior to the men's game that even a 55-year-old such as himself could beat the current top female players when she challenged him to an exhibition match. The match, dubbed "Battle of the Sexes," took place in Texas on September 20th and garnered huge support. There were more than 30,000 spectators courtside and a further 90 million people around the world who watched the game via television. King beat Riggs 6-4, 6-3, 6-3, and, in doing so, single-handedly raised the profile of women's tennis. It was considered a defining moment in the feminist movement of the era.

Even in retirement, King has continued her activism, not only campaigning for gender equality but also the LGBTQ community and inclusivity in the workplace. In 2009, she was awarded the Presidential Medal of Freedom, the United States' highest civilian honor, for her advocacy work on behalf of women and the LGBTQ community. She was the first female athlete to be recognized in this way, which highlights her influence and effect as a campaigner.

King passionately believes it is her responsibility as an athlete to try to make the world a better place, saying, "Athlete activism ... should be celebrated, and not derided ... Our job is to not only lead within our sport, but to help others," and helping others is not only about speaking out, but also actively listening. King has exemplified this on numerous occasions throughout her tennis career and beyond. Even as she nears 80 years old, she continues to be as active as ever in speaking out and supporting other female athletes. King is concerned that not enough athletes use the platform they have been given to speak out and that too many bow to the pressure put on them by their associations, sponsors, or agents to keep quiet, toe the line, and just collect their paycheck. Despite all the obstacles she faced over the years, King is reassured by the changes she has helped bring about. Buoyed by the recent upsurge in female athletes speaking out, she is optimistic that the fight for equality is moving in the right direction and gaining momentum again.

Me, myself, and I

If the 60s and 70s were characterized by athletes taking a stand as social activists despite the often negative impact on their careers, by contrast, the 80s and 90s saw the focus shift towards athletes using their influence to build huge personal fortunes. This shift in focus is not to say athletes no longer took a stand on social and political issues, just that they were generally less vocal or active in conveying their commitment, and there were fewer of them doing it. It is no wonder, as athletes were merely mirroring the prevailing sentiment in society. In the corporate world, companies were single-mindedly focusing on generating value for shareholders, and individuals were chasing success in the form of fancy job titles, huge salaries, and coveted possessions.

The 80s and 90s was the era in which the world of sports marketing flourished, and athlete megastars were born. Athlete endorsements came into their own, and sports agents had their hands full negotiating favorable terms for their clients that would deliver staggering financial returns. In contrast to the activists of the 60s and 70s, the athletes dominating this era tended to be more inwardly focused, looking out for themselves as opposed to taking an active interest in tackling the issues of the day. It was easier to build a likable public persona without challenging the status quo and speaking out on controversial topics.

Michael Jordan, the most marketed athlete in history, epitomizes this era. Jordan achieved remarkable success as a basketball player, competing in the NBA for 15 years and winning six championships with the Chicago Bulls. In 1999, he was named the greatest US athlete of the 20th century by ESPN, and he is considered to have been instrumental in popularizing the NBA around the world in the 1980s and 1990s.

In 2014, Jordan became the first billionaire player in NBA history, largely thanks to the many successful product endorsements he has with brands such as Nike, Gatorade, Coca-Cola, Chevrolet, McDonald's, Wheaties, and Hanes, to name a few. Over nearly four decades, he has earned $1.7 billion from endorsement deals alone, most of which have been made since he quit playing.

One of Jordan's biggest and longest-running endorsements is with Nike. The relationship started back in 1984 with a deal that changed sports marketing forever when Nike offered Jordan a deal that would earn him $500,000 annually. Until then, the previous highest contract in basketball was James Worthy's agreement with New Balance worth $150,000 per year.

As is the Nike way, the brand lent its marketing muscle to growing the Jordan brand and ensuring a return on its investment in the rising NBA star. A signature sneaker was launched, the first of its kind in the world of sponsorship. The sneakers not only bore the Jordan name but also sported highly visible black and red colors instead of the customary white sneakers worn in basketball up to this point. Not happy with this departure from the norm, the NBA reportedly fined Jordan $5,000 every time he stepped onto the court wearing his new Air Jordan 1 sneakers, but this only played into Nike's hands and ensured that the "banned" sneakers achieved instant notoriety. Whether or not this is a completely accurate account of events has been questioned over the years, but, whether truth or folklore, it propelled Jordan to super-stardom and built the empire of branded apparel deals that followed in its wake.

The Air Jordan sneakers had an edginess about them and, thanks to tantalizing images of Jordan mid-flight on the court, the idea that there was something special about the sneakers took hold. The follow-up Air Jordan II released a year later, was the first to feature the iconic Jumpman logo, which has since become the visual identity for the Jordan brand and has been used for product endorsements far beyond the basketball court. Each year since the launch of the Air Jordan, Nike has released a numbered edition sneaker. To date, there have been 34 iterations in addition to numerous special editions and re-issues, and sales continue to be as strong as ever. By 1991, sales had amounted to $200 million a year, and, fast forward to today, Air Jordan is a $3.1 billion global business for Nike. Nearly two decades after his last NBA game, Jordan is still reportedly the highest earner in the NBA, higher even than Lebron James and the current crop of stars.

Jordan was a singular sportsman who built a global reputation for doing things his way. He, together with Nike, single-handedly changed the athlete landscape and alerted the world to the power of sports personalities to drive profits through product endorsements. The athlete, not the product, became the focus of the relationship, and the brand communication and building one's brand became paramount. Today, nearly two decades after his final NBA game, Michael Jordan still enjoys 98% awareness levels, has a net worth of around $2 billion, and is one of the world's highest-earning athletes of all time. Jordan showed the path to a fortune built on endorsement earnings long into retirement that has since been followed successfully by global sports icons across nearly every sports code.

The extent of Jordan's financial success is almost unbelievable and is a vivid portrayal of the behavior at the time. Athletes were single-minded in their commitment to being the best they could be in the competitive arena, and endorsement deals were more forthcoming and lucrative if athletes did not rock the boat. Cultivating a likable image to the world was far easier if athletes kept quiet about their political views. A 1993 Nike commercial, featuring Jordan's fellow NBA player Charles Barkley, encapsulates the thinking at the time with Barkley proclaiming, "I am not paid to be a role model. I am paid to wreak havoc on the basketball court."

And no one was better at this than Michael Jordan. His performances on the court were legendary, and his image, both on and off the court, was very carefully constructed to appeal to a broad range of people and attract leading brands for endorsement deals. It has only been since he retired from professional basketball that Jordan has begun to speak out on issues and support issues that are close to his heart. He has even admitted, "When I was playing, my tunnel vision was my craft. I was a professional basketball player, and I tried to do the best I could. Now I have more time to understand things around me, understand causes, understand issues and problems, and commit my voice, my financial support, too."

In the past five years or so, Jordan has lent considerable support to addressing police violence against African Americans. Just this year, in the wake of George Floyd's death at the hands of a police officer in Minneapolis, Jordan spoke out, calling it a "tipping point" for African Americans, and made a $100 million donation to organizations support-ing racial equality. Jordan has also donated significant sums to multiple hurricane relief funds. He has supported medical clinics in at-risk communities while continuing his longstanding support of the Make A Wish Foundation, where he has granted more than 200 wishes to terminally ill kids.

Jordan's change of heart is perhaps partly linked to the changes brewing in society at the turn of the century because it was at this time that businesses were beginning to re-evaluate their role in society, and many athletes were, in turn, doing the same. While the 80s and 90s had seen many athletes shy away from using their voice to speak out—either because they feared it would hurt their career or because the lure of fame and fortune took precedence—the 2000s have seen a marked resurgence in athlete activism. Although still earning huge amounts of money, both from endorsements, salaries, and prize money, more and more athletes are now boldly using their profile and influence to take activist stances on a wide range of social justice issues. The difference this time around is that they have the widespread vocal support of their fans behind them.

From me to us

The world may be divided by language, religion, and culture, but it is increasingly global through platforms like the internet. Sport, and the athletes who give it a personality and cult following, have incredible power to unify and mobilize fans into action. The internet and social media have only exacerbated this to unprecedented levels.

The athlete activism we see now is different from the past. Today, people expect athletes to have a voice, and they are critical if they do not. And sponsors know that to pull the plug on an endorsement deal because an athlete has taken a stand on something often ends up alienating consumers and negatively impacting their brand. That is not to say that today's athletes always have it easy when they voice their opinions. Many sports federations still adopt a knee-jerk reaction and try to shut athletes down instead of openly engaging with them. But today's athletes are composed, self-assured, and committed. It is not a publicity stunt for them. They are in it for the long haul. Athletes do not back down because they know they have the power and hordes of people who gravitate towards them, joining them on their crusade until real change comes about.

Former NFL quarterback for the San Francisco 49ers, Colin Kaepernick, is one of the current group of athlete activists whose actions and opinions have forced people to sit up and take notice, drawing criticism from some circles but gaining respect and support from more. Kaepernick, who is biracial, was adopted and raised by white parents and has had a huge impact on the debate around race, police violence, and politics in sports. He first made a name for himself as an activist when, at a preseason NFL game in August 2016, he refused to stand for the singing of the national anthem to protest racial inequality. To explain his actions, he said, "I am not going to stand up and show pride in a flag for a country that oppresses black people and people of color. To me, this is bigger than football, and it would be selfish on my part to look the other way."

Through the 2016 season, Kaepernick continued to protest, drawing both support and condemnation from all corners—fellow NFL players, fans, politicians, and celebrities. By 2017, his quiet protest had expanded into something much bigger, with several players on each NFL team kneeling during the anthem and athletes from other sports showing their support as well, causing Kaepernick to fall out with the NFL owners. His actions sparked a national debate and even elicited an angry response from President Trump, who called for all kneeling NFL players to be fired.

Come 2017, Kaepernick was without a team. He firmly believed his exclusion from the draft was at the hands of the NFL. In September 2017, he filed a grievance against the NFL. He claimed that its owners had "colluded to deprive Mr. Kaepernick of employment rights in retaliation for Mr. Kaepernick's leadership and advocacy for equality and social justice and his bringing awareness to peculiar institutions still undermining racial equality in the United States." The NFL tried to dismiss the grievance, which was denied as an arbitrator felt Kaepernick had presented sufficient evidence to support his claims. It was only in February 2018 that the NFL and Kaepernick finally agreed to a confidential settlement. Kaepernick never got another NFL contract and remains without any formal job offers to participate in the league.

Nevertheless, despite limited support within the NFL, Kaepernick continued to make headlines. He appeared on the cover of the December 2017 issue of GQ as its "Citizen of the Year '' where he was lauded for his determined stand and likened to Muhammed Ali—both willing to risk everything to make a difference. He also received the Sports Illustrated Muhammed Ali Legacy Award, which is bestowed on former athletes and sports figures who embody the ideals of sportsmanship, leadership, and philanthropy as vehicles for changing the world. And he was chosen as a finalist for TIME Magazine's Person of the Year designation. He appeared as the face of Nike's "Just Do It" 30th-anniversary campaign with the phrase "Believe in something. Even if it means sacrificing everything." A far cry from Nike's Charles Barkley "I am not a role model" campaign of the 80s.

The Colin Kaepernick story highlights how polarized society is currently. The public reaction in 2016, from both sides, was overwhelming, ranging from racist tweets and death threats to an outpouring of support and accolades. In June 2020, we witnessed another surge in protests, brought on by the public outrage across America, and indeed the world, at the killing of African American George Floyd by a white policeman in Minneapolis. Sports leagues and athletes, from LeBron James and Michael Jordan to Serena Williams and Naomi Osaka and many more, came out in condemnation of the systemic racism that still exists in America today and called for meaningful change. Kaepernick's name came up again to highlight that, sadly, nothing much has changed since he spoke out about the very same issues in 2016. If Kaepernick's protests had led to meaningful dialogue and positive reform around issues of racial inequality, perhaps America would not have erupted as it did in 2020.

While Kaepernick became the beacon for the rights of minorities in 2016, it is the NBA basketball player, LeBron James, who can be credited with being a consistent force on the issue of racial inequality. Alongside Michael Jordan, LeBron James is regarded as one of the greatest basketball players of all time. Contrary to Jordan, LeBron always felt compelled to use his profile to speak out. He has willingly tackled issues of racial inequality, police shootings, and even Donald Trump. James' activism, which is often expressed through his clothing, really took shape in 2012 when he and his Miami Heat teammates wore hoodies to protest the shooting of Florida teen, Trayvon Martin. Then, in 2014, he wore an "I Can't Breathe" T-shirt in a tribute to the killing of Eric Garner, a New York man who had shouted these words while dying in a police chokehold. Having gained a reputation as an influential spokesperson against racial injustice, LeBron was criticized in 2016 when he failed to speak out against the police killing of Tamir Rice. The criticism seemed to spur him on to become even more outspoken, and, in 2018, he boldly introduced his new LeBron 15 sneakers—an all-black shoe with the word "EQUALITY" stitched in bright gold, highly visible letters across the back. His footwear had become the embodiment of his inspirational activism alongside his on-court performances.

Nowhere has LeBron James' influence been more apparent than in his spat with Fox News host Laura Ingraham in 2018. Her "Shut up and dribble" response to James' criticism of Donald Trump sparked a national controversy and got the attention of the collective sports world. Ingraham had hit out against one of the most popular and influential names in sports, and it did not sit well with greater America. James responded with a quiet, yet powerful message, a single Instagram post using the phrase "I Am More Than An Athlete," captioning it with the hashtag #WeWillNotShutUpAndDribble. He knew that with his social media reach (35.4 million followers on Instagram, 40 million followers on Twitter, and 22.6 million on Facebook), he is a powerful man. He could make such bold statements knowing that he had the respect and support of millions of people around the world. In the end, it was LeBron James who silenced Laura Ingraham and those who agreed with her.

Following Ingraham's comments, James acted with renewed energy in the activism space. During the 2018 NBA Playoffs, a time when James habitually stopped his social media activity completely, he crafted a unique approach to keeping his activist presence alive while remaining true to his annual tradition. In a genius move, James gifted his Instagram page, along with his 35 million followers, to young activists looking to send a message to a wide audience. His page became a symbol of social activism, with teenagers posting an array of messages on his story almost daily, covering issues ranging from climate change to school bullying. James has since gone on to create The Shop, a show on HBO that gives athletes the chance to speak their mind freely and serves as a way for James to extend his activist platform to other athletes and celebrities. It provides a safe space for these influencers to have an honest conversation about the culture of society today without their words being edited and cut to fit someone else's narrative.

James continues to lead the fight for college athletes to be fairly compensated for the revenue they generate for college sports. At the other end of the education spectrum, he is spearheading the establishment of better education opportunities in vulnerable areas such as Akron, Ohio, where he grew up. In 2018, he opened the I Promise School, a public elementary school in Akron. The school is a game-changer for at-risk youth in his hometown as it provides free tuition, free meals, job placement services for parents, and guaranteed tuition to the University of Akron for all students who graduate.

James understands that he is one of the most powerful voices in sport, and he is more than happy to use it to good effect. People respect what he has to say, and because of him, other athletes feel emboldened to take up the activism mantle as well. Athletes today will not be silenced. They hold power, and they know it.

The rise in athlete activism has not been confined to American athletes. Following several racist incidents in European soccer, we are now seeing a growing cohort of players in Europe challenge racism in ways that have not been done before. One of these is Raheem Sterling, arguably the standout English soccer player of the current generation. His is a measured but urgent voice on the issue of racism both within soccer and outside it. In 2019, he called out the English media for its repeated negative and distorted portrayal of young black soccer stars and urged them to "do better" and to "look up and tune in" to the world around them. Sterling's influence as an unofficial spokesperson for his generation of players is on the rise. Never one to shy away from controversy, Nike moved quickly to partner with Sterling and launched a campaign in December 2019, with the strapline "Speaking up doesn't always make life easier. But easy never changed anything."

Another strong voice is that of Marcus Rashford, the Manchester United forward. In the summer of 2020, as many UK families struggled financially due to the pressure caused by the coronavirus, Rashford single-handedly led a campaign that forced the government to change its policy regarding free school meal vouchers during the school holidays. Thanks to Rashford's efforts, 1.3 million school children did not go hungry during their summer holidays.

The Power of Group Action

Individual activism is one thing, but the potential impact that can be achieved through group action is far greater. With this in mind, Common Goal was launched in August 2017, with the support of Spanish and Manchester United soccer player Juan Mata. Common Goal is a pledge-based charitable movement whereby professionals in the soccer industry pledge 1% of their annual salary towards philanthropic resources around the world. The rationale is that soccer is a global game with more than three billion fans and 265 million players, giving it unprecedented reach, influence, and cultural value. Creating Common Goal serves as a way to forge a link between players, managers, fans, organizations, brands, and soccer-for-good organizations so that all can work together to tackle the most pressing issues facing society today and achieve more together. It has the potential to be hugely impactful, and Juan Mata is to be commended for his commitment to spearheading the movement aimed at forming a lasting connection between soccer as a business and as a tool for social change. The number of players, coaches, and other high-profile people in the world of soccer who have signed up is increasing steadily. As of June 2020, there were 468 members from 139 organizations. It will be interesting to see if, in time, more big names feel inclined to join, either due to public pressure or a growing personal conscience regarding their role as a changemaker in society.

In a similar vein, Global Athlete, an international athlete-led movement that aims to inspire and lead positive change in world sport, was established in February 2019 to listen to, engage with and empower athlete groups to speak up and address the disconnect that exists between athletes and sports leaders. Amongst other achievements, the movement has helped athletes to challenge the IOC regarding Rule 50 of the Olympic Charter, whereby athletes are prohibited from any form of protest during the Games, arguing that silencing athletes should never be tolerated. The success of Global Athlete in giving athletes a voice highlights the desire among athletes to help shape the world around them, not only within the structures governing sports but in wider society as well.

Women speak out

One of the most powerful displays of collective athlete activism played out in the USA Gymnastics sex abuse scandal of recent years and the case against Larry Nassar, thanks to the 156 courageous women and young girls who shared accounts of the sexual abuse they had suffered and stood together demanding justice.

Nassar was the former USA Gymnastics (USAG) team doctor and sports medicine physician at Michigan State University who had sexually abused young gymnasts under the guise of medical treatment spanning 20 years. In March 2016, things finally began to unravel for Nassar when the Indianapolis Star ran a report on USAG and its systemic failure to protect its young athletes from sexual abuse and report allegations against coaches to the relevant authorities.

The report prompted Rachael Denhollander to file a criminal case against Nassar, and from there, the floodgates opened. A further 125 women filed criminal complaints against him, and over 300 more filed civil suits against Nassar and the organizations that employed him and turned a blind eye to his actions even after being alerted to his behavior.

Nassar was sentenced to 175 years behind bars, but he was only one part of the issue as many more cases of sexual misconduct from coaches and other staff within the sport came to light. USAG, as the custodian of the sport and with ultimate responsibility for its athletes, was severely criticized. Current and former gymnasts found their collective voice, calling out USAG for its lack of accountability and demanding change as well as some measure of justice for what they went through. With nine high profile Olympians among the survivors, their voices led to a shakeup at USAG, including the resignations of board members and senior officials and the adoption of new policies to protect its athletes. This unprecedented momentum of empowerment crushed USAG's reputation. Its sponsors left, and, in December 2018, USAG filed for bankruptcy—potent testimony to the power of modern-day athletes and the influence they hold. These brave athletes were honored as a collective at the 2018 ESPYS with the Arthur Ashe Courage Award, which was a fitting recognition of their bravery in speaking out. Seeing 140 women take to the stage to receive the award was a powerful image of survival and strength.

Olympic gymnasts Aly Raisman and Simone Biles have continued to speak out and demand more. They want more transparency from USAG and wholesale changes within the entire system to ensure the safety of gymnasts in the future. They believe USAG's bankruptcy filing and its proposed $215 million settlement are just USAG's attempt to hide from further public scrutiny, delay justice to the victims, and make the whole mess go away. The emboldened voices of the more than 500 athletes who have sued USAG are not going to let that happen.

Aside from the collective voice of female athletes, perhaps one of the most powerful singular voices in women's sport today is Serena Williams. Together with her older sister, Venus, she has transformed women's tennis with her athleticism and strength and paved the way for other women of color in sports in general. It was Venus who was instrumental in getting equal pay for female winners at Wimbledon in 2007, and she continues to encourage women, in all spheres of society, to believe in themselves and to ignore limitations that may be placed on them by others. Meanwhile, throughout her career, Serena has advocated for women's rights and equality, not shying away from calling out discrimination in tennis. She has spoken out against double standards in sports, the gender pay gap, sexist remarks, racial discrimination, and also body shaming. While Serena acknowledges the great strides that have been made across sports, she realizes that there is still so much more to be done. With her legion of fans and a huge following on social media (11 million on Twitter and 12.2 million on Instagram), Serena is a force to be reckoned with, and when she speaks, the world takes notice.

In the world of athlete activists, 2019 belonged to soccer star Megan Rapinoe. As co-captain of the U.S. Women's National Soccer team, she was instrumental in her team's win at the 2019 FIFA World Cup, but this is a small part of what got the world's attention. She is a confident and highly eloquent speaker on a range of causes, so much so that she has even been described as this generation's Mohammed Ali. The World Cup win only served to catapult her from soccer star to global activist for women's rights and LGBTQ issues.

After the World Cup victory, Rapinoe and her teammates sued the U.S. Soccer Federation over unequal working conditions and pay for female athletes. Overall, the public has been hugely supportive of the team and, wherever they go, they are greeted with chants of "U-S-A! Equal pay!" Their protest resulted in the federation agreeing to a mediation process to implement future changes. However, they still appear to be dragging their heels on the issue of equal pay.

Around the world, spurred on by Rapinoe, other women's teams have found their voices too, also demanding to be paid more in line with their male counterparts. In Nigeria, women soccer players held a sit-in at their hotel to demand unpaid salaries, Ireland's female soccer players threatened to strike, Australia did so, and Norway signed an equal pay agreement.

Rapinoe describes herself as a "walking protest," and being in the public eye for her controversial statements is not new territory for her. She was one of the first white professional athletes to show solidarity with Kaepernick and the first to do so on an international stage, which helped to turn a ripple of discontent into a wave that swept the entire country. She has also been an outspoken advocate for LGBTQ rights. She is adamant that gay relationships need to be normalized. She is fearlessly open and honest about her sexuality and her lesbian relationship with Sue Bird of the WNBA's Seattle Storms despite concerns of fan fallout and endorsements drying up, none of which has materialized. They were the first openly gay couple to appear on the cover of ESPN Magazine's Body Issue.

Looking back on 2019, Rapinoe is quick to say that the World Cup win was not nearly as rewarding for her as the way her team was able to transcend sport and use their platform to address inequalities on and off the field. Her recognition as the Sports Illustrated Sportsperson of the Year, only the fourth woman to win the award unaccompanied in more than six decades, is indicative of her influence.

Athletes as environmentalists

It is not only around issues of social justice that athletes advocate for; they are also starting to become influential agents of change concerning environmental issues too. There is an intrinsic link between sport and climate change, with many athletes seeing its impact firsthand whether on the ice or in the ocean or seeing the huge amounts of plastic waste left behind after an event. For this reason, there is an increasing number of athletes stepping up and spreading awareness of the impacts of climate change and pollution and encouraging others to do more to protect the environment. The long-distance swimmer, Lewis Pugh, is one notable athlete in this space. He undertakes grueling swims in vulnerable eco-systems to highlight their plight. Then there is basketball player Lauri Markkanen, who has pledged to stop eating red meat to minimize his carbon footprint, and tennis player Kevin Anderson, who has pushed for reusable water bottles and a reduction in single-use plastic on the ATP Tour and supports the Trash Free Seas program to fight ocean pollution.

R.I.P. Kobe Bryant

As we ushered in the new year, the world was given another taste of the place athletes hold in society. The public reaction to the untimely and tragic death of Kobe Bryant, in January 2020, was a glaring reminder of the immense power and influence that today's athletes possess.

Bryant enjoyed a hugely successful 20-year career with the LA Lakers. However, his appeal transcended sport—he was loved and admired as an athlete, a leader, a successful businessman, and a committed family man. After retiring in 2016, he was still very much in the public eye, and the widespread outpouring of grief at his death was immense and unlike anything seen before in sports. People from all walks of life and all corners of the world were devastated. Fellow players, like Michael Jordan, LeBron James, and Shaquille O'Neal, were visibly shattered by the news, with Jordan saying he had lost a brother. Across the league, players paid tribute to him, and teams observed moments of silence before games. Madison Square Garden changed its colors to the Laker's yellow and purple, and Staples Center, home of the LA Lakers, became a central place of mourning for fans with thousands leaving flowers, basketballs, and emotional messages.

Fans admired Kobe Bryant for his competitiveness, work ethic, and determination on the court. However, it was his understanding of his capacity to speak on behalf of the voiceless that made him relatable and gained him even more followers. He cared deeply, particularly about youth sports as a tool for human development. He understood the value of sports as a vehicle for change and his role as a global icon in this, using his social network, his international reach, and his credibility to change the world. Bryant's death, and the outpouring of emotion from the public that it elicited, reinforces the space that he and other athletes of his caliber hold in popular culture today. People look up to and take the lead from athletes, which puts them in a commanding position to use their influence with care and impact. Bryant instinctively knew this, which makes his untimely death even more of a tragedy.

Athlete activism takes center stage

Sport has always been a microcosm of society, but athletes have never been as willing as they are now to have a say in how that society is shaped and how sports are governed. Whether as a group or individually, the last few years have seen a marked upswing in athletes using their voices to hold sports authorities to account and to fight for an array of issues.

Social media has changed the landscape for athletes, particularly around social justice movements. It is a powerful tool to bring about solidarity and means that an athlete who speaks out never has to be alone.

With their millions of social media followers, athletes have the power and the support base behind them to shape the narrative, and this is the real difference between the athlete activists of today and those of a few decades ago.

Sports leagues, federations, and governing bodies have been forced to be more open and accepting of athletes voicing their opinions and taking protest action. It has also made corporates revisit their endorsement relationships with athletes. Brands are wanting to attach themselves to athletes whose values and opinions resonate with the person in the street. Simply put, it is no longer *whom* an athlete represents that is important but rather *what* they stand for and what issues they are committed to supporting.

Athletes take their role as activists seriously too. They believe they must use their platform to better society and are particular about the issues they choose to speak out on, ensuring that, in doing so, they are knowledgeable, articulate, authentic, and honest. They know that real change comes from hard work and rational advocacy, not emotional self-indulgence, and they will not be silenced.

KEY INSIGHTS: ATHLETES CONTINUE TO SHAPE THE NARRATIVE

➤ Sport has always been a microcosm of society, reflecting the values of the day and shining a light on what matters most to people at a given point in time.

➤ Sport has the unique ability to inspire and unite people in a way that little else does, and athletes are at the center of that. They command attention. A clear, intentional statement or act of protest by an athlete can be a powerful way to raise awareness, stimulate conversation, and fast track change.

➤ Over time, we have seen three eras of athlete activism. The 1960s and 1970s saw several athletes using their position of influence to draw attention to the issues of the day, often with harsh and lasting consequences. Iconic activists from this era include John Carlos and Tommy Smith, Mohammed Ali, Arthur Ashe, and Billie Jean King.

➤ By the 1980s and 1990s, athletes had become much more commercially focused, and the emphasis shifted to being more about building their brand and maximizing their earning potential through product endorsements, branded merchandise, and the like. It was an era focused on the self, and no athlete encapsulates this era better than NBA legend Michael Jordan.

➤ The 2000s have seen a re-emergence of athletes using their influence to advocate for change, with the biggest influencers being athletes such as Colin Kaepernick, LeBron James, Serena Williams, and Megan Rapinoe.

➤ Social media has changed the landscape for athletes, particularly around social justice movements. With their millions of social media followers, athletes have the power and the support base behind them to shape the narrative; this is the real difference between the athlete activists of today and those of a few decades ago.

LEADING THOUGHTS:
ATHLETES WITH A PURPOSE

LISA ZIMOUCHE   Freestyle soccer star and women's empowerment activist

LISA IS ONE OF AN EXCITING GROUP OF YOUNG FEMALE ATHLETES WHO USES HER PLATFORM TO PUSH FOR GENDER EQUALITY. SHE IS DESCRIBED BY ESPNW AS "ONE OF THE MOST VISIBLE AND INFLUENTIAL TALISMANS IN SOCCER'S FREESTYLE SUBCULTURE."

On her role as an activist and how she wants to make a positive difference:
I think I have been an activist all my life—being in the freestyle industry as the only woman; you have to be an activist. Right now, I want to do more to have a real impact on people, not just share my videos. They have had a big impact over the years, but I want to be out there interacting with young boys and girls, about equality. I want to travel the world and share my experience.

On her mission:
My mission is to work on gender equality, to show that women and men can do the same thing. Having this time at home now because of the coronavirus has given me time to reflect and think about my future and what I can do that will have a real impact. The virus has highlighted for everyone what matters, and it has made me even more determined to focus on what my true Purpose in life is. It is about more than just being famous on social media and getting millions of likes and millions of followers. We must use the time to make a positive difference.

On other activists that she admires and would like to meet:
Serena Williams definitely, she is breaking the rules all the time in tennis. Watching her career over the years, as a black woman in tennis, has been so inspiring for me. Then there are artists like Beyoncé, whose whole career has been inspiring, her work ethic and how she built her independence. I also recently met Ibtihaj

Muhammad, the first Muslim-American athlete to win a medal at the Olympics. She is unbelievable and has done so many things for female athletes and Muslims.

On the progress in sport regarding gender equality:
I think there has been progress, especially in soccer and freestyle sport. If I look back at when I started playing in 2007, people would say I did not belong, but now I see so many women being true to themselves and doing whatever they want to do in soccer and freestyle. In general, there has been huge progress, but there is still a lot more to do. All women athletes must put in the effort, show the progress, and not let the boys make choices for us.

On her vision for gender equality in sports in ten years:
I hope that in ten years, we see that even bigger changes have taken place; that people won't see any differences between girls and boys and that we have fans in stadiums for women's leagues. I hope to see big changes.

KEVIN ANDERSON

Professional tennis player and environmentalist—
US Open and Wimbledon Finalist and
former ATP Top 10 Ranked Player.

KEVIN IS A FIRM BELIEVER THAT LEADING TENNIS PLAYERS HAVE AN IMPORTANT ROLE TO PLAY IN SETTING EXAMPLES AND BEING POSITIVE ROLE MODELS FOR FUTURE GENERATIONS.

On how Purpose became part of his life:
By nature, I have always had a desire to help where I can. Tennis is so focused on the individual, which is necessary to excel and improve on the court. However, a few years ago, I felt I needed to use the platform I had built in the tennis world to do good. I identified a few causes that were meaningful to me—an animal shelter in Delray Beach in Florida where we live, a program called First Serve, also in Florida, and Ocean Conservancy.

On his efforts to stop the use of single-use plastic:
From a personal perspective, I consider myself to be fairly environmentally aware. However, I remember, during the French Open a few years ago, watching a

documentary about plastic pollution in the ocean, and it was a real eye-opener and got me thinking that tennis could be a platform to get the message out. Initially, I thought it was something that could be changed quite easily, but you soon realize that it is not that simple. The world is hugely dependent on single-use plastic, so adopting the mindset that every little bit helps is the way to go because reducing it, even just a little bit, is a step in the right direction. From a Tour level, I have worked with the ATP to see how we can make a difference, and changes have been implemented, but hopefully, in time, we will see even more meaningful reforms. From a personal perspective, I support Trash Free Seas, a program with Ocean Conservancy that focuses on single-use plastics and rooting out plastic from the ocean. It has been exciting to see what they have achieved so far and the impact they have had, and, for me, it will be a lifetime initiative.

On whether the ATP and the players are doing enough:
Up until the last few years, we probably were not doing enough, which is unfortunate, but realizing that we can do more is the first step, and there has been a lot more happening lately. The ATP Finals in London is often a testing ground for new initiatives and is used as a springboard to get other tournaments onboard. (The event has tested things like reusable cups, water coolers instead of single-use water bottles for fans, and reusable bottles for on-court soft drinks for the players.) The players have taken the message to heart on their own, and hopefully, we can bring that passion, awareness, and care together to have a more profound impact over time.

On the process of choosing what causes to support and whether it is better to focus on a few or to be widespread:
There are many needs and many great initiatives to support. I have always tried to give as much of my time as I can because there is value in it for me too. Being on the Tour exposes you to a lot of different issues where we can offer our support and help, and I think that, if time allows, it is important to do it. Even if it is not your sole focus, you can make a difference. Many of the Tour players are happy to give up their time in support of other player's causes and foundations. Hence, many players are giving back, and the Foundations of Nadal, Djokovic, and Federer do a lot, which is inspiring for the rest of the players on the Tour.

On engaging with fans to get the message out:

Raising awareness amongst fans can make the biggest difference. Reducing plastic waste onsite at events is good, but getting fans on board will be even more impactful. For the most part, reaching out to fans and talking about these issues on social media is easy because people want to help, particularly around the plastics issue. It can have a unifying effect, too, which is positive.

THE OLYMPIC MOVEMENT
FROM LOS ANGELES AND BACK AGAIN

The first modern Olympic Games can be traced back to 1896 in Athens, Greece, thanks to the somewhat eccentric Frenchman, Baron Pierre de Coubertin, who saw sport as a way of bridging cultures and building a better world. He believed that a multi-sport event with participating athletes from different countries would promote the ideals of physical, mental, and spiritual excellence along with courage, endurance, tolerance, and a sense of fair play. Over a period of 125 years, the Olympic Games went from being a small fry oddity to a phenomenon of sport and entertainment, a publicity machine, and a project of an almost incomprehensible scale and complexity. Bar cancellations due to the two World Wars and COVID-19, the Olympic Games have been held every four years since 1896, and despite many challenges along the way, the Olympic spirit lives on, placing sport at the service of humanity.

The Olympic Games has a long and storied history. In the age of sport as entertainment in which we now live, where everything has to be a spectacle, capturing views, shares, likes, follows, eyeballs, and ultimately dollars and cents, this kind of event is only going to have more at stake. Alongside the FIFA World Cup, Euro Football Championships, Asian Games, and Commonwealth Games, the Olympics is considered a mega-event and is probably the largest of them all. With size and stakes comes complexity and complications and thus more challenges. But the

Olympic Movement has never shied away from a challenge. It has weathered two World Wars, terrorism, boycotts, and the implications of affairs of state as well as allegations of corruption, opaqueness, elitism, and human rights abuses. There are also many cautionary tales related to the staging of the event, including bankrupting economies, paving the way for a substantial debt crisis, displacement of people and communities, misuse of public funds, and the perception of wastefulness—building infrastructures at high public cost for an event that lasts only sixteen days, but whose aftershocks are felt thirty years after the fact.

Indeed, in the late 1970s, when the International Olympic Committee (IOC) was searching for a host for the 1984 Games, they faced the situation of zero candidate cities. The huge cost overruns at the 1976 Montreal Olympics that left the city with a debt of $1.5 billion, a string of corruption scandals, and a lot of disgruntled residents had made potential host cities wary of bidding. To secure Los Angeles as the eventual host for the 1984 event, the IOC essentially had to throw out their old rulebook and agree to allow the Americans to run the Games their way.

The start of a new era of Olympic marketing

1984 turned out to be an interesting case in that it marked the arrival of big business to the Olympic Movement for the first time. With no commitment of funding from President Reagan's Federal Government at the time of attribution, Organizing Committee (OCOG) President, Peter Ueberroth, set about selling everything. The financial and critical success of the event, despite the boycott by many of the Eastern Bloc countries such as the Soviet Union, East Germany, and Bulgaria, paved the way for a new model of Olympic Games revenue raising. Ueberroth negotiated a $225 million television deal with ABC, the biggest broadcast rights deal in history, and secured the backing of corporate sponsors to the tune of $123 million. The sponsorship program at the 1984 Games became a model for future editions of the event. It also influenced the development of the IOC's TOP Program, which has been a significant revenue generator for the IOC. Rather than accepting a wide variety of sponsors, suppliers, and licensees, the Los Angeles OCOG strictly limited the number of companies who were granted an "official" sponsor or supplier status. Sponsors were required to make much larger contributions, in money or value-in-kind, than in previous years; in return, their exclusive association with the Olympic Movement was guaranteed. As a result of low construction costs, corporate funding, and a lucrative broadcast deal, Los Angeles 1984 generated a profit of $250 million. Following the event, the LA84 Foundation was created to promote youth sports in Southern California, educate coaches, and maintain a sports library using the profits from the event.

Proving that the Olympic Games could be profitable and returning it to some of the cultural foundations espoused by de Coubertin was a big success of the 1984 Games for the IOC. The appetite for hosting was reignited, and for the next 20 years, the number of bids—which had the potential to cost the bid city somewhere between $50 and $100 million without the guarantee of any supported economic "return" that could come with being the successful bidder—gained momentum. For the 2004 edition, ultimately hosted by Athens once more, a total of eleven candidatures passed through a three-round voting process. The following Olympiad saw Beijing triumph over no less than nine other bids while London beat seven other bids for the right to host the 2012 Summer Games.

The events during this time were characterized by excessive commercialism and an almost boastful show of political and economic will rather than a celebration of the "Olympic spirit." The event became a way of rebranding a city and turning the world's attention towards its beliefs and triumphs in an environment where cities could control the narrative. Although the IOC benefited enormously from a financial perspective, it came to be regarded as a monolith of wealth that had lost touch with its soul and humanitarian purpose. Furthermore, the onset of social media meant that controlling the narrative became more difficult for host cities as the public began to speak out.

All that glitters is not gold

And so, the narrative began to shift once more. As evidence from the success of LA84 had encouraged cities to believe in the benefits of hosting, eventually, word began to get around about the pitfalls. A number of problems hampered the Athens Games. There were issues in delivering the project, e.g., only half the venues were ready five months before the event. The empty stands throughout the competitions suggested a lack of public engagement and the high cost of hosting and high public expenditure contributed to the subsequent macroeconomic crisis that has plagued the country for the past ten years. Like Athens, where purpose-built venues fell into disrepair and struggled to attract tenants and patrons, Beijing suffered the post-event white elephant headache. London, lauded for the urban regeneration of East London in the development of the Queen Elizabeth Olympic Park, spent far above its initial budget to get the job done and has been criticized by some for displacing communities. London already faced costly conversion projects to repurpose the infrastructure put in place for the Games, and its much-lauded spending on grassroots sports participation amounted to zero impact five years on from the event.

And, this is just the Summer Games. The budget for the 2014 Winter Olympic Games in Sochi went above 500% of the initial project, and, in addition to white elephant syndrome, faced criticism for environmental degradation and human rights abuses. In a similar vein, Rio 2016 displaced both people, with the destruction of favelas, species of animals, and vegetation for the construction of the golf course that the city certainly did not need—and has also seen its purpose-built venues fall into disrepair. Suddenly the prospect of hosting a sixteen-day party with few obvious rewards for the host city is viewed in a much more sober light.

For the awarding of the 2024 Olympic Games, the IOC had only two bids. The rest had been defeated by the weight of public opinion, through either a formal referendum or just having a successful anti-hosting campaign. Only Paris and Los Angeles remained, the latter having stepped in when the No Boston Olympics campaign successfully killed off the initial American host city nominee. Presented with two ostensibly sound and reasonable bids reflecting the IOC's renewed focus on Games legacy and sustainability that was brought in as part of their 2020 Agenda, the committee took the unprecedented step of awarding the Games for two consecutive Olympics at once.

Not only did this decision save the IOC from having to drum up interest in hosting in just a couple of years, but it also ensured that everyone went home a winner. Bids can be incredibly costly. In years gone by, cities have pulled out all the stops to secure themselves a win. London flew David Beckham and Tony Blair to Singapore to glad-hand all of the voting members of the IOC. London's masterstroke is sometimes cited as the reason behind London's successful campaign for 2012, where Paris had long been the favorite. There can only be one winner. In Singapore, in 2005, Paris was not the only bid that left feeling disappointed; Moscow, Madrid, and New York also walked away out of pocket and empty-handed.

This point is key, although the IOC overlooked it for years. Bidding costs too much money, and only one team comes away with the win. Even if a city does "win," the benefits of hosting are not a given. For projects of the size, scale, and complexity as the Olympic Games, it takes good planning, management, sponsors, and a fair dose of luck to deliver the rewards envisaged at the beginning.

Back to its Olympic roots

That a change was required was evident to the IOC and, following the 126th IOC Session in Sochi in 2014, they convened working groups to tackle the most urgent strategic issues facing the movement. Their efforts identified fourteen key issues under five general pillars with one working group per key point. The working groups consolidated their proposals and, together with submissions from stakeholders within the Olympic Movement, various independent organizations, academics, NGOs, and businesses; Agenda 2020 was born. It was named both for its delivery date and for the 20 + 20 recommendations it produced to shape the future of the Olympic Movement. Ultimately, Agenda 2020 seeks to safeguard the uniqueness of the Games and strengthen the role of sport in society so that the Olympics continues to remain relevant in a rapidly changing world.

Pillar number one, "The Uniqueness of the Olympic Games," addressed bidding procedures, sustainability and legacy, the composition of the Olympic Program, and program management. The result of this work addressed efficiencies and processes, transparency, cost management and cost obligations, sustainability efforts and behaviors, and putting legacy at the center of all hosting activities as key objectives for the Olympic movement.

In February 2018, the IOC adopted the New Norm Initiative, which supplemented Agenda 2020, specifically regarding the organizing and hosting of the Games. The plan put forward more than 100 revisions to the requirements and obligations of the hosting committee designed to reduce the cost of hosting with an emphasis on making the Games affordable, beneficial, and sustainable. It also stressed collaboration, whereby the IOC and its key stakeholders—sponsors, International Federations, National Olympic Committees, and broadcasters—will work in partnership with the organizing committees to ensure this vision is upheld.

Then in June 2019, further changes to the bidding process, including the required revisions to the Olympic Charter, were voted in at the 134th IOC session in Lausanne, Switzerland. This overhaul removes from the Charter the requirement that host cities are elected seven years in advance, abolishes the Evaluation Commission, which is the IOC body responsible for evaluating and reporting on the validity of a bid city's submission, in favor of a Future Hosts Commission. The new commission's mandate is to work with interested cities or regions for as long as deemed necessary to prepare them for eventual nomination as a host at a future IOC session. This change allows cities to be mentored to the point of being equipped to host the Games. It also allows the IOC to ensure that their hosting partners have the right objectives in mind and that their reasons for hosting are aligned with the IOC's own wish to see the Games as affordable, beneficial, and sustainable.

The hosting rights for the Olympic Games have long been awarded specifically to a city, with the Charter specifying that the host city stage all events within its bounds, except in extenuating circumstances. Agenda 2020 relaxes this limitation to allow for events to take place in a city (or cities) outside the host city, notably for reasons of sustainability. In 2019, the Olympic Charter was amended to reflect this. Candidatures from multiple cities, regions, or countries will also be accepted, and the Host City Contract is now called the Host Contract.

The IOC has also specified that, wherever possible, hosts should make use of as much existing or temporary infrastructure as possible. Bids containing plans for new venues and significant construction work should demonstrate a realistic and relevant use of this infrastructure by the host post-Games. Hosts should recognize the need for the Olympic Movement to distance itself from the much-criticized white elephant syndrome synonymous with so many of its events in the past.

Now that the promise of the kind of urban redevelopment and access to sporting facilities that the construction of the Olympic Parks seen in the likes of former hosts Sydney, Athens, Beijing, London, and Rio de Janeiro is no longer on the table, what other motivations exist for cities to host? And how does the IOC sell this idea to their market to ensure that the Games continue? The answer, lurking in the shadows since the mid-fifties, but only recently the buzzword of the Olympic Movement, is Legacy.

Legacy has always mattered to the Olympic Movement in that creating long term benefits for people and cities is tied to the Movement's vision of "building a better world through sport." Despite dating as far back as the foundation of the modern Games, the term legacy was only first associated with the Olympics in 1956 as part of the Melbourne Games. Over time legacy was invoked but was still not a focus nor an obligation of host cities and nor was it a concern for the IOC. It was only from 2000 onwards that the IOC required legacy planning as part of any host city bid, but, even then, it was still not given much thought or commitment. London 2012 was the first Organizing Committee to take particular care in developing and implementing their legacy plan before the staging of their event.

Following the adoption of Agenda 2020, the IOC relabeled its Sport and Environment Commission as the Sustainability and Legacy

Commission and, at the end of 2017, published their Legacy Strategic Approach wherein the Olympic Legacy is defined as ". . . the result of a vision. It encompasses all the tangible and intangible long-term benefits initiated or accelerated by the hosting of the Olympic Games/sports events for people, cities/territories, and the Olympic Movement."

The Legacy Strategic Approach used the UN Sustainable Development Goals as a framework for its objectives with regards to legacy building around the Olympic Games. It established four objectives, namely to embed legacy through the Olympic Games lifecycle; document, analyze, and communicate the legacy of the Olympic Games; encourage Olympic legacy celebration; and build strategic partnerships.

It also highlighted several dimensions through which the scope of Olympic legacy could be framed, namely: organized sport development, social development through sport, social skills, networks and innovation, culture and creative development, urban development, environmental enhancement, economic value, and brand equity.

The idea is that host cities can leverage the booster effect of the Games, the engagement with sponsors, and the chance to engage with their citizens, to make progress on several challenges in both the physical, built sphere and the social sphere. Hosting the Games gives cities the chance to inspire its citizens to engage with Olympic sport, to develop participation in sports at both elite and amateur levels, for performance or health-related reasons. Sport can also be used to draw attention to broader issues; for example, using volunteering opportunities as skill enhancement for future jobs, building expertise and know-how when it comes to staging major events or sporting fixtures, or encouraging the spirit of volunteerism among sporting and social pursuits. Other issues that can be addressed using sport as a vehicle are: improving inclusiveness and social interconnectedness among and between citizens, for immigrants and refugees, and those in precarious social situations living with an impairment.

Then there is also the legacy of urban development, cleaning up soil and wasteland, redeveloping derelict or under-utilized land, and repurposing or refurbishing existing but aging infrastructure and putting it to the service of the general public. There is also the economic legacy of giving local businesses a boost via increased patronage and the opportunity to be a supplier for the OCOGs vast procurement needs and giving the city itself a chance to showcase its wares to encourage local and foreign investment, tourism, and perhaps even skilled migration. Finally, the IOC focuses on educational strategy, using sport as a pedagogical tool on the sharing of the Values of Olympism, to improve academic outcomes, literacy, attendance as well as tolerance, diversity, and inclusive communities. The aim of the IOC framework is for the OCOG to align their strategy with the areas that are the most pertinent to them, considering their needs and capacities, and aligning them with their social climate, citizen priorities, and developmental projects. It is important that such priorities exist outside of hosting the Games and that hosting the Games serves the broader needs.

The fact that there were just two willing participant cities bidding for the right to host the 2024 Olympic Games suggests that the impact of Agenda 2020 is still to be felt. The stakes for the upcoming Olympic Games, in Paris 2024 and Los Angeles 2028, are high as these will be the first events held in full accordance with Agenda 2020. Now, more than ever, the host cities, together with the IOC, need to do a better job of managing their legacy to ensure the long-term sustainability of the Games, both from an environmental and economic standpoint. If they remain the domain of the powerful elite, the Games will struggle to deflect the potent visual evidence that suggests they serve little else but the IOC and the sponsors. Note that the host cities themselves are not a party to that category.

The London 2012 Organizing Committee instigated a long-term legacy plan to span 2008 through to 2014, and it is interesting to measure where things stand. In addition to the expenditure on the infrastructure and staging of the event, the organizing committee allocated £3.8 billion in additional funds towards their legacy program. More than five years down the road, a study by the University of Colorado's Spencer Harris suggests that this investment may not be reaping the rewards it promised. Growing grassroots participation in sport was a pillar of focus and finance from the LOCOG Legacy expenditure. Yet, data from a Sport England survey suggests participation has been flat over the period of the £1.7 billion investment. Given the amount of money allocated to this function, this result is somewhat alarming. Whether this is due to the strategy itself or its implementation is unclear but should be of concern to the organizers of Paris 2024. Paris has allocated $2.3 million to its legacy programs; however, unlike London, this makes up part of their overall $4.1 billion budget.

The Olympic movement setting a new bar

The Paris 2024 legacy plan covers three areas of impact—economic, social, and environmental. The economic legacy is built around the development of critical Olympic facilities in the Seine-Saint-Denis department. This area has a large population with a high proportion of youth aged 18-25 who are cut off from employment opportunities. It is believed that building the Olympic infrastructure in this space will impact many economic sectors, involve a multitude of contractors, and inject new life into the area. From a social perspective, the Paris 2024 team has proposed two projects. The first will develop youth civic engagement by incorporating Olympic values and themes in school and university curricula, and the second hopes to stimulate a culture of volunteerism beyond the Games that will see Paris 2024 volunteers becoming involved in a sports club or federation.

The Games also hopes to increase regular participation in sport by promoting the positive health benefits of sport through the media and improving the accessibility of sporting facilities across the country. The environmental legacy will be felt through the acceleration of a more dense and modern transport system, the lasting transformation of the Seine-Saint-Denis region with new housing units in an area where housing rarely meets demand, and through the Seine River clean up to accommodate the Olympic triathlon and open water swimming events. Also, the Olympic and Paralympic Village will be a model of sustainable development, including 100% bio-based materials, 100% green energy during the Games, 100% sustainable food sources, and 100% of the athletes and spectators using clean transportation during the Games.

Similarly, Los Angeles 2028 is building a legacy plan based on Agenda 2020's guidelines. They have promised a fiscally responsible, values-led Games that reconnects the Olympic Movement with its original Purpose of serving humanity through sport. Ninety-seven percent of the venues used in 2028 will be temporary or existing, leading to significant cost reductions as well as eliminating the risk of white elephant legacies after the Games. Los Angeles will also be the first "energy-positive" Games, meaning that more energy will be generated through renewable sources than is needed to power the Games. From a social perspective, Los Angeles 2028 has committed to investing $160 million in local youth sports in the decade leading up to the Games to advocate for greater participation in sport amongst the youth.

In March 2020, the IOC unveiled its climate-positive vision, which will require host cities to implement lasting zero-carbon solutions at the Games from 2030 onwards. It will no longer be sufficient to reduce and compensate for carbon emissions if the IOC is to achieve its goal of being at the forefront in the field of sustainability. The organization acknowledges that it will need to provide support to host cities to accomplish this goal. However, it is already encouraged by the efforts being made by upcoming hosts Tokyo and Paris, with the former showcasing hydrogen energy and the latter using 100% renewable energy during the event, not to mention LA's pledge to host an energy-positive Games. Then there is also the IOC's contribution to the Great Green Wall Project, the ambitious plan to plant an 8,000km forest of trees across the width of Africa to combat the effects of desertification. From 2021, the IOC will plant an Olympic forest in partnership with the UN Environment Program. As of 2020, thirteen years after the project was initiated, around 15% of the wall had been planted, so there is still a lot to be done.

There is a lot at stake for the IOC over the next decade and, in particular, 2024. Paris will be the first Games staged, having adhered fully to the recommendations of their 2020 Agenda. Should its legacy projects prove inadequate, it will be the IOC with egg on their face, and thus the pressure is on Paris to deliver for the IOC. The two parties' interests are tightly bound.

To ensure the long term future of the Olympic Games, the IOC needs to ensure that cities are still willing to accommodate them, that citizens can endorse the spending of public money on them, and that neither party is damaged from doing so. Any kind of sustainability program, or legacy program in Olympic parlance, needs to be implementable and measurable to be successful. It is critical for host cities to focus their energies specifically enough to make real gains rather than trying to be everything to everybody. They need to aim for profit without being overly commercial, and they must champion regeneration without incurring crippling debt. With so much money and power at stake, applying creativity and finding a better way to make success possible is of utmost importance. Paris has forecast breaking even with their $4.1 billion budget, and, should they succeed, it will be the least expensive Summer Games in terms of costs since Atlanta 1996 some 28 years earlier. Let's hope they succeed.

KEY INSIGHTS: OLYMPIC MOVEMENT RETURNS TO ITS ROOTS

➤ The modern Olympic movement is grounded in a philosophy of life espoused by Pierre de Coubertin in 1894 that places sport at the service of humanity.

➤ The movement became distracted from this philosophy during the 1980s and 1990s when its focus shifted, and it started to place money before humanity.

➤ The IOC's adoption in 2014 of Agenda 2020, its new strategic road map, saw the Olympic movement return to its roots to remain relevant in a rapidly changing world.

➤ Agenda 2020 sets out 40 recommendations aimed at safeguarding the uniqueness of the Olympic Games and strengthening sports' role in society. These recommendations have been transformational and set a new level of expectation for bidding cities that Paris 2024 and Los Angeles 2028 have both embraced and will set a new benchmark for the industry.

LEADING THOUGHTS:
OLYMPIC MOVEMENT ON PURPOSE

MARIE SALLOIS   Director Corporate & Sustainable Development at the IOC
TANIA BRAGA   Head of Legacy at the IOC

THE IOC LEADS THE WAY IN TERMS OF PUTTING SPORT AT THE SERVICE OF
HUMANITY AND THE PLANET.

On what legacy means to the IOC and why it is part of Agenda 2020:
Legacy is not a new concept for the Olympic movement. It is very closely linked to a
vision of building a better world through sport, and the Olympic Games aims to be
a catalyst for positive social change and innovation and an accelerator for urban
and regional development. The word legacy appeared in the Olympic Charter
for the first time in 2003, and that was not completely by coincidence. It was at
the same time as the candidature for the 2010 Olympic Games. The theme for
the Vancouver candidature file was Legacy Now, and the intention was to deliver
benefits to the local population in advance of the Games. Now, ten years on from
Vancouver, we've set new standards in terms of legacy, especially in education,
social inclusion, and the environment. 2015 was also another key milestone in the
Olympic Movement regarding legacy because we launched Agenda 2020 wherein,
we completely changed the approach to the organization of the event. We no
longer ask cities what they can do for the Games; we ask them what the Olympic
Games can do for them. We engage in dialogue with future hosts much earlier
to help clarify their vision and plans to deliver tangible and intangible long term
benefits to their city, its people, and the Olympic movement, and this is how we now
define legacy at the IOC.

On good examples of legacy programs that came out of Olympic Games events:
Vancouver 2010 is one of the best examples of a complete and thorough legacy
approach. It benefited the whole of British Columbia and involved dialogue with
communities in different cities to understand how the games could support and

accelerate social benefits that were a priority for them. That work has continued and has become a social venture that supports different associations and communities in sport, education, and literacy all over Canada.

Another interesting example, albeit an old one, is the Seoul 1988 Olympics. They used the surplus from the Games to create an organization called Korean KSPO Sport Agency, and this has grown to support all levels of sport and now funds 85% of the sport in Korea. It is also responsible for maintaining the Olympic Park, a place for people to gather for sport, culture, and relaxation.

On the extent to which the Legacy Program forms part of the IOC's value proposition to their corporate partners and any partners who have activated around legacy:

More and more of our commercial partners are looking for Purpose-led associations. Just looking at the Tokyo 2020 partners, they have played an important role in engaging with over 90 million Japanese citizens ahead of the Games. For example, Procter & Gamble organized a clean-up campaign at beaches and other places that collected enough used plastic waste to build the Olympic podiums. This Legacy Program has a huge impact on Japan and helps to raise awareness regarding sustainability and waste management globally.

On the IOC's achievements around sustainability:

Since 2015 and the launch of Agenda 2020, sustainability has been a priority across the entire Olympic movement. That does not mean we did not do anything before this, just that it has now been elevated to collective responsibility and is implemented more systematically. We have developed a sustainability strategy that helps to embed sustainability in everything we do. The IOC has to be a role model and leads through five key focus areas—infrastructure and natural sites, sourcing and resource management, mobility, workforce, and climate.

Looking specifically at what we have done, we have worked to reduce our carbon footprint. We are a carbon-neutral organization as we speak, and we are striving to become climate positive. Olympic House, our offices in Lausanne, is one of the most sustainable buildings in the world and has achieved several rigorous sustainability certifications, including the highest LEED Platinum score worldwide. We have a fleet of eight hydrogen cars and a temporary hydrogen fuelling station, the first in Switzerland, at our offices. Sustainability is also built into our procurement process, so a lot is going on at the IOC level, which is important to us for credibility when it comes to discussions with organizing committees and the wider Olympic movement.

The Olympic Games are our most visible platform, so we work hand-in-hand with the organizing committees to make sure we maximize impact in that respect. We have reinforced our sustainability commitments in our Host City contracts and the operational requirements related to the Games. However, we have also increased our support to the organizing committees by providing much more expertise through partnerships we have with the International Union for Conservation of Nature (IUCN), the United Nations Environment Program (UNEP), and the International Labor Organization (ILO). We are setting the bar quite high as we now ask that, starting from 2030, the Olympic Games must be climate positive.

On building collaborations across sport and society outside of the actual Games themselves:

We have huge convening power. If you take into account all the Federations, National Olympic Committees, and athletes, we have a huge impact beyond the Games, which are only visible every two years. We try to join forces and support some of the initiatives that are in line with our strategy. For example, as part of the UN Clean Seas initiative, we are working to address plastic pollution. We also support the Big Plastic Pledge, which is a global campaign, led by the Olympic Champion in sailing Hannah Millsto, to unite athletes and fans around plastic pollution. We have the Sport for Climate Change Framework, which is bringing the sports community together to help address climate change. When we come together as a movement, we have a huge impact.

On what the next ten years hold for the IOC in terms of legacy and sustainability:

We expect to see more ambition and flexibility. Ambition, in the sense that we can expand the benefits well beyond the seven-year preparation for the Games and that many legacy initiatives will last for decades after the Games. Ideally, we would like to be more impactful and long-lasting through a cohesive approach with different hosts of previous Games working together in programs around youth and sport. Also, the key for the future is flexibility, to continue to adapt the Olympic Games to the needs of the host city and the changing needs of society.

On the important connection between sport and the SDGs:
If you look at the Purpose of the Olympic movement and the Games, four SDGs are in the DNA of what we do—those related to health and the health benefits of sport, gender equality, sustainability, and peace. Through the work we are doing in sustainability and legacy, we can broaden our contribution to other SDGs as well and thereby align the work we do with the bigger goals of humanity.

On the IOC's message to sport with regards to sustainability and Purpose:
I would say sustainability and legacy are no longer a choice for many industries, and sport is no exception. With its global reach and universal appeal, sport has a unique power and a huge responsibility to raise public awareness and help the world to do its share of the work to address some of today's critical sustainability challenges.

CHAPTER 7

STORIES FROM THE FRONTLINE OF PURPOSE AND SPORT

On the whole, the business of sport has been slow to adopt the move towards Purpose that has been underway across the corporate sector for the past 20 years. This lethargy is a shame considering the incredible power of sport to engage with a far-reaching fan base, capture their attention, educate them, and shift perspectives. However, there are some excellent examples of forward-thinking individuals, sports properties, organizing committees, host cities, and sponsors that have embraced the opportunity to use Purpose as a key organizing principle. In this chapter, we will share some of these with you, demonstrating that doing good while doing well can work equally well as an operating principle in the business of sport as it does in the corporate sector.

Sport has the power to change the world

The 1995 Rugby World Cup in South Africa is a defining moment in the world of Purposeful sport, largely thanks to the genius of one man, Nelson Mandela. It was possibly the first time that an individual had harnessed the power of sport at an individual country level for the common good of society on such a grand scale. Only a year after the country's first multiracial democratic election, South Africa hosted the global tournament, and Mandela, ever the statesman and visionary, seized this opportunity to bring hope and unity to the once divided nation of South Africa. Fans are fanatical in their support of rugby in South Africa, but, at the time, rugby was seen as a symbol of apartheid, the white man's game. Many of the Indigenous Africans in the country went so far as to support New Zealand's All Blacks rather than South Africa's national team. Furthermore, there was pressure to abandon the team's despised emblem, the Springbok. However, Mandela resisted and managed to leverage the country's passion for sports, to rally the country around the team, knowing that hosting and then winning the Rugby World Cup would unify and heal the divided people of South Africa as nothing else could.

Having returned to international sport only in 1992, the Springboks had played very few international test matches. Yet, during the six-week tournament, they played magnificent rugby inspired by their President and the growing momentum of support from local fans of all race groups. The Springboks opened the tournament by beating the Wallabies (Australia's national team and the tournament favorite), swept through the pool games, then beat Western Samoa and France to advance to a showdown against the All Blacks in the Final. Against all the odds, they won in a nail-biting final that needed extra time to decide on a victor. The final took place in a stadium of 63,000 people, most of whom were white. In a genius move, Mandela arrived dressed in the green-and-gold team jersey and cap, with the once despised Springbok emblem on his chest and the captain's number 6 on his back. He was greeted to tumultuous applause and loud chants of "Nelson, Nelson" and, when he presented the Webb Ellis trophy to the winning captain, Francois Pienaar, the whole country erupted with joy. That image, together with Pienaar's memorable response that the win was for all forty-three million South Africans and not just those in the stadium, is etched in the memory of rugby fans around the world. Spearheaded by Mandela's visionary leadership, the Springbok performance had changed South Africa forever and set the country on the path to meaningful reconciliation.

Off the back of Mandela's masterstroke at the Rugby World Cup, he persuaded prominent South African businessman, Johann Rupert, to create the Laureus World Sports Awards, which celebrated the power of sport. Mandela gave the speech at the inaugural awards in 2000, where he reiterated his message that sport has the power to change the world and encouraged the world's sporting community to take up the challenge. So, the Laureus Sport for Good Foundation was conceived and now supports more than 200 programs in over 40 countries. The Foundation uses sport to help children and young people overcome violence, discrimination, and disadvantage in their lives. Over the last 20 years, Laureus has raised more than $160 million and has helped to change the lives of almost six million young people. It truly is a remarkable organization harnessing the power of sport to create meaningful change. You can read more about Laureus and other Sport for Good organizations in Chapter 8.

It seemed appropriate that nearly 25 years after South Africa's first Rugby World Cup win, it was the Springboks who again lifted the Webb Ellis trophy led by South Africa's first-ever black captain, Siya Kolisi. The Springboks were never expected to win, but, as if ordained by the gods, they reached the Final and pulled off a memorable victory against the favorites, England. The Springbok win provided a much-needed morale boost for a nation plagued by challenges in the last decade. Siya's story, of a once hungry township boy who, through rugby, had transformed his life to become a shining symbol of the country's pride and belief that anything is possible if you work together, was one that resonated with many. Focusing on the pressures faced by many South Africans in their daily lives, the team chose to see their playing rugby as a privilege, something that creates hope, and it worked, with the team ending the tournament with an emphatic 32-12 winning score in the Final.

Siya's story is special and will no doubt inspire a new generation of rugby players and the achievement of dreams outside of sport as well. He has transcended rugby and, from his perspective, is relishing his responsibility as a role model. He is using the World Cup win as a springboard to help impoverished kids in communities across South Africa, particularly those in his hometown of Zwide, so that kids grow up with better learning opportunities and chances to succeed. He has admitted that, in 1995, he was too young to fully appreciate Mandela's words that sport has the power to unite a nation. However, he attests to having now felt it firsthand

and is committed to keeping the inspiration alive. He repeatedly tells the story of the diverse team that he leads—one made up of men from vastly different backgrounds and with vastly different challenges but who are united behind one goal. He urges his beloved country to adopt the same attitude—to look beyond the country's challenges and work towards a better future together. In an interview after the Springbok's win, he made the following comment which sums up the measure of the man that he is and highlights his grasp of the role he can play using sport to promote change, "I can win the World Cup as the first black test captain, but there will be another. To be remembered for all the things that you do and as someone who makes people smile, touches people's lives, that is what should wake you up every single morning."

The Greening of Sport Finds Wings

But let us return to the early 2000s when we began to see the next big move in the sport for good space under the guidance of American environmental scientist Allen Hershkowitz. Hershkowitz worked at the Natural Resource Defence Council (NRDC), one of America's largest environmental advocacy groups. The NRDC needed a far-reaching platform to spread their environmental message, and, on the recommendation of a board member, Robert Redford, Hershkowitz looked to the world of sport. This change of direction turned out to be an inspired move and was the start of Hershkowitz's long and successful role as one of the leading environmental sustainability experts in sport, starting with The Sports Greening Initiative and later the Green Sports Alliance, which he led until 2016.

The NFL's Philadelphia Eagles were one of the first sports teams Hershkowitz worked with, transforming them into one of the greenest clubs in sport. He used newsworthy hooks to shift perceptions around climate change and to educate ordinary people about what they could do to improve the situation. For example, the fact that the Eagles toilet paper was sourced from paper originating in forests that were eagle territories, so the team's supplier was, in effect, wiping out natural eagle habitats! Hershkowitz set about changing the team's toilet paper supplier and then built a comprehensive environmental plan for the team. Since that first intervention, the Eagles have gone on to increase their recycling by over 200% and offset all their travel by financing tree plantings in other parts of Pennsylvania.

Hershkowitz worked tirelessly at the NRDC, developing greening guides for MLB, the NBA, MHL, the USTA, and MLS, as well as numerous sports teams. By 2009 there was such demand for the work he was doing that the NRDC was battling to cope. A separate organization was required to manage the dissemination of information more widely, and so the Green Sports Alliance was founded, starting with six teams from six leagues. Today it is the biggest environmental association in sport, representing over 400 teams, leagues, venues, conferences, and partners, all of whom are dedicated to promoting healthy, sustainable communities around sports. Hershkowitz also helped to establish a similar organization operating out of Europe, called Sports and Sustainability International, and, despite its European roots, it is now a truly international organization with members in 50 countries.

There are essentially three parts to the work Hershkowitz does. The first is to change the operations at the sports venue or league offices to make them more efficient, to reduce their energy use or the waste they produce, and to make them more efficient and lower emitters of carbon. The second component is to change the supply chain, to make venues and governing bodies more conscious of where they are getting their energy or their water from and where their waste is going. Finally, the third element involves engaging with and educating fans and initiating a change in their behavior.

There are many successes one can speak of to highlight the work that Hershkowitz has done. For example, the Seattle Mariners pro baseball team has achieved savings of up to $1.75 million in electricity, natural gas, water, and sewerage changes thanks to reducing the use of natural gas by 40%, electricity by 25%, and water use by 25% since 2006. Another noteworthy example is the Cleveland Indians, who installed a wind turbine capable of generating roughly 40,000-kilowatt-hours of wind energy per year while also implementing a recycling program that reclaims about a quarter of all the venue's waste.

Sport has been a hugely successful platform for Hershkowitz to drive the sustainability message. He explains the reason simply—"In the US, only 16% of citizens follow science but 80% follow sports every day in every newspaper across the country. The opportunity for those of us who are trying to promote environmental literacy and reduce the cultural polarization around the climate change conversation is to embrace sports. In fact, it would be ridiculous to ignore it. It is a spectacular platform! Furthermore, it is also viewed as being non-partisan and non-political and the supply chain for sport reaches across all sectors of business and society. If you've got the Yankees saying climate change matters...then the marketplace is going to get the message. Frankly, I think the sports and sustainability movement is one of the most vibrant sectors of the environmental movement globally."

Sports Organizations and Host Cities Seize the Opportunity

Both the South African example of Purpose in action and the tireless work spearheaded by Allen Hershkowitz around sports greening draw on the foresight and influence of inspirational individuals. However, the impetus can come from a variety of sources—the event organizing committee, the sport's governing body, or even an event's host city—as the next examples show.

The IOC has always had a humanitarian focus, as was highlighted in Chapter 6, and, since the late 1960s, organizing committees have considered the issues of environmental impact and social inclusion to varying degrees. However, it was the 2010 Olympic Games in Vancouver that prioritized these issues and set new benchmarks for sport, sustainability, and social legacies. Like many other Olympic Games before it, Vancouver 2010 accelerated significant improvements in terms of transport, infrastructure, and housing in the city. Construction plans focused on creating social and environmental benefits that would last while also minimizing costs through the reuse of existing infrastructure. Vancouver was the first Olympics in history to have an Official Supplier of Carbon

Offsets as one of its sponsors. Together they put in place a carbon offset program to offset 118,000 tons of direct carbon emissions related to the Games from things like construction, travel, and even the cross-country torch relay. Vancouver was also the first-ever host city to establish a non-profit organization devoted to the creation of community legacies. This organization was called 2010 Legacies Now and worked on over 1,250 initiatives to benefit more than 400 communities in British Columbia. Today it has changed its name to LIFT Philanthropy Partners and still works with social purpose organizations across Canada.

With Vancouver having set the bar, London 2012 followed with an ambitious long-term legacy plan. London was the first organizing committee to include sustainability principles in absolutely every aspect of its planning, construction, and execution. The London organizing committee (LOCOG) also allocated £3.8 billion in additional funding towards a legacy program, which served as further evidence of its commitment to the Games having a lasting positive impact on the host city. LOCOG embarked on an extensive education campaign encouraging people to reduce their energy usage, recycle more, grow their food, and do more physical activity. Also, all venues for the London Games were made of at least a quarter of recycled materials, the use of temporary sites was more than at any previous Games, and it was the first 'public transport' Games which saw all spectators arrive by public transport, walking, or cycling.

During the event, there was a 34% reduction in venue energy use, saving the equivalent of 31,000 tonnes of carbon dioxide, and 100% of the event waste was diverted from landfills. One of the event's most notable achievements was the creation of the Olympic Park through the regeneration of a once derelict and polluted industrial area to the East of the City. The area has provided local communities with a huge urban parkland space that has stimulated increased levels of social integration and economic activity. Despite some criticism that London 2012 failed to live up to all its sustainability promises, the event was declared the most sustainable Olympic Games ever and won gold in the Environmental and Sustainability category of the 6th International Sports Event Management Awards. It was also the catalyst for the development of

ISO 20121, an event management standard that helps to ensure that all events, no matter their size, leave behind a positive legacy in terms of economic, environmental, and social benefits with minimal material waste, energy consumption, or strain on local communities. Since 2012, all Olympic events are now required to adhere to the standards set out in this framework.

Purpose can be equally successful when motivated by a host city, as shown in the example of the 34th America's Cup, which took place in San Francisco in September 2013. San Francisco has been voted the greenest city in the USA, and, to ensure that sustainability was prioritized in the hosting of the 34th America's Cup, the City insisted that a commitment to sustainability was written into the Host City Agreement. The event pledged to understand its impacts, reduce any that were potentially negative, and maximize legacy benefits. Sustainability was built into every single aspect of the event planning and execution thanks to extensive collaboration between the City and the America's Cup Event Authority (ACEA). The vision was to deliver a model sustainable sporting event that left a positive legacy, and, as our detailed case study shows, it more than delivered on this vision and demonstrated that it is indeed possible to stage major events with sustainability and Purpose at the core.

CASE STUDY
THE 34TH AMERICA'S CUP

How San Francisco delivered the most sustainable America's Cup by going carbon neutral, having zero waste, and being Purposeful.

San Francisco prides itself on its active commitment to the principles of sustainability—from protecting the air, water, and the San Francisco Bay area, to leading innovative efforts to combat climate change and advance environmental justice. From July to September 2013, the city hosted the 34th America's Cup and used this global platform to promote the City's visionary and thorough approach to sustainability.

The America's Cup is the world's premier sailing race and the oldest trophy in international sport. It consists of multiple racing events and concerts over a period of weeks, culminating in the America's Cup Finals. The event brings huge benefits to a host city as it attracts millions of visitors and spectators, creates jobs, and generates a sizable economic impact. In 2013, San Francisco hosted the event, with the vision of delivering a model sustainable sporting event that left a positive legacy in the local community and on the sport of sailing as well as highlighting to the rest of the world that San Francisco leads the way in sustainability.

From the initial planning stages through to the final race, the City of San Francisco partnered with the America's Cup Event Authority (ACEA) to execute the event in a way that supported the city's environmental policies and its programs that promoted social equity and the protection of human and ecological health. In every way, the event supported the City's commitment to waste less and recycle more, to reduce greenhouse gas emissions, and to stimulate the local economy through job creation and generating a substantial economic impact.

The ACEA sustainability plan covered five broad themes:

1. **Energy & Emissions:** To optimize the use of energy and minimize associated air emissions through efficient planning and technological innovation.

2. **Resource Efficiency:** To maximize natural resource and land-use efficiency, minimize waste, and sustainably source products and materials.

3. **Natural Habitats:** To protect biodiversity, habitats, and wildlife.

4. **Inclusion:** To provide an inclusive and welcoming experience for event spectators and the event workforce and to maximize legacy benefits for the City's residents and businesses.

5. **Engagement:** To raise sustainability awareness and to foster pro-environmental behavior and sustainable lifestyles.

Under each theme, several programs were implemented. Concerning **energy and emissions**, ACEA looked for and capitalized on opportunities to avoid or reduce energy and emissions through design decisions and contractor and vendor agreements. For example, a fleet of hybrid-electric vehicles was provided by Lexus, the event's Official Car and Sustainability Partner, and a wide array of sustainable transport options were made available for visitors. Also, the America's Cup Village made use of solar security lights, which saved an estimated 12 tons of greenhouse gas emissions. The event prioritized local sourcing of food to minimize energy and emissions associated with transporting food. Temporary materials were used in construction to reduce the energy consumption and carbon impact of manufacturing and, thanks to a partnership with Offsetters, the event's Official Carbon Credit Supplier, it was able to be carbon neutral.

ACEA was equally committed to **resource efficiency** through strategies and activities that minimized or eliminated waste and promoted the wise consumption of water and energy in the areas of construction, food and beverages, and hospitality. The commitment to zero waste went beyond recycling and waste diversion by promoting the prevention of waste through design considerations and choice of materials. Over 9 tons of plastic film was separated from the event waste stream for recycling, avoiding sending this material to landfills. All vendors were required to source and deliver products, materials, merchandise, and services in the most sustainable manner possible, having regard for the environment as well as social, economic, and ethical issues. For example, food vendors were required to consider packaging, single-use plastic, and the health and nutritional value of their offering and then also dispose of excess food at local shelters or programs that fed the hungry.

In terms of **protecting biodiversity, habitats, and wildlife**, ACEA was careful to minimize and mitigate any potential negative impacts on habitats and wildlife during both event preparation and staging. A Boater Guide to the San Francisco Bay was published, which provided guidelines to boaters for using the water in the most eco-friendly way, e.g., how to protect local sea life and how to avoid sensitive habitats. Also, the America's Cup Sustainability Credit program was created to allow all event stakeholders the opportunity to offset their carbon emissions and provide a legacy for the Bay area; merchandise partners donated proceeds from the sale of official America's Cup apparel and memorabilia towards the event's sustainability credits; 24 beach cleanups along the Bay shoreline were organized; plastic bottles and balloons were prohibited from all event venues to prevent marine debris and litter; an education program was also implemented that increased public awareness and understanding of marine conservation and, lastly, the Clean Boater Pledge campaign provided information to mariners on how to keep San Francisco's water 'clean and green.'

The event's sustainability plan also included a commitment to **providing an inclusive and accessible event** that showcased the Bay Area's diversity, businesses and innovation, natural environment, thoughtful leadership, and a strong sense of community in ways that maximized the legacy benefits for the City's residents and businesses. For the first time, the event was held near an urban waterfront, which meant that there were multiple places for free and accessible waterfront viewing of live racing at close range. For those not able to attend, there was TV coverage and live streaming online. The America's Cup Village provided a communal space for visitors, teams, and spectators that included free viewing areas, hospitality, retail stores, and an interactive spectator engagement area that highlighted the connection between sailing and protecting the ocean. ACEA and event delivery partners fostered partnerships with local businesses, restaurants, retailers, manufacturers, and building suppliers to maximize opportunities for all to be involved in and benefit from the event and to deliver lasting community benefits. The Youth Involvement Plan allowed for learning opportunities and internships at all phases of the event planning and delivery, and there were volunteer opportunities for hundreds of residents.

Engagement strategies were created to promote sustainability awareness and to foster pro-environmental behavior in a variety of areas, including travel, marine protection, and zero waste. The Healthy Ocean Project was the cornerstone of the efforts in this regard. It involved an educational and call-to-action campaign to engage people around protecting and restoring the ocean. All Official Partners of the event were encouraged to adopt sustainable behaviors when activating their association with the America's Cup, and several of them embraced this in highly engaging and effective ways.

The 34th America's Cup embraced Purpose at all levels, modeling best practices in sustainable event management and demonstrating that an event of this scale can deliver lasting benefits for society, the economy, and the environment. There were many sustainability successes from the event, not least of which was that more than 18,000 pounds of litter was removed from the San Francisco Bay shoreline, more than 85% of event waste was diverted from landfill, and the event was carbon neutral. The City was integral to implementing the many sustainability initiatives. It showed how a host city, organizing committee, and event sponsors could come together very effectively to deliver a Purposeful event. ∎

The City of San Francisco again showcased its Purpose credentials when it hosted the Super Bowl 50 in 2016 and delivered the most commercially successful, shared, most participatory, sustainable, and most giving Super Bowl ever. The event redefined the Super Bowl experience across many disciplines—fan experience, technology, innovation, and culture—all underpinned by sustainability and a focus on community. The vision was to use the Super Bowl as a platform to do good for the benefit of the entire Bay Area, and specifically, people living in disadvantaged communities, by philanthropy, by engaging local businesses to participate in the Super Bowl economy, and by promoting sustainable principles. The Host Committee more than delivered on its vision. Super Bowl 50 set a new bar for global sporting events and how they can embrace sustainability and still deliver a successful event. You can read more about Super Bowl 50 in the case study in Part 3.

Sports Events that are getting it right

A year after Super Bowl 50, the 2017/18 Ocean Race also showed the world how an event could successfully lead with Purpose. There is an obvious link between sailing and ocean health, which is why The Ocean Race organizers saw the potential to use their event as a platform to engage with people and shift behavior around the ocean and its preservation. And so began their journey into the world of Purpose, starting with a landmark Science Program that saw all seven boats participating in the nine-month race in 2017/18 being fitted with a scientific device to collect critical data on ocean health.

The Science Program consisted of three elements. The first element concerned the gathering of meteorological data—temperature, wind strength and direction, and barometric pressure—which is critical to developing a better understanding of future weather patterns and the potential impact of climate change. The second element involved the use of drifter buoys, which were essentially floating sensors equipped with satellite communications equipment to transmit information on ocean composition and currents. Thirty of these were deployed in very remote ocean areas along the route. And the third element saw selected boats carry groundbreaking instruments on board to test salinity and other key metrics for ocean health. Microplastics sampling was carried out to collect data on microplastic concentrations in the most remote oceans on the planet. Disturbingly, out of the 86 samples taken, 93% of those analyzed contained microplastic pollution. The Science Program was a unique collaboration between ocean research scientists and sailors and has been praised for its significant contribution to an increased understanding of ocean health, particularly in remote areas. It is to be expanded for the 2021/22 edition of the race to gather more scientific information that can shape ocean restoration projects.

Since 2017, The Ocean Race has gone on to further embed sustainability into all its operations under the mantra 'Racing with Purpose' to accelerate ocean health restoration through a range of actions and tangible outcomes. Together with its event Partners, 11th Hour Racing, Bluewater, and Volvo Cars, The Ocean Race will deliver a broad range of initiatives for cleaner and healthier seas over the course of the next edition of the event. They are embarking on an education drive, hosting 12 Ocean Race Summits around the world, as well as innovation workshops that will serve as a solutions exchange platform to come up with tangible actions to improve ocean health. They are also introducing a curriculum-based school learning program to ensure that children understand the damaging impact of plastic pollution on the world's oceans and how they, too, can be part of the solution.

The commitment to Purpose also extends to event production and the participating teams. The Ocean Race is working closely with stakeholders at each stopover city to ensure that they adopt sustainable practices at the race village and inspire visitors to play their part as well. Race teams are also being asked to look at more sustainable boat building practices and to have a minimum of 30% of renewable energy onboard their boats.

Since embarking on its hugely successful Science Program, The Ocean Race has embraced Purpose to the extent that it now impacts every single thing that they do, from operations to stakeholder engagement to securing financial and in-kind support from its Partners. It truly is one of the best examples highlighting the power of Purpose in sport.

In the same way that The Ocean Race has put ocean health restoration at the heart of its sustainability efforts, the world of motorsport uses Formula E, a city-based, single-seater electric car motor racing championship, to drive a powerful message around air pollution. The World Health Organization estimates that seven million people die from air pollution every year, making it one of the biggest killers on the planet. Electric vehicles are one of the best solutions to reduce urban air pollution. By actively promoting electric mobility and alternative energy solutions, Formula E is helping to raise awareness and shift behavior towards an alternative way of living that is better for the environment.

Formula E's vision is to accelerate change towards an electric future, one race, and one city at a time. Its races are merely the platform from which to drive this Purpose. There are over ten races per season in cities across the world, and Formula E works hard to have a positive impact in the host cities. Getting their support to embrace sustainability is usually easy since many cities see a Formula E event as a great way to advance their city mobility plans or as the ideal platform from which to kickstart one. City support is also enhanced through community engagement and ensuring that each event leaves a legacy. Invitations are extended to local schools, universities, and charities to attend races so that the local community can see first-hand that it is more than just a competition, and there is a much bigger message at play. Formula E also hosts tailor-made conferences in the different host cities where key stakeholders come together to look at mobility and its impact on city planning and explore what solutions can be put in place to improve city infrastructure for a future with electric vehicles.

According to Julia Palle, Formula E's Senior Sustainability Consultant, the key to Formula E's strategy is the delivery of sustainable events by measuring the CO_2 emissions at events and implementing reduction measures to offset this. In addition, waste recycling and plastic reduction programs are implemented at each event. Its partners also offer vital support in enabling Formula E to embed sustainability in all its activities, e.g., DHL, the logistics partner, helped to create the race calendar since they understand transport and how to maximize efficiencies in terms of transportation and logistics.

Using sport as a platform, Formula E delivers a compelling message to a growing audience. Formula E has gained a huge following since it was launched only six years ago, with 400,000 spectators per season attending its events and over 410 million people tuning in to watch on television each year. What is even more exciting is that it is capturing the attention of a younger audience—72% of its followers are under 35 years—making it one of the highest performing sports platforms in terms of attracting younger fans. And these younger fans are keen to embrace a cleaner future and are more open to a switch to electric mobility.

Intentions, not size, are what matter most

The move to Purpose does not necessarily require size and stature to make an impact, as the example of Forest Green Rovers (FGR), a 130-year old Gloucestershire-based (UK) soccer club, demonstrates. FGR is the world's greenest soccer club, and yet they compete in the fourth tier of English soccer, a far cry from giants like Manchester United, Liverpool, and Chelsea.

In 2010, the Club ran into financial difficulties and asked a local businessman, Dale Vince, to step in and help them. As the founder of Ecotricity, a green electricity provider, Dale was well versed in sustainability and applied this mindset to his management of the Club. He set about building sustainability into every aspect of the Club's operations, from transport to energy to food supply.

The Forest Green Rovers sustainability plan had five key objectives, namely, to become a zero-carbon Club (which was achieved in 2018); to reduce energy and water consumption; to reduce waste and emissions produced by FGR and maximize its recycling efforts; to reduce the environmental impact of its grounds maintenance, and to reduce the ecological impact of stadium management. To achieve these objectives, the Club had to retrofit several eco-technologies around the ground, e.g., the installation of 180 solar panels on the stadium roof, which helps the Club to generate 10% of the electricity needed to run the stadium. The pitch was modified to become an entirely organic pitch, free from pesticides and irrigated with rainwater—a world first in sports. It is serviced by a robot mower, known as a 'mow bot,' that uses GPS technology to guide it around the pitch and is powered using solar energy. To reduce emissions from travel, the players use carpools, sharing lifts to and from training and matches, and they have access to 11 electric vehicles that were secured through a partnership deal with Nissan. Carpooling has helped the Club eliminate roughly 135,000 kg of CO_2 each season. The stadium also houses a fast charger where the squad and members of the public can recharge their electric vehicles for free using renewable energy. FGR is the first club to only serve a meat-free and environmentally sustainable menu at its grounds, thereby supporting local suppliers while also cutting down on food miles and lowering emissions.

In addition to these greening initiatives at the Club, there are bigger ambitions to spread the message of sustainability to the wider world of soccer and sports in general. As such, the Club helps other sports organizations around the world to reduce their carbon footprint and regularly engages with fans around sustainability, encouraging them to change their behavior. Furthermore, in 2018, FGR became one of the founding organizations of the UN's Sport for Climate Action Framework that aims to raise awareness and support programs in sports that meet the goals of the Paris Agreement to fight climate change. Vince has since been appointed as a Climate Champion for the UN, a platform he plans to use to encourage sports fans and teams globally to make a real difference around climate change.

Corporate Brands Leading with Purpose through Sport

Cable sports channel, ESPN, has long been a believer in the role sport can play in drawing attention to and shifting perceptions on important social issues. For years the company has been a shining example of how sport can be used to positively address society's needs through strategic community investments, cause marketing programs, collaboration with sports organizations, and employee volunteerism while also utilizing its diverse media assets to amplify its message.

CASE STUDY
ESPN: THE WORLD'S MOST PURPOSEFUL SPORTS CHANNEL

How ESPN has embedded doing good in its corporate strategy and operations to bring to life the company's mission statement to "Serve the sports fan. Anytime. Anywhere." and to demonstrate that doing good can also result in doing well.

Over twenty-five years ago, Jim Valvano, former basketball coach and ESPN analyst, was battling cancer and formed the V Foundation. ESPN worked hand in hand with the V Foundation to fundraise for cancer research. That support became a culture carrier for ESPN for decades, with nearly everyone at the company feeling a strong connection to the Foundation. Spurred on by the success of this collaboration, then President of ESPN, George Bodenheimer, called for the creation of a robust corporate social responsibility program that would build the business while also making a meaningful impact on the community.

Dubbed "The Worldwide Leader in Sports," ESPN lives and breathes sports 24 hours a day. The company's mission is to "Serve the Sports Fan. Anytime. Anywhere." So, to bring that mission to life, the ESPN Corporate Citizenship team, led by Kevin Martinez, developed a sophisticated and outcomes-based philanthropic strategy aimed at enhancing and driving the company's core competency: sports.

Martinez began the journey by establishing specific, measurable criteria with partner organizations. At the top of this list were two key qualifiers: a commitment to providing access to sports for underserved youth; and the demonstrated capacity to maintain long-term programs to build leadership skills and empowerment through sport. They collaborated with innovative and accountable nonprofits, colleagues in every major professional sports league, as well as advertisers and respected Thought Leaders in the industry, to establish a philanthropic investment portfolio. Their North Star was the goal of enabling one million people to access sports in five years.

In tandem with the social objectives, the ESPN Citizenship team established clear deliverables to help build the business by enhancing key relationships, growing sports fans, showcasing powerful stories, engaging employees, and driving reputation. They did this all while helping the most vulnerable in the community of sports build a better path to the future. Achieving the business objectives took a bit more time.

Growing sports fans

For ESPN, reaching a younger audience is mission-critical, and research has shown that the more kids enjoy sports at a young age, the more likely they are to be sports fans as adults. By helping to increase youth sports participation, ESPN could grow the sports fans of the future. More importantly, ESPN could contribute positively from a societal perspective because being active keeps kids healthy, keeps them in school, improves their grades, and builds skills like perseverance, teamwork, accountability, and leadership. To help achieve this goal, ESPN teamed up with several nonprofit organizations whose primary mission was to get kids, who may otherwise not play sports, into the game. Five years into the strategy, ESPN had helped 1.7 million people gain access to sports and had provided 218,000 coaches with the training and tools they needed to keep kids in the game. That's over a million people who now have the important life skills that sports develop, and over a million people who have built a foundation as a sports fan.

Enhance business relationships

ESPN is a company that is built on relationships. Relationships with the sports leagues in the form of billions of dollars in media rights packages. Relationships with affiliates and cable carriers who transmit the ESPN networks. Relationships with advertisers who use the platforms to promote their products and initiatives. Relationships with athletes who are interviewed each day, and relationships with sports fans, who consume the content.

All of these relationships are infinitely important to ESPN, and building, growing, and fostering each of them is critical and ongoing. They are unique in that they have relationships with most industries and with competing brands within those industries. ESPN's community programming creates a way to bring them all together around a common cause or shared interest. ESPN's bullying prevention program,

Shred Hate, is an excellent example of this. This program saw ESPN, X Games, and MLB collaborate and, in so doing, leverage new audiences, create shared content, and utilize each other's assets in ways that benefited the partners far beyond the coverage of baseball games.

Driving Revenue

The effective application of Purpose in an organization can demonstrate that doing good can also result in doing well, and the ESPN Citizenship teams do this in the form of sponsorships with advertisers who have a mutual interest in a community program or cause. It is a win for the advertiser, who uses ESPN's expansive platforms, and it is a win for ESPN, who benefits from the advertising revenue and the shared message to sports fans.

Reputation Management

In terms of enhancing brand reputation, ESPN's Sports Humanitarian Awards, honoring those using the power of sports to create social good, play a big role. These awards, developed in 2015, were created with three goals in mind. Firstly, to strengthen ESPN's relationship with the professional sports leagues that sponsor the program and submit nominations for the awards; secondly, to create an avenue to showcase positive stories in sports across ESPN platforms; and thirdly, to raise funds for the V Foundation, which was the show's beneficiary. All of these goals contributed to enhancing ESPN's reputation and showcase ESPN's commitment to telling positive stories in sports.

Powerful Storytelling

With a TV and digital audience that reaches as many as 212 million Americans per month, ESPN's reach is expansive. And when they use their voice and platforms to reach audiences with stories of inspiration, heart, and Purpose, it has an impact far beyond what the statistics may show.

Cause-related content can be found on ESPN via public service announcements, editorial reporting, in-game coverage, and multi-media platform integration and is another unique way that ESPN supports organizations. This multi-platform approach was especially exemplified in ESPN's "Don't Retire, Kid" campaign in 2019 in response to a partnership with the Aspen Institute and 20 sports organizations as part of Project Play 2020, which sought to address factors leading to the decline in youth sports participation. "Don't Retire, Kid" created awareness about why kids are dropping out of sports and drove parents and coaches to helpful resources to keep kids playing longer. ESPN used nearly all of its platforms to showcase the issue, with compelling editorial content on ESPN's digital, social, and linear platforms. The campaign was featured on ESPN's highest-rated programming and generated over 322 million impressions in less than a month as well as receiving a 99% positive sentiment on social media. There is no doubt that ESPN has a meaningful voice, and when they can use it to spread messages of hope and inspiration, everyone benefits.

Employee Engagement

Employee buy-in to a company's Purpose strategy adds authenticity and impact. In the summer leading up to ESPN's 40th anniversary in 2019, the company created the "40,000 Acts of Service" initiative to inspire employees to give back to sports fans through service to others with the collective goal of logging 40,000 acts of service to celebrate the company's milestone. Weekly pop-up stations were set up on its Bristol, Connecticut campus so employees could perform various acts of service on-site, from packing back-to-school backpacks to collecting sports equipment. Over 80,000 acts of service were carried out overall and shifted employee perceptions on how they can serve others to create positive change—big or small—in their communities.

Unified: ESPN + Special Olympics

ESPN's partnership with Special Olympics is perhaps the best example of the company's application of Purpose to achieve social and business impact. The decades-long relationship between the two shifted up a gear in 2013 with the entrepreneurial program called Unified Sports, which pairs an athlete with intellectual disabilities with an athlete without disabilities on the same team to foster inclusion and friendships. Together, ESPN and Special Olympics set about getting more kids with disabilities to play sports, which saw a phenomenal 172% increase in athlete and teammate participation (to 1.8 million people) and a 464% increase in the number of Unified Sports coaches (to nearly 119,000) between 2013–2019. ESPN also ensured that the incredible and inspiring stories of Special Olympics athletes were covered across its media channels, giving athletes with disabilities the exposure they deserved. The partnership drove additional revenue for ESPN with the sponsorship of the Special Olympics, World and USA Games coverage from companies including Bank of America, Coca Cola, and Microsoft...new advertising dollars and new relationships built from a common interest in ending discrimination against people with intellectual disabilities. Finally, ESPN's collaboration with Special Olympics has also driven employee engagement with more than 300 employees helping to carry the torch for the Special Olympics Unified Relay Across America in advance of the Los Angeles World Games in 2015 and a number continuing to regularly volunteer as Unified coaches or participants in Special Olympics events. You can read more about the Special Olympics in our Thought Leadership interview with Tim Shriver in Chapter Four.

Purpose sits at the core of everything ESPN does as a business. It is embodied in the company's mission of service anytime, anywhere; harnessing the unifying power of sport to inspire social good. It is an integral part of their exceptional storytelling. It is key to their relationship with the leagues and sponsors; it engages and unites employees, and most importantly, it is positively impacting the lives of people across the world. ■

Harnessing the Power of Sport Through Collective Effort

As the examples we shared show, sport has a role to play in the world of Purpose because of its global fanbase of billions who are engaged and receptive to conversation and because all sports impact the sustainability of the planet. Whether big or small, sports organizations and events contribute to climate change in several ways—energy use, construction, associated travel, waste, and catering. As the global fight against climate change escalates, it is time for the sports community as a collective to stand up and play its part. To this end, the UN Sports for Climate Action Framework was co-developed by the UN and the IOC and was launched in December 2018. The Framework urges the sports community to unite in creating a climate action plan for sport and provides a strong platform for the sports sector to play a more prominent role in meeting the challenge of climate change and inspiring its fans to do the same. It supports the aims of the Paris Agreement, signed in November 2016, which are to intensify the actions and investment needed for a sustainable low-carbon future.

The UN Framework has two overarching objectives, namely to achieve a clear trajectory for the global sports community to combat climate change and to use sports as a unifying tool to drive climate change awareness and action among global citizens. There are five guiding principles that members must commit to as signatories to the Framework; these are—to promote greater environmental responsibility, to reduce overall climate impact, to educate for climate action, to promote sustainable and responsible consumption, and to advocate for climate action through communication.

Any sports organization or team can sign up in support of these principles regardless of where they are currently at with their own environmentally responsible endeavors. They just need to state a commitment to these principles and then demonstrate ongoing progress over time—through strategies, policies, and procedures—to implement them. So far, more than 100 organizations have made this commitment. It remains to be seen whether the various signatories embrace its principles and implement meaningful change across the board so that we are on track for the net-zero emission economy by 2050 that global leaders agreed to in Paris. One certainly hopes they do!

Just as sports greening bodies in the USA have sought to guide sports organizations and teams to be more sustainable, so too did the French Ministry of Sports, together with WWF France, launch the Charter of 15 Eco-Responsible Commitments in January 2017. Each year, around 2.5 million sports events take place in France, which represents 2.5 million opportunities to place sport at the service of the planet and hence the Charter to guide sports event organizers in France to be more environmentally responsible when staging their events. The priorities underpinning the Charter's commitments include responsible purchasing and food sourcing, waste recycling, control of water and energy consumption, sustainable mobility, preservation of biodiversity, accessibility, and promotion of gender equality in positions of responsibility. The Charter has been signed by more than 80 sports bodies in France, including Paris 2024, and is a clear demonstration of the growing movement around sports as a force for good.

France also hosted the first Global Sports Week gathering in February 2020. The platform was created off the back of the increased awareness of sport's cultural and societal influence and emerging trends that would impact sports in the future. Around 2,000 global leaders and change-makers in sport and business gathered in Paris to collaborate and work towards accelerating changes that will shape the future of sports. The energy and commitment displayed in Paris suggest that sport is perhaps finally waking up to its enormous potential as an agent of change.

Driving the Agenda for Women's Sports

With the growing popularity in women's sports, we are seeing more female athletes come forward and speak out on the issue of gender equality to level the playing field. Nowhere was this more evident than at the 2019 FIFA Women's World Cup, which will be remembered both for the awesome winning performance from the US Women's National Soccer Team (USWNT) and for the extraordinary demonstration of the power of women's sport to be about much more than just the game. Athletes, sponsors, fans, and the media all stepped up to make the most of the US Women's National Soccer Team's showing in France, to drive home some important social messages around equal rights and fair play.

Several sponsor campaigns took up the theme of gender equality, e.g., Commerzbank, sponsor of the German national team, ran an ad entitled "We play for a nation that doesn't even know our names" and highlighted varying levels of discrimination and lack of reward and recognition for the women's team relative to the men's national team in Germany; and Nike's emotional "Dream with us" ad aimed to mobilize young women and encourage them to take part, not just in soccer, but in sport in general.

The event itself was a huge success with record numbers of fans tuning in to watch the matches and applaud the high standard of entertaining soccer on show. And yet, despite all the ad campaigns and the delightful brand of soccer, the winning US Women's team still earned only $250,000 each vs. the more than $1 million that a winning US Men's National Team would stand to earn were they ever to win the tournament. This disparity extends to all levels of the sport. According to data from the International Federation of Professional Footballers, 49% of professional female soccer players do not receive a salary even as the industry generates over $500 billion a year.

As discussed in Chapter 5, Megan Rapinoe led a unified group of women's soccer players leveraging the FIFA Women's World Cup as a platform to drill home their point that female players are not being treated fairly by the US Soccer Federation (USSF), and that they deserve to be paid the same as their male colleagues. The team filed a gender discrimination lawsuit against the Federation over unequal working conditions demanding at least equal playing, training, and travel conditions, equal promotion of their games, equal support and development for their games, and equal pay. The lawsuit sought more than $66 million in damages.

The polarized responses by the media and fans to the team's activism have been interesting. As has become the norm in US culture today, not everyone was supportive of Rapinoe and the team's behavior—several media commentators sided with the Federation, and labeled Rapinoe and the team as unpatriotic and not the kind of role models we want for our children. One media platform went as far as to headline a story, "We all wanted to love the USWNT, but the team, led by foul-mouthed Megan Rapinoe, disgraced society." But some came out in support of the team and helped to amplify their message to a deafening crescendo. Appearances at the ESPYs and on major morning and late-night television shows proved to be a perfect platform to amplify the team's message further.

Despite the detractors, there were a significant number of supporters for the team—not least of which are a vocal and growing group of fans, who took it upon themselves to amplify the team's message with lively chants of "Equal Pay" from the stands during games and after the tournament at the Canyon of Heroes Parade and the sold-out stadiums where the team played on its victory tour.

The fans took their show of support a step further by coming out in huge numbers to purchase the official replica USWNT home team jersey. In the process, they established a new record for the number of soccer jerseys, men's or women's, ever sold on the Nike website in one season. And it was not just women buying the jersey—record numbers of men did so too, in a show of male solidarity with the women's team and, by extension, their cause.

Team sponsors also came out in support of the team. P&G's Secret deodorant brand gifted the players $529,000 to help close the earnings gap and then went a step further by taking out a full-page ad in The New York Times urging the USSF to "be on the right side of history and take this moment of celebration to propel women's sport forward." The brand went on to urge the USSF to be a beacon of strength and end gender pay inequality. Given how reluctant sponsors have traditionally been to challenge their rights-holding partners, Secret's actions are profound. They reflect a growing recognition amongst brands that the fans expect them to stand for something more than just profits—even if that means putting otherwise-lucrative relationships at risk.

The whole issue around how much the USWNT team members are paid and how they are treated is a complicated affair, but that is beside the point. The USSF's attempts to defend themselves have fallen on deaf ears, with the court of popular opinion painting them as the bad guys in this story. At the time of writing, the dispute is still ongoing and, judging by the USSF's latest insensitive response that male players deserve more because they have "more responsibility" and the men's game "requires a higher level of skill," it is likely to get even more ugly. One can only conclude that the USSF must be living in a success bubble of their own making, or they just don't care—or if they had been more in touch with what is happening around them in society, they would have seen all this coming and reacted more proactively. But they did not, and instead, they have been forced to play defense and catch up. It is such a wasted opportunity for them, for they could have been the heroes in this saga.

It would seem that the first rumblings of change are finally taking hold in some areas of women's soccer, though, with UEFA launching its

"Time for Action" campaign in May 2019. This campaign is a dedicated women's soccer strategy that has committed to double women's representation in soccer across Europe in five years. And UN Women signed a memorandum of understanding with FIFA, also in 2019, to develop a sports policy, raise awareness about gender equality, and use soccer as a tool to empower women and girls with the idea that, as the world's most popular sport, soccer can play a meaningful role in closing the gender gap.

When Things Go Wrong

As so many of our examples demonstrate, Purpose needs to be embraced on every level if it is to be credible, authentic, and impactful. Gestures that don't appear to be genuine or contradict other actions or are perceived as window dressing will be noticed and torn apart by fans as some brands and athletes have had the misfortune to experience. In today's world, where social media can be leveraged in a matter of seconds to call out a brand, one poor decision can be critical and if you, as an event, brand, organization, or athlete, decide to stand for something, let it play out consistently and thoroughly.

As great as the Nike "Dream with us" ad was a rallying cry for gender equality in sports, it fell flat next to the revelation, from six-time Olympic Gold Medalist Allyson Felix, that Nike did not guarantee female athletes a salary in the months surrounding pregnancy and childbirth. In response to Felix's op-ed in the New York Times on the subject, not typically a brand to make such blunders, Nike quickly announced that it was changing its policy on pregnancy in sponsorship contracts. The policy now ensures that female athletes are not adversely affected financially during pregnancy for a period of 18 months. Furthermore, Nike cannot terminate an athlete's contract even if she decides not to compete due to pregnancy. Nike's turnaround was too little too late for Felix, who declined a multi-year renewal partnership with Nike and instead signed with Athleta, The Gap's B-Corp-certified, ethical women's athletic wear brand.

In another example of sponsor activism, Athleta took full advantage of the opportunity to sign Felix as a way to signal its commitment to championing women and girls. It was interesting to see Athleta state that it sees its partnership with Felix as a means of changing the way that sponsors contracts are structured with women athletes across the board; in other words, to leverage the opportunity to change a system that treats women unfairly. The lesson here, for any athlete, brand, or organization, is that one's words need to be consistent with one's actions. If they are not, you will be found out.

MasterCard's campaign around the 2018 FIFA World Cup might have arisen from a positive, Purposeful intention but shows how easily good intentions can unravel if Purpose has not been well thought through. The brand pledged to donate 10,000 meals to starving children in Latin America for every goal scored by Messi or Neymar Jr during the tournament. There was an immediate outcry on social media with fans criticizing MasterCard for resting the fate of starving children on whether multimillionaire soccer players scored a goal. MasterCard was urged to donate the money regardless of goals scored—"If you've got the money @MasterCard, just give it away anyway," one tweet suggested. MasterCard might have had good intentions, but the campaign was in bad taste and out of touch with public sentiment around global concerns. The execution just didn't ring true with fans. MasterCard was forced to withdraw the campaign and ended up donating the meals but under a cloud of negative sentiment. The learning is clear—being Purposeful does not automatically translate into positive brand PR, and, for it to be seen as genuine, there needs to be a logical and authentic link between brand and Purpose.

Another example worth highlighting is the online dialogue between climate change activist Greta Thunberg and tennis legend Roger Federer that took place at the start of 2020. This example is interesting because there are lessons to be learned on both sides. Federer came in for some flak from Thunberg for his long-standing relationship with Credit Suisse when she tweeted about the bank's $57 billion funding to fossil fuel companies and then finished her tweet with "@RogerFederer do you endorse this? #RogerWakeUpNow." Thunberg deliberately used the Federer name to heighten awareness around the issue (Federer has a twitter following of over 12 million people). He responded in his usual level-headed manner, expressing great admiration for the youth climate movement and that he was open to "innovative solutions" to climate change. He expressed appreciation for the reminder of his responsibility as a private individual and an athlete and committed to engaging with Credit Suisse on the issue.

The incident is an important reminder to athletes that they are held to a higher standard by fans and that every sponsorship they enter into speaks to who they are and what they stand for. If a sponsor's Purpose and business practices are not aligned with the athlete's Purpose, then it will be criticized by fans. But equally, the confrontation also highlights a lesson for activists that they need to be mindful of exploiting athletes because of their popularity. Thunberg's message had a lot more traction because she linked Federer's name to it, and yet Federer himself has never attached his name to the issue of climate change; this is not to say he has not used his position of influence for Purposeful endeavors. Quite the contrary, Federer's foundation has played a huge role in supporting early childhood education in Southern Africa for the last 16 years and has changed the lives of nearly two million children. When confronted about his response to Thunberg, Federer suggested that he had been misused by Thunberg, saying, "When I help one person, I am criticized for not doing it for others . . . I can't be everywhere; I can't do everything." He went on to say he believes attacking others is not the best approach to bring about change. Fair enough.

KEY INSIGHTS: THE FIRST MOVERS IN PURPOSEFUL SPORT HAVE SET THE STANDARD

➤ While the business of sport has been slow to adopt the move to Purpose, there are some great examples of forward-thinking sports properties that have embraced the opportunity to use Purpose as a key organizing principle.

➤ The 1995 Rugby World Cup was the first out of the gates with President Nelson Mandela recognizing the power of sport to change the world, in this case, as a launchpad for the New South Africa.

➤ The greening of sport in the USA followed, inspired by the greening of the NFL's Philadelphia Eagles and the environmental partnership between MLB and NRDC that led to the creation of, amongst others, NBA Green, NHL Green, and the Green Sports Alliance in 2009.

➤ The 2010 Vancouver Winter Olympic Games and 2012 London Summer Olympic Games were next up.

➤ The City of San Francisco voted the most sustainable city in the USA, made its mark, requiring that the 34th America's Cup be delivered as the first carbon-neutral and zero-waste event ever.

➤ The Host Committee for Super Bowl 50 in 2016 delivered the most commercially successful, shared, sustainable, and giving Super Bowl in history by leading with a Purpose of improving the lives of young people in the Bay Area, a record that still stands today.

➤ The Ocean Race embraced ocean health as its Purpose in 2017/18 to great success. Based on its successful approach, the strategy has been carried forward to the next edition of the race under the title "Racing with Purpose."

➤ Formula E's reason for being is to promote a future of electric mobility and renewable solutions to combat the issue of air pollution. Launched in 2014, the Series is now six years old, and its following continues to grow.

➤ Forest Green Rovers, a UK-based soccer club, leads the way as the world's greenest soccer club thanks to the club owner, Dale Vince, and his efforts to change the way the Club is run.

➤ Sport has a role to play in a Purpose-led world, and by uniting behind a common Purpose, more can be achieved hence the establishment of the UN Sports for Climate Change Framework in December 2018, which supports the aims of the Paris Agreement. It creates a climate action plan for sports and provides a strong platform for the sector to play a more prominent role in meeting the challenge of climate change and inspiring its fans to do the same.

➤ Countries like France have gone further, through the creation of the Charter of 15 Eco-Responsible Commitments, which guide French event organizers to stage environmentally sensitive events.

➤ The growing popularity of women's sports has led to an increase in female athletes speaking out on issues of gender equality, and we are finally starting to see positive changes in this regard.

➤ Some have tried to embrace a more Purposeful approach but failed—Mastercard's campaign at the 2018 FIFA World Cup in one example.

LEADING THOUGHTS: PURPOSE AND SPORT

ALAN JOPE
CEO at Unilever PLC

UNILEVER IS ONE OF THE WORLD'S LEADING EXAMPLES OF HOW TO EMBRACE PURPOSE AT AN ORGANIZATIONAL LEVEL AND IS A MEANINGFUL INVESTOR IN SPORT.

On the sports industry's understanding of Purpose:

I will contextualize that by saying we have seen a seismic change in what marketing is in the last few years. Before this, the branded consumer goods industry did not change much in the way mass-market brands sold in mass-market channels using mass media. Technology has allowed that model to be disrupted, and we now have to talk to very much more tightly segmented groups of consumers. Thanks to technology, people can screen out advertising that is not relevant or interesting to them. So, we are shifting a lot of our marketing mix away from forced consumption of advertising messages into content that people choose to engage with—and the best content for that is passion points.

It was the realization that we needed to shift our marketing away from interruption-based models of advertising to content-based models rooted in people's passion points that led to us stepping up our engagement in sports as part of our marketing mix. We are still not a big player in sports marketing, we are still feeling our way in and learning how you do it, but the way to think about it is that it is a passion point for many people. And we want our brands to show up in a relevant way in that space.

On how sport serves Unilever's commitment to Purpose:

There is a spectrum, I think. The best example would be something like Dove Men+Care working with global rugby. The Dove Men+Care platform is about the importance of men having a caring role in society and breaking out of the stereotypes of machismo. The focal point of it is men caring for their children, and one of the things that the brand has done is campaign for paternity leave for men because we know that men feel more connected as fathers when they take paternity leave. This sense of caring and respect is consistent with rugby's values of respect for your teammates, yourself, the game, the rules, and the officials. Having world-class rugby stars talk about their caring role as a parent as well has been unbelievably good for the Dove brand, and so, in that regard, it is a very good fit.

Another example would be Rexona, also known as Sure, whose Purpose is borne out of the context of too many people leading sedentary lives. Rexona believes that the more you move, the more you live, so the brand is trying to get more people involved in grassroots sports. They have got involved in dance groups and pop bands but are also using soccer as a platform to encourage people to move more.

The idea is to use sponsorship to drive positive behaviors and positive actions as opposed to just driving brand awareness. We want our sponsorships to synchronize 100% with the Purpose propositions of our brands, and we are much more interested in the content that can be generated through the sponsorship than simply the awareness that can be generated through signage and badges.

On the extent to which Unilever's partners in the sports world understand Purpose:

We have been impressed with the rugby unions around the world and the various soccer clubs and associations with which we partner. They authentically seek to understand what the brand need is and what the brand is trying to do and, as we have become more sophisticated in how we think about sport and sponsorships, so too have our sports partners become more sophisticated about understanding what they are trying to do with brands. When we get approached by sports assets that simply pitch it on the cost-effective, awareness building proposition, it is a very easy no.

On what sports can do better when it comes to Purpose:

I think it is exactly like one of Unilever's brands, and that is to understand authentically how the intrinsic nature of that sport can contribute back to society or the environment. By illustration, Unilever does not believe in corporate philanthropy. We do not believe in a corporate foundation because just giving money away is not sustainable. We are only interested in driving our brands harder in a way that they genuinely give back to society or the planet. For it to be authentic and durable, we have to have a long-term mindset. Sports franchises and teams need to find the same thing. If a sport announced that, as part of its work, they were going to donate to a good cause, that is not Purposeful. When a sport understands how it can genuinely help in a community or on a societal issue, then it is going down the right track. It is a question of whether Purpose is truly integrated into the work of that sport or that team franchise, or is it something that has just been bolted on, and, if it is just a bolt-on, then it is not of value to Unilever.

ALLEN HERSHKOWITZ

Chairman and Founding Director at
Sport & Sustainability International

ALLEN IS A PIONEER OF THE SPORTS GREENING MOVEMENT AND HAS BEEN INSTRUMENTAL IN MUCH OF THE STRIDES MADE BY SPORT IN CONTRIBUTING TOWARDS A MORE SUSTAINABLE PLANET.

On why sport is an excellent platform through which to educate people on climate change:

The opportunity for those of us who are trying to promote environmental literacy and reduce the cultural polarization around the conversation related to climate is to embrace sports. It would be ridiculous to ignore it. It is a spectacular platform that is viewed as being non-partisan and non-political, and the supply chain of sport involves every industry. If you have got the Yankees saying climate change matters and we want energy-efficient technology, or we want healthy food, or we want safer chemicals, or we want to recycle paper, then the marketplace is going to get the message. Frankly, I think the sports and sustainability movement is one of the most vibrant sectors of the environmental movement globally. Having worked with NGOs in this space for 40 years now, I feel I am making more progress than I have ever made.

Advice to businesses or organizations considering an environmental philosophy in the sports space for the first time:

If you are not sustainability literate, you are not going to succeed as a leader in the business sector today. That is not just my opinion. It is widely recognized now that sustainability reporting is increasingly demanded by investors, by the public, by the media, and by players and fans as well. The key thing is that, while it is the right thing to do, it does not mean it will be embraced by business because the ruthlessness of the market does not go away just because you have good intentions. It has to out-compete the bad stuff. What I do is work with organizations to help them develop sustainability plans and, to implement them, we have to show how sustainability advances profitability and enhances the brand, basically how it helps the organization achieve its goals more effectively. We are not going to combat climate change only through ethical behavior and philanthropy, though, sustainability has to be seen as essential to the business of sport to make a real difference.

Sports organizations are especially attuned to the sentiment of unity. Every business wants customer loyalty, and nothing compares to the loyalty that sports teams have. It is passed down from generation to generation. There is an allure to sports where people self-identify with their team and feel like a participant in a game. So the sports industry leadership has to pay attention to public sentiment, and, right now, 80% of people in the United States believe climate change is real, and over 70% say sports organizations should do something about it. Organizations, therefore, have a responsibility to do something, and those numbers are only going to go up as the consequences of environmental challenges become more and more impactful on our lives.

On whether the relationship between sport and climate change is a global phenomenon or restricted to certain regions:
There is no question that there is now global awareness of environmental issues in a way that we have never had before, but it is probably greater in some regions than others. Australia and Europe are better than the United States, where there is more climate denialism. Also, the political system in Europe, of proportional representation, means that there is a greater ability for the environmental community to influence government policy in Europe than in the US. We have also seen evidence of the relationship between sport and climate change in Pakistan and the Middle East, where FIFA had to move soccer games to a different time of year due to heat, or Europe, where the science of climate change is mobilizing the population.

On the UN Framework Convention for Climate Change (UNFCCC) and its effectiveness as a global platform to mobilize sport around environmental issues:

I am very supportive. I think the work we did in North America inspired the UN to create it. One of the first things I did when I was officially appointed to the Yankees is to have them sign the UN Framework. They were the first team in North America to do so. The Yankees are not known for being a left-wing environmental advocacy group. They are rather known for their commitment to excellence and performance. But when they signed up, suddenly other leagues and teams felt compelled to do so as well—the NBA, the USTA, AEG (venue owners in the US), Golden State Warriors, and the LA Kings.

It is a complicated business trying to get a sports league or team committed to sustainability as a business practice, and it takes work. There are three barriers to sustainability—technical barriers, financial barriers, and cultural barriers, and the latter are the most challenging. The most important thing we can do is instigate a cultural shift in attitudes and expectations about how we relate to the ecosystems that give us air to breathe and water to drink. We have to change attitudes; then money gets allocated to invest in new technologies to bring about change.

ANNE-CÉCILE TURNER   Sustainability Director at The Ocean Race

WITH ITS "RACING WITH PURPOSE" POSITIONING, THE OCEAN RACE IS ONE OF THE BEST EXAMPLES AROUND TODAY OF PURPOSE IN ACTION IN A SPORTING CONTEXT.

On how The Ocean Race came to be a Purpose-driven event:

The initial thought was for The Ocean Race to be a platform for change engaging all stakeholders because the beauty of sport is that it talks to a lot of different people. We wanted to use sailing as an exciting driver to talk about wider subjects which, in our case, was the ocean and its preservation. This idea came to us in 2016, when people were not as aware of sustainability and its benefits as they are today. It took a lot of convincing initially, but now everybody understands the value, not only for the ocean but for the community as well.

Summing up what The Ocean Race's Purpose is in one sentence:
Our vision is to accelerate ocean health restoration.

On The Ocean Race Science Program:
Boats in The Ocean Race go to the most remote places, areas where sailing isn't traditionally done. So, the idea was for our boats to carry a scientific device to study the ocean, and we had microplastic sampling on board. It was really helpful for the scientific community to use sailing boats as a platform for observation. However, it was also very helpful for the media because, as soon as we landed at a stopover, we had a lot of media attention about challenges facing the ocean.

The science program had much success in the last race, but the journey was not an easy one. I had to fight against the status quo against technology that was preventing us from doing what we wanted to do, but now we influence the whole fleet, which is good, and it is done in partnership with the sailors as well. For the next race, we will gather, as a minimum, the same data as before, but we are also exploring more to see what else is feasible within the boundaries of technology.

On how the Ocean Race has embraced sustainability from an operational perspective despite the challenges of taking place over so many months and visiting so many different parts of the world:
Of course, you cannot use your voice if you do not walk the talk, so we took the initiative to have parallel programs, one that was communicating the issue through our platforms and the other that was putting our house in order. We formed a great partnership with 11th Hour Racing (an organization that works with the sailing community to advance solutions and practices that protect and restore ocean health). We have additional partners, such as Blue Water and Volvo cars, who all helped us to find a team of professional experts in sustainability, who understood ISO 20121 (the event sustainability management framework).

We then took a picture of the situation to understand all the impacts, and we now calculate absolutely everything, and we are reducing and optimizing along the way. It has been quite mindblowing in terms of results because we have managed to reduce single-use plastic by 85% simply by optimizing the supply chain, and we are encouraging our stakeholders and host cities to do the same. Communication is key to engaging all stakeholders in the journey.

On the importance of Partners:

In the beginning, embarking on this sustainability journey was a financial risk for the organization. Then Partners came on board to help us deliver the program, and we did things in a parallel manner. There was a very strong commercial value and a very strong impact value, and that is what we sell and communicate to Partners.

In terms of sponsorship and the commercial aspects of sustainability, we are asked about our sustainability work more and more in meetings with prospective sponsors. I would say 90% of the time, there is a discussion about sustainability because we have such a strong program, and the world of sport is awakening to that. Many people want to do something, but we have already done it. It is about creating measured and tangible results with which people want to be associated. We also have a new sponsorship strategy where it is not only about putting a logo somewhere in the race but also to drive down the impact and to use it as a showcase for sustainable innovation.

The race has seen many changes recently—a different ownership structure, a different name, but still, the same vision, Racing with Purpose. On looking forward to the next edition of the race in 2021/2022 and how it is going to evolve:

This time sustainability is completely integrated within the organization. The look and feel and the brand work that has been done by the marketing team encompass the notion of circularity. We are launching a secondary school program that replicates the primary program in the languages of the host cities; we are launching a series of Ocean Race Summits, 12 across the world, that are also aligned, and we are adding innovation workshops. These are industry-led workshops, basically, a solution exchange platform that will not only inspire but also create roadmaps for action.

Not only is the event committee taking care of its actions, but it is also influencing the behavior of others that they interface with, which is great progress:

We cannot stop within our boundaries. What we do is open source. Our education program is available for free online. The scientific data collected onboard our boats are contributing to the global database of information alongside other work from the scientific community. There are lots of collaborations in the sailing world, and workshops facilitate a more structured way to collaborate and accelerate change.

On the importance of Purpose to the Ocean Race:
Purpose is embedded at the heart of the organization. It affects everything we do, from the way we operate to the way we engage with stakeholders, the way we communicate, the way we fund the event, and it is driving our success. As people start to understand the role of the ocean and realize that, although there is so much we do not know, the ocean plays a crucial role in all our lives, even if you live in a city or desert. It gives you half the oxygen you breathe, and the Ocean Race is willing to contribute to understanding the value of the ocean and the need to preserve it. It is working with stakeholders to accelerate its restoration.

Advice to sports properties, sponsors, and athletes thinking they would like to embark on this journey of Purpose but are not quite sure how to go about it:
I would say first look, not only inside, but outside as well because a lot is happening already. There is no need to reinvent the wheel as there is a lot of knowledge that is completely transferable. Look at organizations such as Sport and Sustainability International (SandSI). I am part of the organization, and they are bringing together the world of sport to provide tools and platforms to collaborate.

Then, take a picture of your organization, identify your values, and look at the reason you do what you do. Involve management because if top management is not engaged, it is never going to work at the scale and in the spirit that is needed. Use professionals in the areas where you do not have the skills and expertise in-house. Create sustainability criteria because we all need to be using events to make things change. And my last point would be to engage your partners and your stakeholders along the way.

JULIA PALLÉ   Senior Sustainability Consultant at Formula E

FORMULA E, WHICH FOCUSES ON RELEVANT FUTURE TECHNOLOGY AND PROMOTES THE ADOPTION OF SUSTAINABLE MOBILITY IN CITY CENTERS, IS SEEING EXCITING GROWTH AND DELIVERS A COMPELLING MESSAGE ON CLIMATE CHANGE AND AIR POLLUTION.

On Formula E's Purpose-driven approach and how it is relevant for the 21st century:
Establishing Formula E has been an organic process. The world did not need another motorsport series, but it did need a way to show that mobility is an issue in our cities

because of the air pollution it creates. Air pollution is the number one killer on earth at the moment—every year, the equivalent of the whole population of New York City dies due to air pollution. So, we are using the electrification of transport and the benefit it brings to society to create this motorsport series that can help to capture people's minds and raise awareness on the dangers of air pollution.

On the challenges when Formula E first started:
In the beginning, no one believed that electric cars were fast, fun, attractive, and reliable enough for an exciting motorsport series. However, we have proven, season after season, and by pushing the technology, that it is possible. I think our product is really exciting, and the fact that our events keep growing is a sign of achievement and a great example that you do not need to compromise performance to be sustainable.

It was essential to show that we were walking the talk and that our efforts to embed sustainability in the DNA of the championship were credible. That is why we decided, very early on, to certify Formula E against the Sustainable Events International Standard (ISO 20121). We knew that, to be legitimate, we had to, not just say it ourselves, but that an independent international body had to recognize it as well.

On the importance of Formula E's sustainability positioning to attract sponsors and partners for the events and teams:
When partners come to us, sustainability is of paramount interest, but the beauty is that they do not want to stick their name and logo on our event. They are interested because they have their sustainability strategy, and they see us as a platform to tell their story. For example, Allianz is our fan zone partner, and they supported our plastic reductions program by developing a reusable water pouch together with free hydration stations for fans at our events. In just one season, we managed to save more than 200,000 plastic bottles from landfills. For me, this is a fantastic example of creating shared value with a sponsor.

On Formula E's important collaborations with organizations other than corporates:
One of the most important partnerships we have developed over the last year is with the United Nations. We showcase their program, #BeatAirPollution, which is a

perfect match with what we are trying to achieve—creating and raising awareness on air pollution issues.

We work with UNEP, the United Nations Environment Programme, to reach as many people as possible to make them understand that this is a big issue that touches everyone and is killing millions of people. One of our best drivers, Lucas Di Grassi, is an ambassador of the program, which has been an amazing way to reach out to younger people and get them fascinated on the topic. Last summer, we sent Lucas to New Delhi, probably one of the most polluted cities in the world, to see with his own eyes what air pollution means and what its impacts are. We have made a documentary film about it, and the images of people being surrounded by polluted air with no way of protecting themselves were very powerful. It has been extremely well received by our fans and the public in general.

On moving from a focus on driving awareness to driving a change in behavior, changing the way people engage with mobility:
Changing behavior has always been one of the key things that the Championship aims to achieve. Our mission has three key pillars—pushing the technology, which is normally the reason motorsport exists as the races are like a technical laboratory, then changing perceptions. We use the race as the vehicle for this. We get people excited, and when we capture their imagination, we also send the message around the benefits of electric mobility. Finally, there is the infrastructure pillar and the fact that we have collaborations with host cities and businesses to make sure that the right infrastructure is implemented across our cities to make change a reality.

On whether they are starting to see the impact of the strategy yet, even though it has only been six years:
Yes, we are. We have realized that when people get exposed to Formula E as a product, their propensity to become interested in the topic of sustainability is greater. So, for us, it shows that the message is received and that it is working. We want people to have our message of sustainability as a takeaway from watching or attending one of our events. We want them to have a different perspective on the lifestyle they can have. Our message is a lot wider than just encouraging electric mobility, we offer vegetarian options at our food stalls, and we have initiatives to

reduce plastic pollution and showcase that waste recycling is simple and achievable on an individual level.

Advice for an organization who wants to embark on a sustainability journey:
I would advise them to think through what their Purpose is and how they can make a difference to the world. It is a difficult question, but it is essential to address. How are you different? What are you doing to make a difference to the world by your product or service? It might involve going deep into your strategic perspective and could lead to completely refocusing your strategy to make sure that you remain relevant. And then, once you have done that, you need to make sure you walk the talk. You cannot just put messages out there around your Purpose because that is not robust.

ANNA ISAACSON   Senior Vice President of Social Responsibility at the NFL

THE NFL RECOGNIZES ITS ROLE AS A COMMUNITY ORGANIZATION THAT HAS A RESPONSIBILITY TO USE ITS INFLUENCE TO AFFECT CHANGE.

On the business rationale for adopting a more Purposeful approach:
Companies are trying to do well by doing good, and it is also important for the NFL players to be seen for the men that they are, which is charitable, community-driven, good husbands, and good fathers that give back to the community. The NFL leadership was at the forefront of recognizing that there was a positive business impact to doing this type of work, but also a responsibility that the league has as a community organization to give back.

On defining the Purpose of the NFL:
We see our Purpose as being to inspire fans and make our community stronger and better. That is pretty broad, so we have been working hard over the last six months to put out a Purpose statement that unifies all the things we are doing. It came out of the Huddle for 100 campaign that we launched in 2019 in celebration of our 100th season and rallied fans to volunteer 100 minutes of their time for work in their community. It brought the entire league together and allowed us to tell a cohesive story.

On the focus areas of the NFL Foundation:

The focus of the NFL Foundation is narrow and broad at the same time. It is narrowly focused on youth health and wellness and youth football support, and then, from a broader perspective, it is focused on the communities that support our game. We created the Play 60 health and wellness campaign for kids in 2007, and we had no idea where it would go, but it is a natural fit for our brand and our players. They can talk easily about the importance of being active for 60 minutes a day. When you find something where everyone across the league can speak to it, then you have got a winner.

On the NFL's potential to have an impact around issues of social justice:

The NFL has always been tremendously committed to our communities, particularly underserved communities. A couple of years ago, when we faced challenges around the national anthem, we started having in-depth conversations with NFL players about the issues that exist in our country. It became clear to everyone that these issues were not just player issues; they were issues that we all face. These issues were something where the NFL could put a stake in the ground and support what the players were doing and make an impact. It took some time to determine where specifically we wanted to be because social justice is pretty broad, and it is defined differently by many people. Our definition is that we are trying to reduce barriers to opportunity. We focus on education, economic advancement, police and community relations, and criminal justice reform.

On where the sport for good movement is going and what we are likely to see over the next ten years:

I think we are going to see continued and deeper integration as well as higher expectations from companies and their consumers in terms of what they are doing to give back. I do not think it is going anywhere; I only see it increasing. We have been held accountable by our fans, but I think more companies are going to see that come to fruition as well. I think we are going to see more partnerships between sponsors and leagues, and we are going to dive a lot deeper with our partners to do good. We are going to partner with like-minded organizations, on the for-profit or the nonprofit side, and bring these campaigns to life in an even bigger way.

Advice for anyone thinking about getting started in this space for the first time:
Research to see what other organizations are doing, make phone calls, and reach
out to people who have done it before. It is easy to get information, whether it is
online or just picking up the phone. This industry is small, and people are willing to
help.

SCOTT JENKINS

Board Chair at Green Sports Alliance and
General Manager at Mercedes Benz Stadium

THE GREEN SPORTS ALLIANCE HAS BEEN HIGHLY SUCCESSFUL
IN MOBILIZING VARIOUS STAKEHOLDERS IN SPORT TO EMBRACE
SUSTAINABILITY FOR THE GOOD OF SPORTS AND LOCAL COMMUNITIES.

On the role of the Green Sports Alliance today:
Just about every team or league in professional sports in North America is a
member. We have a growing Collegiate membership and strong corporate support.
So, we have increased significantly. The first time we did a summit ten years ago,
it involved about 2-3 months of planning, and we had 70 people there, and now,
we anticipate 500–600 people at our annual summit. It is always a great couple
of days to get together, share ideas, and celebrate the good work that is being
done. The conversations have evolved over the years, and there are currently three
pillars driving our activities—the financial, the social, and the environmental. We
have robust conversations about what we can do to address issues and how we can
advance things quickly to achieve change.

On the initiatives that the Green Sports Alliance engages in:
We have a monthly webinar where we take a topic and invite our members to
listen in. We create playbooks and case studies to share with our members of
what individual teams, leagues, and venues are doing. We work closely with our
corporate partners and our supply chain to provide solutions. We try to make it
very practical.

We talk a lot about sport's potential to influence society and set a good
example. However, the priority list for sports is huge, and sometimes being
environmentally responsible is not as high a priority as it should be. Hopefully,

though, with more people talking about what we are doing, it will all start to tie together. One of the challenging things with climate change is that it is not seen in daily life but, I think with the SDGs demonstrating that there are things we can all do as a community to drive positive change, it creates a connection. We need to build strong communities because that is what gets people to act. I am a great believer in collaboration, and people getting more done together than they can alone. Is it naïve of me to dream that, one day, big chunks of the sports industry will come together and collaborate around joint initiatives to address climate change issues?

On sport's perceived reluctance to embrace Purpose:
Probably because they are a bit apprehensive and think it is too risky. But I do not believe there is a risk if you are going out and making a positive difference in your community. I think, overall, there is a reticence about being too aggressive in measuring environmental impact and making commitments to reduce impact and being held accountable for that. The UN Sport for Climate Change initiative is crafted to account for that and kudos to the teams that have signed up because they have made a statement, and that is part of leadership, and you do not lead without taking some form of risk.

On the move to Atlanta and the construction of the Mercedes-Benz Stadium:
Right from the beginning, it was clear this stadium was going to be noteworthy from an architectural standpoint. It is also stunning from a technology standpoint; it is cutting-edge from a food and beverage program, and it is in the heart of Atlanta alongside public transit. It is a stunning building that is LEED Platinum certified and built the right way. It is energy-efficient and water-efficient.

On the challenges of operating the stadium:
When large groups of people come together, it puts our daily consumption habits under the microscope. It is not just sports that consume a lot, we do the same in our everyday lives, and we tend to walk away as if it will just magically go away. But, if we stop and open our eyes, there is a major impact that we can make. Our big focus now is to make it a zero-waste stadium. We have made some really good progress, and our private event business has been zero waste for a year. But, now we are trying to expand that to the whole stadium.

RICARDO FORT   Head of Global Sponsorships at The Coca-Cola Company

COCA-COLA IS AT THE FOREFRONT OF THE PURPOSE MOVEMENT AND
SUCCESSFULLY INTEGRATES ITS PURPOSE VISION ACROSS ALL FACETS OF
ITS BUSINESS, INCLUDING ITS SPORTS INVESTMENTS.

**On how Coca-Cola's sustainability commitments play out in the way the
company activates its sponsorships:**

We use our sponsorships to tell stories about what is important to the company,
and sustainability is important to us. Regarding recycling, we have been managing
waste at global events for a long time. At the FIFA World Cup and Olympic
Games, all the waste is recycled by us as part of our Without Waste initiative.
Sometimes we go beyond waste management, like at the 2014 FIFA World Cup
in Brazil, where all the seats for the new Maracanã stadium were made using
recycled plastic from our products. For the 2018 Winter Olympics, we worked with
the organizers and government to treat water supply in the Pyeongchang area.
For the Torch Relay for the 2020 Tokyo Olympics, we helped with the design and
manufacture of the uniforms, which were made from PET bottles.

Looking at women's empowerment, we sponsor a team of 30 global athletes,
two-thirds of whom are women. There are Olympians, Paralympians, and Special
Olympians, and they all get paid the same, and their rights are the same. It is
very different from the approach of other companies who give a lot of money to
a superstar and not as much to their up-and-coming athletes. The same applies to
every event or organization that we sponsor; we make sure that there is equal pay
amongst men and women. When US Soccer recently claimed that its female players
do not have the same ability as the men, so should not be paid equally, Coca-Cola
was the only sponsor who spoke out and said this was not right.

So, in essence, our sponsorships help us to magnify our commitment to water,
packaging, and women's empowerment. Events allow us to tell better stories about
what Coca-Cola is doing in areas that are important for our business, and they also
help the organizers deliver a better event.

On fan reaction to Coca-Cola's plastic reduction initiatives:

When people are made aware of what we do, their reaction is always very
positive. We have done this for years without talking about it. We did it because

we knew it was the right thing to do. It is an engagement process, and we know that people's perceptions of the company will improve when they know about it.

On whether the sports community is making it easy for Coca-Cola to tell its sustainability stories through its sponsorships:
I do not think it is a case of being easy or difficult. It is more a choice of the sponsor as to what stories to tell but, all of our research shows us that consumers, particularly young consumers, are interested in sustainability. If you merge sustainability with sports, you have twice the chance of success. We are lucky because we have global relationships, and we can tell global stories that we believe are meaningful everywhere.

On whether the sports category as a whole is doing enough to contribute towards building a sustainable future:
It is hard to say if we are doing enough because we can always do more, but more often than not, these days, companies are using sports to tell stories about Purpose. If you look at global events, a lot of the development that you see in the local communities of host cities is driven by these events. Look at the Olympic Games in Brazil and what it did for urban mobility, and London 2012 and what that did for the improvement of the neighborhood in the East End. If you go event by event, you can pinpoint certain things that would never have happened without sports.

JOANNE PASTERNACK
Former Warriors and 49ers Foundation Executive Director and President and Chief Impact Officer at Oliver Rose

THROUGH HER WORK AT THE SAN FRANCISCO 49ERS AND THE GOLDEN STATE WARRIORS, JOANNE HAS DEMONSTRATED HER UNDERSTANDING OF THE CRUCIAL ROLE THAT A TEAM CAN PLAY AS A FORCE FOR GOOD IN THE COMMUNITY.

On the highlights of her work with two of the leading professional sports teams in the Bay Area and the interaction of sports and doing good in the community:
When I started at the 49ers, there was no synergy between the work that the Community Relations Department was doing, our corporate partnership activations,

and the off-the-field activities in which our players were engaged. So, we started to look more proactively at what we could do with our community partners and corporate partners and where we could bring them all together to create meaningful programs. We found that these partnerships became so much more impactful overall. Allowing our corporate partners to align their business and philanthropic practices in a way that made sense felt truly authentic.

On the extent to which the community programs factored into the sponsors' decision to support the 49ers and the Warriors:
Our corporate partners felt a sense of pride, not just to be aligned with our on-field or on-court performance, but also with the tremendous work we were doing in the community. And the fact that we were being recognized, not just on a local or national level, but on a global level for groundbreaking work and for the type of impact we were having, fills us with honor. Our players were not just going out to make appearances and sign autographs or take pictures with kids. We were rolling up our sleeves, getting to work, and building meaningful, long-lasting partnerships. For example, at the 49ers, we had a multi-year investment with Chevron to open up the Science, Technology, Engineering, and Math (STEM) Leadership Institute, which was the first of its kind. It started as a three-year partnership and has continued, with hundreds of students benefiting from it.

On creating a plausible link between sport and science and technology:
It is rewarding to connect your brand with something that captures attention and elevates your brand to a level of visibility that it would not otherwise have had. Going back to science and technology, when I was 12 years old, I was not particularly interested in physics and, although I was a good student, I was much more interested in figure skating. When my physics teacher told me that figure skating was all about physics and that I should be interested in it because physics enabled me to move, spin, and jump on the ice, suddenly, physics became fascinating to me, and I wanted to learn more. To have that spark at 12 years old is something that I have never lost, and I remember it when we are looking at ways to bring a topic to life for a corporation or a nonprofit. When you put a story to something that is not as popular or as easily understood by the general public, it suddenly comes to life.

On the benefits of such programs to the team:

The 49ers are now able to offer consulting services to other teams globally who are looking to launch similar programs. The reason other teams are interested in it is that they see that it not only generates goodwill, but it generates revenue and opportunities for them to launch similar partnerships with corporations.

On how the role of athletes in society has changed:

It has changed tremendously, mainly due to social media, because it gives players a platform to share messages about things that are important to them and for others to gain a sense of who they are and align with that. Every single athlete has a unique background and a unique story to tell. Since 2011, we have looked at how to engage our athletes in the causes that are important to them, to help athletes feel more connected to our aligned brands. For example, 49ers player Joe Staley, whose mother is a librarian, is passionate about literacy. He has done numerous events around Early Childhood Literacy because it is something he knows a lot about, and that makes him passionate. If you can create something that will drive momentum towards your brand in an authentic way and enhance the corporate partner's visibility at the same time, then you have a win all around, and it creates the renewals for those partnerships.

CLEMENTINE PAINTER   Senior Manager of Strategic Planning at adidas

PURPOSE SITS AT THE HEART OF THE ADIDAS BUSINESS, PARTICULARLY AROUND THE ISSUES OF PLASTIC WASTE, BREAKING BARRIERS FOR GIRLS, AND INCLUSION. THE BRAND USES SPORT AS A PLATFORM TO BRING ITS COMMITMENT TO PURPOSE TO LIFE AND TO CREATE POSITIVE CHANGE.

On adidas' belief that sport can play an important role in changing people's lives:

At adidas, we live and breathe sports as part of our everyday lives. Yes, we produce shoes and clothes but, we also know that sport is central to every culture and society and is core to an individual's health, confidence, and happiness. If you look at a soccer match or the Olympics, events like that, you realize that sport has the power to inspire and unite people from diverse backgrounds. We work every day to inspire and enable people to harness the power of sport in their lives, using our athletes and the communities they are impacted by to bring role models to people who might not have the chance to have role models in their everyday life.

On the strategy around ending plastic waste and how this plays out:
From as far back as 2015, we have been looking at ways to reduce our plastic waste. Back then, we produced a shoe made entirely of recycled polyester, and, now, in 2020, we will produce 15–20 million pairs of these shoes compared to 11 million pairs in 2019, so it is growing every year. From a product perspective, this was the start, and we have since expanded our focus to other areas like the cotton we use. We have also produced our first fully recyclable running shoe, Futurecraft Loop, which has been tested internally, and we plan to launch it in 2021. Ultimately, we would like a regenerative loop, where we create products made from biodegradable material. It is not only about the product though. We also carry our message of sustainability through our communication strategy.

On the strategy around breaking barriers for girls and how this plays out:
Our strategy speaks directly to the idea of using sport to bring about change. We partnered with streetfootballworld to increase the participation of girls in all sports. We chose this because, by high school, many girls have dropped out of sports for several reasons, and our intervention hopes to increase their access so girls can enjoy the same benefit as boys get out of sports. The name, streetfootballworld, is misleading because the organization is a network of nonprofits who use any kind of sport to bring everybody together. Our goal is to impact more than 50,000 girls in five years, so it is a long-term project for us. We want it to go beyond sport too. Sport is the starting point, but we want to give these girls the skills they will need outside of sport to have the confidence to be the best version of themselves.

On the lessons learned and advice for other sports brands who are skeptical about Purpose:
I think Purpose is becoming increasingly important for consumers and employees. If Purpose is at the core of the company, it can be inspiring for employees and consumers. If anyone is skeptical, I would say look at the examples of companies

who are doing good and see the benefits that they derive from it. Even small acts can lead to bigger things. I would say do not hesitate to partner with an expert who can help you to shape your Purpose.

KELY NASCIMENTO-DELUCA
Filmmaker, advocate for women's soccer, and eldest daughter of Brazilian soccer legend Pelé

KELY HAS PRODUCED A GROUNDBREAKING DOCUMENTARY, WARRIORS OF A BEAUTIFUL GAME, WHICH HIGHLIGHTS IMPORTANT ISSUES FACING WOMEN IN SOCCER TODAY AND ADVOCATES FOR GREATER GENDER EQUALITY.

On the background to her documentary:

I came to this project because of a young Brazilian woman I met through my brother-in-law. He had spotted her talent while at a youth soccer camp in Brazil. He eventually managed to arrange for her to come to America on a scholarship where she did exceptionally well, later captaining the Brazilian U20 National Team and attending the University of Florida on a full soccer scholarship. Her incredible story made me realize that there was no path for young women in Brazil to make a career in soccer, and so, around 2015, I started researching women's soccer, and I was shocked at what I found, which compelled me to want to tell the story. The really interesting thing for me was how soccer was just a mirror for the state of women in general in different countries, and it made me think that we needed to tell the story in a bigger context. Tell the young girl's story, but within it, we needed to tell the wider story about women's soccer.

On the commitment to make the film benefit soccer and help bring about change:

When we decided to make the film, one of the most important things for me was that the film needed to work for soccer. So, I signed MOUs with five grassroots soccer organizations that allow them to use the film after its release to generate money and, if not money, then to generate awareness. My idea was for the film to serve as a public service announcement to get people talking and making changes. I do not believe that these films do anything in and of themselves. What they can do, though, is inspire people to do things and to change. They can give young girls out there a little extra energy, or an extra push.

On the progress made in women's soccer recently and what the future holds:
The one thing that gives me great hope is that when things are not exposed, there is very little chance for them to be resolved. But how women's soccer has come to the forefront in the media recently and how public opinion is now also starting to play a role is wonderful to see. Once you start telling stories, then there is more accountability, and that leads to change. I think it is going in the right direction, but there are many barriers, mainly due to the lack of women in power at all levels of the game and in the media. It is about changing the narrative at the top. If there were more diversity in the room, there would be more opinions.

Advice to corporates who are hesitant to support women's soccer:
I would encourage them to be the first major corporation to support women's soccer. Be the next Nike! It is not even about doing anything altruistic. The men's game is saturated, but there is an incredible opportunity to support young female players. Currently, male athletes are the rock stars, but how long will it be before women athletes are the rock stars that everyone admires? Nobody ever made a mark in this world by playing catch up.

SPORT FOR GOOD COMES OF AGE

Sport For Good, Sport for Development, Sports Based Youth Development, Sport for Peace are all names used to describe a practice that has emerged over the last twenty years, where sport is used as a platform to bring about positive social outcomes for people and communities.

While the participants in these Sport For Good programs directly benefit from the physical activity connected with sport, they also benefit directly from the life skills, life values, and other educational benefits that are often an integral part of these programs.

The communities where these people live, most of them underserved or neglected, also benefit from these programs as they are often focussed on changing behaviors that otherwise are a burden on these communities.

Historically, these programs have relied on philanthropic funding to support their missions. However, this is starting to change as more and more Sport For Good organizations begin to think through how they can be of value to sports properties, sponsors, and athletes looking for opportunities to activate their Purpose.

Sport For Good organizations operate at just about every level of society. There are those with a worldwide remit like streetfootballworld, the world's largest Soccer for Good network with over 140 network members across the globe that reaches over 2 million underserved kids each year.

Another global example is the Laureus Sport For Good Foundation that supports over 200 Sport for Good organizations in over 40 countries and has directed more than 160 million Euro to benefit over 6 million kids around the world.

While organizations like streetfootballworld and Laureus support organizations addressing multiple social issues, there are also Sport For Good organizations focussed on addressing specific issues. For example, the Women's Sports Foundation tackles issues related to gender equity in sports, and Peace And Sport focuses on peacebuilding through sport. Some organizations operate at an ultra-local level focussed on serving a single local community.

The Global Goals have become a focus of the Sport For Good sector in recent times as its actors have recognized that the work they are doing contributes to one or more of the 17 Goals. They provide a great framework around which the actors can demonstrate their contribution to building a sustainable future.

Beyond Sport is an organization that was set up in the last decade to lean into and support this emerging sector. Beyond Sport promotes, supports, and celebrates the use of sport to address social issues in communities around the world through events, sharing of best practices amongst sport for good organizations, and by providing funding support to projects addressing a range of social issues. BeyondSport.org is a great resource for anyone wanting to understand and follow the Sport For Good sector and its actors. As of April 2020, Beyond Sport had listed 2,822 Projects from 2,690 Organizations in 154 Countries across 56 Sports.

The Sport For Good sector is making great strides and doubling down on its ability to address social and environmental issues, rebuild communities, and provide people from underserved communities with the chance at a better life. However, it has not yet done a good job of quantifying the economic value of the contribution of Sport For Good as a sector to society. Just like we can value the economic impact of a sports event to society, we need to be able to do the same for Sport For Good.

We are working on developing such a model at 17 Sport, which we hope to use as a lever to increase the amount of investment that the public and private sectors put into Sport For Good programs, just like the environmental movement has been able to do by placing a value on the environment's Natural Capital. If anyone would like to join us in this effort, we would love to hear from you.

We are huge proponents of the Sport For Good movement and the efficacy of their methodologies, so encourage our partners to involve Sport For Good organizations as an important component of any collaborative effort around sport. We recently partnered with Global Sports Week to launch the GSW Booster Program through which, each year, we will support the efforts of nine Sport For Good organizations to help them scale their impact by providing them with access to our expertise and networks. The cohorts in the first year of the program include some amazing Sport For Good organizations from all corners of the planet, including FundLife, O Megot, 49ers EDU, Baba Au Run, ENGSO Youth, La Recyclerie Sportive, Parikrma Foundation, Sourire D'Un Enfant, and Terres En Mêlées. Each of these organizations is doing something innovative to leverage the power of Sport For Good, and we are excited about the potential they each have to make a real difference.

In addition to the Sport For Good organizations mentioned above, our other favorites include Women Win, Soccer Without Borders, Right To Play, Skateistan, Play Rugby USA, Coaches Across Continents, Sport dans la Ville, Play International, Waves for Change, Magic Bus, and Girl Up.

KEY INSIGHTS: SPORT FOR GOOD ON THE UP AND UP

➤ Sport For Good is a practice that has emerged over the last twenty years, where sport is used as a platform to bring about positive social outcomes for people and communities.

➤ These programs typically address underserved or neglected communities and provide vital benefits. In addition to the benefit of physical activity, participants also gain life skills, life values, and other educational benefits.

➤ Historically, these programs have relied on philanthropic funding, but this is starting to change as these organizations demonstrate their value to sponsors, athletes, and sports properties.

➤ The UN Sustainable Development Goals have become a focus of the Sport For Good sector in recent times as its actors have recognized that the work that they are doing contributes to one or more of the 17 Goals.

➤ Sport for Good organizations can be multi-functional in reach, such as streetfootballworld and Laureus Sport For Good Foundation, or focus on addressing specific issues, such as Women's Sports Foundation and Peace And Sport.

➤ While the Sport for Good movement has made great strides in addressing social and environmental issues, it has fallen short in quantifying the economic value of the contribution of Sport For Good as a sector to society.

LEADING THOUGHTS:
SPORT FOR GOOD

TIM SHRIVER　　Disability rights activist and Chairman of the Special Olympics

THE SPECIAL OLYMPICS AND ITS MESSAGE OF INCLUSIVITY ENCAPSULATE
ALL THAT IS GOOD ABOUT THE IMPACT SPORT CAN HAVE IN EDUCATING
PEOPLE AND SHIFTING MINDSETS AND BEHAVIORS. THE EVENT'S OATH—
"LET ME WIN, BUT IF I CANNOT WIN, LET ME BE BRAVE IN THE ATTEMPT,"
SAYS IT ALL.

On the start of the Special Olympics and the inspiration behind it:
The main distinction about the founding of Special Olympics that is different
from many other sports organizations is that it was based on a desire to solve a
social, cultural, and political problem. In contrast, most sports organizations are
based on joyful, recreational, and physical reasons and then, only later, do some
organizations ask what problem they can look to address. We had a problem,
and sport was the solution. Our challenge was that hundreds of millions of people
around the world had been closed out and treated as sub-human. A small handful
of advocates, mothers mostly, began to rebel against the structure and the
institutionalization of disability, the isolation of these children, and the denial of
healthcare, education, and employment. It was a massive problem that almost no
one saw, and my mother, along with many others, started working in every way she
could to change this. She would visit doctors, politicians, educators, and employers
asking for help, guidance, or funding. Getting nowhere, she looked to sports as
a solution that would bypass the expert community and engage average human
beings, and she tried to end the isolation that way. So, in the 1960s, she started
summer camps, which continued until 1968, when the first Special Olympics were
held in Chicago with the idea of ending the distance, separation, misunderstanding,
and horrifying oppression that separated people with an intellectual disability even
from their own families. Her vision was that if we play together, we can begin to
change the country and change the world.

On the first gathering for the Special Olympics:

The first event looked very much like the events look today. The summer camps were recreational and sporting, and my mother would bring in great athletes to do coaching, as well as high school and college kids to volunteer and play in teams with kids with intellectual disabilities. Children came to my mother's house, and, on a big sprawling field there, she had ponies, obstacle courses, and soccer games. We started practicing the core message that continues in Special Olympics today, which is to try and close the distance that separates us from one another by playing sports, training, competing, learning and developing new skills, meeting and joining with teammates. The very simple dimensions of sport were extraordinarily powerful in ending this stigmatization and the terrifying fear we have of one another, in particular people with intellectual disabilities.

From those first summer camps, she expanded around the country, and by 1968, she realized that these camps could do more, or more accurately, what these kids with intellectual challenges could do. She saw them swim when people said they couldn't swim. She saw them compete when people had said they couldn't; she saw their smiles, and she saw their mothers come and say how proud they were of their child. She saw the teenagers who were volunteering have their whole minds changed, their hearts changed, and have their lives transformed by the simple gift of sport.

It made her think that this was not just sports; it was an Olympic sport. People laughed and ridiculed her for thinking that these forgotten people could be attached to the word Olympic, one of the most aspirational brands in the world. However, no one can look at a Special Olympics athlete without some level of wonder at the personal challenges that these athletes have overcome. Fast forward to today, and we celebrated our 50th anniversary a few years ago. We are in 190 countries with over a million volunteers who run over 100,000 games every year.

On how these events have become part of the community's everyday life:

Our athletes look forward to these events all month, sometimes all year, but you also hear the same thing from the people with no disability. The giant insight of this movement is that unified by sport, both sides benefit equally. When we play on the same football team or volleyball team or run in a relay race together, we release those fears that separated us from one another and, similarly, the athletes themselves say that they have been able to overcome this enormous shame. All of a sudden, they feel the power of developing a skill, proving to them what they are capable of achieving. So, while it may look like a swimming race or a track meet, do not be deceived because it is a classroom on the transformation of the human spirit.

On how the concept of Inclusive Games and Inclusive Schools plays out in practice:

Our work now includes what we call Special Olympics Unified Sports, which means bringing people with and without intellectual disabilities into the games together, and we see this booming in school sports and sports clubs in Europe. So, just as there is a boys' basketball team and a girls' basketball team, there is also a Special Olympics Unified Sports basketball team representing a high school. Why not see this as a standard expectation, not the exception that a school or club would be represented by, not just the elite athlete, but also the Special Olympics athlete performing his or her unified sport together with his or her non-disabled peers. The Inclusive Schools program is a way to teach inclusion without needing a book.

On the broad-based stakeholder approach that has been used to grow the Special Olympics movement and the breadth of partners involved:

I like to explain to people that, in business, you develop an intellectual property or product, and you try to retain control of it, but our goal is to give it away. We offer this platform, these very simple rules of engagement, to the world, and several organizations and people champion it.

Our goal is to point out that there is a great deal that the volunteer can do to change the world. Volunteering is where my mother was so smart. Normally, an organization would see volunteers as a nice-to-have and paid staff as critical, whereas my mother was the opposite. She felt that people who volunteer give from their heart and not for compensation, and this was the energy that would most powerfully expand the message and the mission of the movement.

On the Special Olympics funding model:

We raise money in different ways around the world. In China, we rely on our partnership with government institutions, whereas, in the USA, we rely mostly on contributions from ordinary people who give $25 or $50 a year because they believe in what we are doing. We also have corporate partners who help us amplify our message and provide funding support. We rely on the big sports leagues like the NBA and the NHL, who have been great supporters, not just giving talent, but also financial resources and training facilities.

On the principle of exclusivity with regards to corporate sponsorships and how that plays out in the Special Olympics ecosystem:
We have exclusive sponsors in categories and by geographies and for events, but our sponsors tend to come to us with a slightly different lens. They are looking to us to help their employees get involved in something that gives them a sense of Purpose and connects their brand to something meaningful. They are relying on us to communicate to their customers what their values are because there is not a brand in the world that is not trying to figure out how to combine their focus on the financial bottom line with an emphasis on the social, civic, and cultural bottom line. We can be very helpful to them in that regard.

On the concept of doing good while doing well:
I do not think we will make it on this planet if we do not figure out how to put those two together. It is not an optional, feel-good experience for a few companies to do. Doing well and doing good is the new exigency of the 21st century if we are going to save our planet, community, families, children, and health care. We can no longer afford businesses who see themselves as pure commercial entities with nothing but a financial bottom line, and the rest of the interests of humanity be darned. That doesn't work anymore.

On whether this concept of doing good while doing well applies to sports as well:
I think the same rules apply. I do not believe we can build huge events and spend huge sums of money without regard to issues relating to the environment, society, inclusivity, and participation. The value and credibility of sports hinge on whether or not we are allowing men and women with and without disabilities into our sports communities. The economics of sport depends on whether or not we are speaking to a new generation and in the language they demand of us environmentally, culturally, and socially and it all comes down to inclusivity.

Too much sport is based on elite models. It does not make sense to tell children, at age 12 or 13, that they are no good, which is what we do now. Most kids stop playing sports at that age because someone has told them they are not good enough. What kind of an organization has, as one of its organizing principles, the elimination of 80–95 percent of the people who want to participate as a goal? But that is what has happened, and it is crazy, counterproductive, and misguided. We have to turn some of those paradigms on their head. We have got to make sports accessible to every kid.

On learnings and insights gained along the way in terms of embracing Purpose:

I wish we had done more work upfront, and particularly with the onset of digital media, to push the stories and voices of our athletes because I think they have so much to share. We are still lagging in the capacity to retain, sustain, and mobilize our volunteers, so I wish we could improve there, and I wish we could develop the confidence to ask for financial resources. We need to adopt the mindset that people should be lucky to be able to give to this movement rather than be burdened by it. Maybe, when we do that, we will get more of the financial power that can help us grow.

On the hopes, dreams, and long-term vision for Special Olympics:

I have one very concrete one. I hope every school or sports club in the world will have not just a young men's program and a young women's program, but that they will have a Special Olympics Unified Sports Program. I hope that someday if you meet someone from Rio de Janeiro, Paris, Cairo, or New York City and you asked them about playing on a Special Olympics team in their community, it would be just an ordinary thing that children did.

BENITA FITZGERALD MOSLEY

Olympic Gold Medalist in the 100m
hurdles and former CEO at Laureus
Sport For Good Foundation USA

BENITA IS ONE OF THE MOST RESPECTED PEOPLE IN THE SPORTS INDUSTRY
AND, THROUGH HER POSITION AS CEO OF LAUREUS USA, USED SPORT
TO IMPROVE THE LIVES OF YOUNG PEOPLE, PARTICULARLY YOUNG GIRLS,
ACROSS AMERICA.

On the issue of gender equity and women's sports:
I have been a direct beneficiary of the pioneers of women's sports, the likes of
Billie Jean King, Donna De Varona, Anita France, and more. I certainly was inspired
by the Wilma Rudolphs of the world when I was competing as a track athlete and
knew that they had paved the way. It was apparent to me early on that I needed
to give back and pay it forward so that other women could benefit as well. I have
been involved in the Women's Sports Foundation for many years and have been
cognizant of promoting, supporting, and advancing women in all fields.

On the progress made in terms of the gender balance in sport:
It has been a remarkable success so far. If you look at Olympic sport, when I
competed in Los Angeles, female athletes made up 23% of the athletes in the
Games, and we are almost at the 50/50 mark for Tokyo, where 49.6% will be
women.

On the definition of Sport For Good and its value proposition to society:
It is sport that is intentionally used to develop life skills that are going to help kids
be successful beyond the playing field. It has high quality, well-trained coaches who
can deliver content to these kids once they have been hooked into the sport and
delivering programs that will enhance their educational outcomes, career outcomes,
physical and mental health, and create a sense of social cohesion within the
community at large. It is about so much more than just providing kids with access to
a ball. It is for children to receive the attention and support of caring, well-trained
adults that help protect them and shield them from life's trauma and to help them
steer clear of some of the impediments to their success.

On what kids experience through one of the Laureus Sport for Good Programs:
Generally speaking, it is a safe place for a child to go. It is the consistent presence
of teammates and adults who care about their safety and well-being. It is a fun
environment, playing a particular sport or doing a specific physical activity, and
kids are usually challenged, not only to improve on the playing field, but off the
playing field as well regarding their grades, their attitude, and their behavior. And
it has to be done intentionally through a well-thought-out program led by someone
who has the proper training and is providing the appropriate environment for those
children.

**On Laureus as a very intentional intervention that focuses on the social and
emotional development of kids using sport as a platform to get them engaged:**
When Laureus works with communities on the ground, we try to help local
organizations build capacity so they can serve more children and serve them better.
By creating this ecosystem of organizations, youth, and Sport For Good leaders in a
particular community who are all focused on bettering themselves by learning from
each other and simultaneously improving the community around them, then magic
happens. The Sport for Good platform is not only about doing good things for
individuals or the kids themselves, but it leads to good outcomes for the society and
the community in which they live and operate.

**On where the opportunities are for sport within an environment that is calling
for organizations to stand for more than just profits:**
There is a lot going on in the sports philanthropy space. It is many people, with
athletes and teams and leagues and companies all having their initiatives, and
everybody wants to attach their brand to some unique thing. We all mean well. We
are all trying to help kids and communities. However, I think there is an opportunity
for us to band together in a more strategic way to have an even greater impact,
serve even more people, and go from doing a bunch of activities to having a huge
impact. At Laureus, I think we would like to be the catalyst that helps make that
happen.

OLGA HARVEY Chief Strategy and Impact Officer at Women's Sports Foundation

THE WOMEN'S SPORTS FOUNDATION (WSF) HAS BEEN DEDICATED TO ADVANCING THE LIVES OF GIRLS AN D WOMEN THROUGH SPORTS FOR 45 YEARS.

On the origins of the Women's Sports Foundation (WSF):

Billie Jean King started it in 1974, and, ever since, we have been dedicated to advancing the lives of girls and women through sports and allowing them to realize their power to reach their potential through the benefits of sports. That mission has endured over the years, and we have made huge progress. In some ways, though, we are just getting started because there is still much work to do.

On the role of Title IX and how it was a transformational piece of legislation:

Title IX is also known as the 37 words that changed everything. These words are: "No person in the United States shall, on the basis of sex, be excluded from participation or be denied the benefits of or be subjected to discrimination under any education program or activity receiving federal financial assistance."

The legislation speaks of much more than sports, but it provided enough of an opening for activists back in 1972 to say that they were not going to hold back any longer. At the time, the number of girls playing organized sports at the high school level was very low, and the numbers did not grow immediately because of the legislation. Monetary support was still needed to enforce it, and it took time for organizations to start working towards greater equity.

Title IX has several parts to it, and for an organization to comply, you do not have to meet all the requirements, but you have to show that you have equitable funds allocated towards both men's and women's programs. It is very multi-dimensional and, if you can show that you are working towards it and constantly improving, then you are given a pass. In June 2022, it is the 50th anniversary of Title IX, and it is shocking to see that nearly 90% of colleges still do not offer athletic opportunities to female athletes proportional to their enrollment, so we are not there yet in terms of equal opportunities for boys and girls in Collegiate Sports.

But complaining is not productive. You need to look at the progress that has been made too. We have gone from one in 27 girls playing sports to 60% of girls now doing sports at high school, so that is progress. In 1971, there were just under

300,000 playing opportunities for girls, and now we are at almost 3.5 million, which is huge. One of our goals leading up to the 50th anniversary of Title IX is to make a strong push to close the gender participation gap. It is not a zero-sum game, and that is an important point. We are not taking away from the boys; we want both boys and girls to have the opportunities.

On the Equity Project as the organizing model for the next ten years:
The WSF produced the Chasing Equity research report to provide a starting point for the new decade to identify what has been done and what still needs to be done in the gender equity space. It sets out different focus areas, the first of which is access to sports and physical activity for girls at a grassroots level. While the numbers are climbing, there are still lower numbers of girls playing sports than boys. They are dropping out at higher rates than boys, especially in that middle school age group, and even more dramatically amongst girls of color who have fewer playing opportunities and more barriers for participation, whether socio-economic, safety, transport, or support from parents. Our second area of focus is Title IX and its role in driving gender equity and where that needs to improve. Then we also look at mental and physical health and safety. Mental health, safety from sexual abuse, and injury prevention are all important because they have serious ramifications on the progress we are trying to make in other areas. Another area of focus is leadership, pay equity, and workplace bias. We look at equal pay for equal work and the ability of women to make money playing professional sports, to leadership opportunities, both in coaching and in the business of sport. Finally, we look at the disparity in media coverage of men's versus women's sports.

We feel that now is the time to make progress, and our long-term vision is to ignite a movement around equity that gets both organizations and individuals to engage in this work. We launched The Equity Project on March 8th, 2020, on Women's Day, and asked every individual who cares about equity to join and take a pledge to do their part. Every week we send out calls to action, asking people to do little things that could end up in an aggregate moving the needle. We are also working with bigger organizations on projects where we can have a more immediate impact, through a change in policies or practices that can lead to lasting change.

On the future and what the environment will look like in ten years:
I am bullish. I think the time for gender equity is now. The recent news of the US Women's National Soccer Team pay equity battle, and the Federation's response that women are not worthy of the same pay as the men's team is a setback. However, the fact that so many people responded so quickly in support of the Women's team shows that we are on the cusp of big changes and that the nation is ready to look at equity in different ways. I think we are going to have huge momentum to swing the other way, and in 2030 it is going to be a very different conversation. Growth in women's sport will be exponential, not at the expense of boys, but by opening up the opportunities to play, to participate, to win, to lead, and to benefit from sports.

DEAN KAMEN   Inventor, engineer, and Founder at FIRST

DEAN HAS SUCCESSFULLY USED SPORT AS THE PLATFORM TO PROMOTE AND ENCOURAGE LEARNING IN SCIENCE AND TECHNOLOGY.

On when he first recognized the power of creativity, invention, and technology as a solution to many of life's challenges:
So many kids never see how exciting and powerful technology can be and how enabling it can be to give somebody career options in a world that is getting more and more capable with technology, but also more dependent on people who understand it. So, I started FIRST intending to create more innovators in science and technology. And, from humble beginnings, it has grown into something fairly significant.

I realized that kids love sport, so I based it around sport, creating a double-elimination tournament, and until the last sound of the final buzzer, no one would know who has won. I realized that if I could get all the trappings of sports and package it in a way that kids could feel like they could participate, then the interest would come, and, this time, it would be a sport where every kid on the team could turn pro.

I approached 20–24 big companies and asked them to adopt schools in their local community, saying that they needed these kids for future jobs. I told them about my idea to create a sport around tech, but that I needed superstars from the world of tech, just like the stars in football and basketball, to help create a passion amongst kids for tech. I managed to get 20 or so high-tech companies on board. Our first season was a short, intense six to eight weeks, where all the teams got together in a high school gym in New Hampshire for a tournament, and everybody loved it, and the corporate sponsors loved it. Each year it grew, and, after ten years, we were doing regional events every weekend. We now have about 80,000 schools involved, roughly 200 universities that sponsor our teams, and 3,700 corporate sponsors.

An explanation of FIRST Robotics and how it works:
Every year we change the kit, we change the game a little. We still use the same size playing field, which is roughly half the size of a basketball court. We change the rules of our game every year because we do not want the returning teams to have an unfair advantage over new teams. In the first week of January, we unveil the field and the theme, which might be the ocean, so a big blue field, and we dump onto it, say soccer balls, and they represent pollution. We take the teams at each event and put them into alliances with robots that compete against each other. So, for example, the coalition that collects more soccer balls in the two-minute round wins the round. Extra points are awarded if the robots put the balls into recycling bins or shoot them up very high into other kinds of containers.

Each team gets an identical kit of parts (motors, controllers, and computers), and they have to build a robot. They are only constrained in terms of length, width, and height. They have 6-8 weeks to build a robot to accomplish the goal. At the end of their build season, they attend a regional event every weekend in March, bringing their robot to the event, and they'll be put into random groups of three and play eight or nine rounds in a round-robin process. It ends with a three-day event where, on the final day, the top-seeded players get to pick a partner who they then stay with for the quarterfinals, semi's, and final so the fans can get to understand them and get behind them. They have very competitive final rounds at the regional events, and then the winners from these rounds go to the Championship event. These have gotten so big that, last year, we had to have it over two weekends, in Houston and Detroit, and we had probably 50,000 people show up in each city with 700–800 teams.

On the measure of success being the difference it is making in the world rather than how many people know about it and watch it:

The kids on our teams are making a huge difference in the world, starting in their own lives. But it frustrates me that we could be making a much bigger difference in the lives of tens of millions more kids just in this country and we could, with that number of kids and the technical expertise they develop, be solving the world's problems more quickly. We need more smart people focused on applying better technologies more rapidly, and the best way to do that is to get kids interested while they are young. Our job is not to make FIRST better but to make it more available.

BEN ASTIN
Managing Director at Lionsraw

LIONSRAW IS AN INCREDIBLE ORGANIZATION THAT RECRUITS SOCCER FANS TO VOLUNTEER THEIR SERVICES IN TRANSFORMING NEEDY COMMUNITIES AND CREATING OPPORTUNITIES FOR CHANGE FOR DISADVANTAGED CHILDREN.

On the creation of Lionsraw:

Lionsraw started ten years ago in South Africa after our founder, John Burns, wanted to change perceptions around the reputation of English soccer fans as hooligans. He had the idea that, while fans were on tour following the English team around, why not try and mobilize these supporters to do good across the world? The premise is that we take fans to a major tournament and base ourselves in a host city during the group stages, and on the days where there is no game to watch, we do some good, usually volunteer work with youth in the area. But we do not just stop there; we build a legacy by creating a 501c3 charity status, and then we continue the work even when the World Cup is over. We now have continued work going on in South Africa, Poland, Brazil, and France.

On how many people have been on this journey with Lionsraw:

We have probably had over 1,000 volunteers who have been on a World Cup Legacy Tour. Once the tournament is over, we still put on trips to go back to that location to support the work we are doing there.

On how the process works:

The fans drive it. No federation or corporate sponsor is involved. We set up logistics and manage that, but the fans pay their way. They have decided to go to the tournament and do something different while there. I have been to tournaments and followed the team around and had an amazing time, but this is something completely different, and I can honestly say that it was much much more rewarding when I went to Brazil with Lionsraw. It changed my life and how I view soccer and how it can affect and change people's lives.

What Lionsraw is working on now in 2020:

We have got some exciting things happening. We have been in the US for the last six years, mostly working with supporter groups of club teams, but we have now pivoted into National Team supporters. We created a partnership with the American Outlaws, an incredible organization with 200 chapters across the country and 30,000 members who follow the US Men's and Women's National Teams across the world. Together, we have created a program called American Outlaws Impact that is looking to give a national scope to the community work already being done at a local level.

On plans for the upcoming FIFA World Cup in the US in 2026:

About 12 months ago, together with the American Outlaws, we started thinking about a bigger, national project and came up with the great idea to start building fields, or at least to create spaces that kids can play on, especially in low-income areas. With the World Cup coming, it seemed perfect to link our plans to the event and have a six-year build-up and then organize a Lionsraw Legacy Tour at the 2026 World Cup as a big celebration of all the fields that we have built over the last six years. And this is how 26x26 was created. We are going to develop 26 fields in 26 low-income areas across the USA, Canada, and Mexico before the 2026 FIFA World Cup. We have a vision for 26 community transformations, bringing development and economic strength to communities built around the soccer field.

On using the infrastructure, once the field is built, to improve lives in the community over the long term:

We have been really lucky over the last 18 months to meet organizations that have come on board as a National Partner. I met LISC, a nonprofit standing for Local Initiative Support and Cooperation. They have had a 20-year relationship with the NFL and built over 350 sports fields with them, which is quite amazing. I told them about 26x26, and they jumped on board. Then we also have another partner called streetfootballworld, a global nonprofit that has worked with FIFA on its legacy programs for the last 12 years. We are building a strong foundation of nonprofit partners that are going to see this project home.

On using soccer as a tool to build stronger communities:

We are looking at the field as the first part of a project that will bring prosperity to a community or at least some element of positive change. We will partner with community groups and local stakeholders who will be able to prove how they want to use the field. Then we will supplement these organizations with modules to teach kids about soccer, healthy eating, building self-esteem, and things like that. We are also looking at a program that covers the business of soccer.

On how 26x26 will be funded using LISC's funding model:

We are hoping for corporations to come on board and support us, and a few Foundations as well. We want partners, not sponsors, organizations that will get involved and have a say in what will be built in these communities. The corporates will cover the operational costs and the last quarter for all of the fields. We will be looking to leverage as much as we can get out of people to bring their local services to the project. Through their innovative funding model that draws on public and private sector money, LISC brings capacity and real muscle to the project that puts it on the map.

On what else is happening in the Sport For Good movement that is interesting and will be worth following over the next ten years:

I like the Common Goal movement. It is a great idea that gives sports pros an easy platform to get involved and do good. Putting money into a central pot to develop grassroots soccer on a global scale is highly ambitious but also fantastic.

Along the same lines, I think there is space for fans to do something similar because fans are also invested in the game and want to see it better. I see this collective fundraising and collective social impact around the game being quite big and prominent in the years to come, and I think that is one thing that is going to be interesting to watch unfold.

CHAPTER 9

WHERE SPORT AND PURPOSE ARE HEADING, AND WHY IT MATTERS. WHAT'S NEXT?

Sport is a platform with immense power, and with that comes tremendous responsibility. We believe it is time for sport to act on that responsibility and maximize the use of its platform to effect lasting positive change—whether socially, environmentally, or economically. Purpose needs to be more than a nice-to-do and must move beyond simply doing less bad towards actively doing more good through sport; to be a net positive influence on the planet and everything in it. It must be embraced as a central organizing idea by athletes, sports properties, federations, and leagues. We believe those that do so will be the winners over the coming decades, and those that do not will become irrelevant.

Fans, particularly the younger millennials and Generation X fans who are notoriously difficult to reach, are actively looking for ways to be engaged in doing good alongside their favorite sports teams, leagues, and athletes. Super Bowl 50's "Play Your Part" campaign that rewarded fans for their sustainable actions, illustrates a positive community-based mindset that involved fans in doing good and thereby built deeper engagement with them. Another good example is Ipswich Town Football Club's "Save your Energy for the Blues" campaign that incentivized fans to adopt energy-saving behaviors in their homes to offset the Club's annual greenhouse gas emissions.

Progressive thinkers in this space are looking for opportunities to build Purpose coalitions that include multiple sport and business stakeholders, including sponsors, athletes, sport-based nonprofits, and sports properties, recognizing that we can get more done together than we can alone. We see growing confidence in the nonprofit community to engage with and leverage off the business of sport to amplify their impact. Streetfootballworld's Common Goal initiative that provides the soccer community with a platform through which to do good is a great example of this, as is their partnership with EA Sports and their FIFA game. Soccer players and coaches currently make up the bulk of those who have taken the Common Goal pledge to donate 1% of their earnings to put back into Football For Good initiatives. However, the signing of a virtual soccer star, Alex Hunter, to the movement added a whole new audience to the nonprofit, which will hopefully translate into more people taking the pledge, whether they generate income from soccer via the pitch or the console. The collective power of coalitions like these will begin to play an even bigger role as we realize that we need to work together if we are to make significant progress in addressing the challenges facing society.

Inspired by the examples of the likes of LeBron James, Megan Rapinoe, and Colin Kaepernick, we have seen a significant increase in the number of athletes and teams raising their voices and leveraging their platform to draw attention to issues and change behavior while also building the value of their brands. Whether it has been reacting to being let down by sports authorities or their sponsors or speaking out about gender equality or racism, athletes are increasingly aware that their fame and credibility can inspire change in society. The Athlete X Brand Summit in Los Angeles in 2019, which was designed to equip athletes with strategies, insights, and learnings to help them be as successful off the field of play as they are on it, reinforced that it is time for athletes to step up off the court and do more than just dribble.

Athletes who do speak up can and will face challenges, and so they should. They are not immune to criticism. And, just as we are all different, so too are athletes, and there is more than one athlete voice. Athletes have different interests and different views on the world, just like us all, so they must accept being both lauded by some fans and challenged by others. However, they do not deserve to be exploited by fans or discredited by their organizations, as was the case with Colin Kaepernick.

With 30% of the Top 100 sponsorship spenders in the world considered Purposeful brands, more and more brands are starting to activate their Purpose through their sports sponsorship platforms and, at the same time, align their commitment to the Sustainable Development Goals with their sports investments. As the Goals move into mainstream consciousness, we are likely to see even more of this. Brands know that this is the right thing to do for the future sustainability of their business and to keep their customers and employees loyal. Within organizations, we are going to see greater collaboration between Chief Marketing Officers, Chief Sustainability Officers, and Community Relations leaders to ensure companies know what Purpose to embrace and how best to communicate those commitments through their marketing channels and sponsorship assets.

Sponsorship innovator, Coca-Cola was already showing the way in 2018 as the activation of its FIFA World Cup sponsorship demonstrates, and others will no doubt follow. As part of the activation, Coca-Cola partnered with Walmart, the One World Play Project, and musician Justin Derulo to donate 100,000 unpoppable One World Futbol soccer balls, to organizations around the world using soccer to improve people's lives. The company then went a step further in linking its sponsorship to doing good by supporting Swedish midfielder Jimmy Durmaz, when he was subject to a wave of racial hatred and threats on his Instagram account after Sweden's loss to Germany in the 2018 FIFA World Cup. Coca-Cola Sweden joined thousands of Swedish fans showing support and taking a stand against racism in the viral campaign #backdurmaz.

Another brand leader in this space is Danone, with its global youth soccer tournament that reaches over 2.5 million kids, aged 10–12 years, from 32 countries, making it the biggest youth soccer tournament in the world. The Danone Nations Cup has put Purpose at the core of its event strategy with its "One Planet. One Health" vision that reflects their belief that the health of people and the planet are interconnected and aims to engage the next generation in the conversation on how to build a more sustainable and fair future for all.

The event is much more than a soccer tournament for the kids who participate as it uses the platform of sport to transform its participants into world citizens who go on to lead positive change in their communities. There are four key areas relating to Purpose that the event focuses on: one, to deliver a sustainable tournament with a reduced environmental footprint; two, to promote a healthy lifestyle by educating kids on healthier eating and drinking habits through workshops, educational games, and sessions with a nutritionist; three, to promote the principles of inclusion, diversity, and gender equality (the all-girl tournament created in 2017 is a step towards addressing this); and four, to provide access to safe drinking water for children. Around 50% of schools around the world do not have access to safe drinking water. Through a partnership with the nonprofit, Watering Minds, Danone aims to provide access to safe drinking water for over 100,000 kids.

As further evidence of the event's commitment to Purpose, the Danone Nations Cup joined the Common Goal movement in February 2020, thereby committing 1% of its total budget as well as 1% of all future sponsorship revenue from partners to the campaign. In addition, kids participating in the Danone Nations Cup get to vote on which of the Sustainable Development Goals they want Danone to act upon going forward.

If there are still some corporates out there who need convincing, consider this: Purpose-led sponsorships have been shown to outperform traditional sponsorships on several fronts. According to data from Performance Research, corporate support for social causes is the biggest driver of purchasing decisions by 72% of consumers, which is almost double that of sport sponsorship at 32%. There are numerous examples to illustrate this. Lloyds TSB's backing of the 2012 London Olympics was leveraged around its Purpose-driven Local Heroes campaign that provided school sport opportunities to more than eight million youngsters. Post-event research revealed that 40% of customers aware of the bank's Olympic sponsorship would likely recommend the brand to friends and family. And this number jumped up by 15% for customers aware of TSB's Olympic sponsorship *and* the Local Heroes community overlay. Across the Atlantic, US Bank, the fifth-largest commercial bank in America, launched a new sponsorship strategy that focused on Purpose-driven activation programs to ramp up its "Power of Possible" brand positioning and, as a result, has seen a 30% increase in consideration amongst customers.

The key to all of this is authenticity on the part of all stakeholders. Choosing a Purpose that rings true to your brand and then committing to it for the long haul have always been important. However, they are now doubly important to deliver real, lasting social or environmental impact as a legacy. Once-offs do not work anymore. You need to play the long game, and your actions need to be consistent with what you say like never before.

The message in all of this for executives running the business of sport is clear: Fans, athletes, and sponsors are all getting on with it, with or without you. They expect sport to stand for something more than just profits and will make sure you know about it if you do not. Purpose is not philanthropy or CSR—this is about embracing Purpose at the center of your organizational DNA and giving this Purpose authentic expression through every aspect of your sports business. Sponsoring brands are looking to partner with sports properties, organizations, teams, and athletes to maintain relevance in the communities in which they operate, and they are demanding that Purpose deliverables be built into the contractual obligations of the assets they sponsor. Contractual Purpose deliverables are no longer a nice option to have for corporates. They are mandatory in any rights package, so sports bodies need to get on board, and fast, or else sponsors will walk away.

On the plus side for sports organizations, rights holders, and athletes is that their commitment to act more Purposefully can be monetized. Integrating Purpose as a key commercial driver within their organizations or brand platforms can open up new business models, new partners, new revenue streams, improved efficiencies, and reduced costs. Rightsholders, who have already embraced Purpose, like Formula E and The Ocean

Race, are excellent examples of how Purpose can be monetized through new sponsorship categories.

Another great rights holder example is Rugby World Cup France 2023. The organizing committee's vision is to create a new blueprint for the Rugby World Cup by delivering an event that is built around sustainability as well as cultural and social inclusivity. Already they have launched a bold and ambitious manifesto that puts community engagement and sustainability at the heart of their event strategy while also promoting unity through diversity and celebrating rugby's values in a national and international societal context. An important element of the strategy is to use the event to highlight local French produce across each of the regions, from farmers to chefs and local independent artisans, thus exposing the 600,000 foreign visitors to the best of French produce and boosting local economies. The event also has ambitious plans to implement an environmentally friendly mobility plan. So far, their commitment to Purpose has received positive support from sponsors and the community, and it only remains to be seen how successful their endeavors are, come 2023.

It is vital for funds to be allocated for impact measurement and evaluation to track the difference being made in the world on an ongoing basis. Meaningless measures about brand impressions are not a barometer for success in the world of Purpose. What is needed now are science-based approaches to measurement to pass the public's smell test. This approach starts with clear goals and objectives upfront and credible, impartial measurement tools that stand up to scrutiny. Fans and brands want feedback on the real positive change that a Purpose-led strategy can deliver. You can read more about measuring impact in Part 3 of this book.

What do we see as the biggest challenges or risks standing in the way of Purpose becoming mainstream in sports? Two issues come to mind. Firstly, the shortage of skilled and experienced experts that understand the world of sport, business, and Purpose in equal measure and can build and deliver business-driven Purpose programs in sports. A different mindset is required to make a move from the traditional eyeballs-driven, profit-driven sponsorship approach to one that builds a strategy around

Purpose. Secondly, there is a risk that Purpose continues to be treated as a form of CSR as opposed to a management philosophy or a strategic organizing principle resulting in underperforming programs that undermine the validity of Purpose as a management philosophy.

When sports organizations, host cities, event organizing committees, teams, leagues, and athletes consider their vast reach and ability to engage fans, they should also consider their ability to build a Purpose-led vision that all stakeholders can support. Brands today are looking to sport not just to create brand impressions and memorable experiences but, more so, to build deeper loyalty by enabling initiatives that make an impactful and lasting difference in people's lives. The way sport rose to the occasion during the COVID-19 crisis of 2020, to support relief efforts in various ways inspires us to believe that sport can and will begin to truly embrace the collective good that it has the power to do. In the process, sport will build a more resilient, robust, profitable, and relevant business model and a better world for all.

KEY INSIGHTS: THE NEXT DECADE WILL BE THE DECADE OF PURPOSEFUL SPORT

➤ It is time for sports properties, athletes, and brands to move beyond simply doing less bad to actively looking for ways to do more good through sport. Sport is one of the most powerful platforms available to lead the transition to a sustainable future.

➤ We believe that sports properties and athletes that embrace Purpose beyond profits as a central organizing idea will be the winners over the coming decades, and those that do not will become irrelevant.

➤ Progressive thinkers will be looking for opportunities to build Purpose coalitions that include multiple sport stakeholders, including sponsors, athletes, sport-based nonprofits, and sports properties, recognizing that we can get more done together than we can alone.

➤ Fans are actively looking for ways to be involved in doing good alongside their favorite sports teams, leagues, and athletes.

➤ The sports sector's increasing adoption of Purpose presents an exciting activation opportunity for brands through their investment in sport. Consequently, we will see more brands activating Purposefully and incorporating their alignment with the Sustainable Development Goals. The next decade will be the decade of The Goals.

➤ We will also see more sponsors discontinuing sponsorships that do not afford them the opportunity of driving Purpose through their sponsored asset. Purpose deliverables will be a mandatory part of the contractual obligations of the properties and athletes that they sponsor.

➤ Properties and athletes should be looking for ways to monetize their commitment to act more Purposefully and integrate Purpose as a key commercial driver within their organizations or brand platforms—new business models, new partners, new revenue streams, improved efficiencies, and reduced costs.

➤ Authenticity has always been important. In 2020 and beyond, it is doubly important, as is a long-term commitment to deliver real, lasting social and environmental impact as a legacy.

➤ Budgets need to be allocated to impact measurement and evaluation to track the difference being made in the world on an ongoing basis. Science-based approaches to measurement are now vital.

The biggest challenges or risks to Purpose in 2020 are:

➤ The shortage of skilled and experienced experts that understand the world of sport, business, and Purpose and can build and deliver business-driven Purpose programs.

➤ Purpose still being treated as a form of CSR as opposed to a management philosophy or strategic organizing principle resulting in underperforming programs that question the validity of Purpose as a management philosophy.

➤ Purpose-washing and dilution of trust amongst fans as a result of Purpose commitments being made and not being kept.

LEADING THOUGHTS:
LOOKING AHEAD

SEBASTIAN BUCK   Co-Founder and Strategic Lead at enso

WITH CLIENTS LIKE GOOGLE, MATTEL, AND THE KHAN ACADEMY, ENSO IS
ONE OF THE MOST RESPECTED SOCIAL IMPACT AGENCIES IN THE WORLD.

On the role of sport to build a more sustainable future:

There are too many sports companies, clubs, teams, and leagues who believe they
are defined by their existing business model and current revenue streams—for
example, a TV-based audience business, an entertainment company that interacts
with people as latent fans who are there to be served content. They have got too
attached to their business model such that they have not thought harder about what
is the true essence of what they provide, which is about togetherness and a sense of
shared interest, shared values, and shared experience. If they could think in that more
elevated way, then they would embrace the business opportunities of today and the
future and be better aligned with deeper human needs. It would involve switching
from thinking of people as an audience, which is a very passive mindset, to thinking
of people as a community who are there to be entertained, yes, but are also part
of something bigger. People want to feel a sense of belonging, they want to feel
connected to their city and other people to a shared endeavor, and I think that opens
up massive business opportunities as well as social impact opportunities for sport.

**On the tendency for the sports industry to adopt a functional approach to their
business model:**

If you take my personal experience of sport, I am a Southampton FC fan, but
Southampton has not won anything since 1976, and, sadly, I cannot go to a game
every week anymore. I still get up every Saturday morning to watch, but there
was a period in my life when I would take a two-hour train ride each way from
London down to Southampton to watch the game on Saturday. Winning was nice

and was part of why I wanted to go but, an even bigger part of it was to be with thousands of other people, singing the songs and going to the pub before and after the game. It was that entire communal experience, the shared journey that touches people deep inside in a much more meaningful way than the bragging rights of winning. Southampton has not won anything in my tenure of following them, but my life is much richer for having been part of the journey.

On the premise that Purpose does not apply to sport:
Any organization of humans has to be animated by a Purpose, or it is missing its potential because humans are emotionally driven creatures, and Purpose is one of the most important ways of cueing emotion. So, to think of Purpose as nice to have is just missing the point.

MATTHEW CAMPELLI   Founder and Editor of The Sustainability Report

THE SUSTAINABILITY REPORT IS AN ESSENTIAL SOURCE OF INTELLIGENCE AND INSIGHT FOR SPORTS PROFESSIONALS COMMITTED TO ENHANCING THE ENVIRONMENTAL, SOCIAL, AND ECONOMIC SUSTAINABILITY OF THEIR ORGANIZATIONS.

On the evolution of Purpose and how sport and Purpose are being integrated:
A few years ago, sustainability in sport was separate from the intrinsic business of sport, and it was paid lip-service to by the major sports organizations and by sports media as well. We are now seeing a handful of forward-thinking organizations, leagues, and clubs incorporating sustainability as a core part of their business and seeing it as a way for them to engage with fans and develop more streams of income. It is still in its infancy, but I think we will see more organizations pick up the mantle as they see their counterparts doing well out of it.

On who is applying Purpose well:
There are always the go-to examples like Forest Green Rovers that immediately come to mind, but there are others. For example, World Athletics are trying to install air quality monitors at all of their certified tracks. They are doing a lot around air quality at their open road events and marathons because air quality is

a real issue for them, particularly running in cities. These organizations are picking a Sustainable Development Goal or an issue that is intrinsic to their sport and then trying to do something powerful around it.

On whether it is an accurate assessment to say that sport is 5-10 years behind business in its adoption and understanding of Purpose:
I would say so, but it is difficult to put a length of time on it. Sport is substantially behind Fortune 500 organizations that rely on customers because sport sees itself as slightly separate from other businesses. Sport's strength is also its main weakness. If someone is a follower of a particular sport or club, they have got a real emotional attachment to that club. If the club does things that are not ethically, environmentally, or socially good, it is more difficult to break that bond than it would be to stop buying from a company. As a result, sport is possibly more complacent and has not put those practices into place in the same way that other businesses have.

On any examples of innovative ways that sports properties or teams are addressing the operational supply chain side of things when it comes to sustainability:
I think some of the more interesting projects relate to renewable energy and how stadiums are being powered. In Amsterdam, at the Johan Cruyff Arena, they have recycled old Nissan batteries and are using them in their stadium to store wind and solar energy that they generate. What is not used on match days is sold back to the grid. So, not only are they using clean energy when they are playing matches, but they are selling excess energy, and that is generating income for them. It is a great example of doing more good than bad by being a net positive contributor to the energy grid.

On the drive from fans for leagues and clubs to be more Purposeful:
The social piece is also gaining in importance because the makeup of fans is changing. In previous generations, fans cared more about the results on the pitch than anything else. However, I do think fans are beginning to vote with their feet and are becoming more acutely aware of how their sport or team can impact the community around them, not just environmentally, but socially as well.

On how Purpose is impacting the negotiations between rights holders and potential commercial partners:
One of the first things potential sponsors want to know these days is what the Club is doing environmentally or socially. It is not about getting eyeballs on their logo; it is about being involved in something and working together on activations that do some good in the community.

On whether there is an increased interest in the SDGs as a framework for sports and their sponsors to work around:
I think sport is behind in that respect. The SDGs are quickly becoming the language of business, but whether this is filtering down into sports, I am not sure yet. It is very nascent in sports, and I do not think you will find many sports executives actively thinking about the SDGs.

On trying to quantify the impact sport could have on the SDGs:
We tend to fall back on the Nelson Mandela phrase that sport has the power to change the world, but we do not do anything to quantify what that means. If we did try to do so, we would see that sport has a massive impact on many of the SDGs. The Commonwealth Secretariat is trying to put together a metric to measure the SDGs concerning sport and sports development, so that could potentially be a way that we could measure that kind of impact going forward.

On how athletes have become more vocal and are using their influence to drive change:
If you want to be an athlete who stands out in the minds of fans today, you are going to have to be an activist. Athletes are in a privileged position. I get that they have worked hard to get there, but it is still a position of privilege, and they are role models whether they like it or not. If there is something they truly believe in, then they should stand up and talk about it.

On the professional practitioners in the sports space and how the sports industry is progressing towards embracing Purpose:
I think we are going to see more sustainability roles in sport popping up, which is a good thing. There are already people at ballparks and stadiums doing

a lot of greening work. These are the professionals who care about sport, the environment, and society, and they are trying to move the needle and are doing a really good job.

A lot of it comes down to governance. Sport is a very short-term focused industry in many respects, always focusing on the next event or the upcoming season, and long-term planning, particularly regarding the environment and society, is limited at best and non-existent at worst in many sports. I think there is a gap to bridge in the kind of governance it takes for sports to catch up to other industries. It is going to need people in leadership positions to understand the issue and opportunities.

On the UN FCCC and its likelihood of being an effective measure for sports to get behind sustainability:
The UN FCCC for Sport was set up with good intentions and calls on sports bodies to come forward and commit to doing five things to address climate action with the ultimate aim of becoming climate neutral at some point down the line. Its success will depend on the organizations that sign up. Overall, I think the UNFCCC is a positive step for sports, and I hope it is successful.

On the road ahead and whether, by 2030, sports will have risen to the challenge to play a more meaningful role in its contribution towards a sustainable future:
I hope we will have seen the wholesale adoption of sustainability in sport; that it is not only the major sports leagues and organizations that have sustainability officers or teams ensuring that everyone within the organization is working towards sustainability goals. I hope sustainability has become the language of sport. That sport will have evolved because some sports are in danger of becoming irrelevant if they do not change and engage fans, young people in particular. There are many things now occupying young people's time and attention. Look at the growth of esports as one example, and I think several sports are in danger of losing that engagement. Things like climate action and the SDGs could be good ways to get this younger audience on board.

LEW BLAUSTEIN   Founder of GreenSportsBlog and EcoAthletes

GREENSPORTSBLOG IS THE LEADING BLOG AT THE INTERSECTION OF
GREENING AND SPORTS, WHICH GIVES LEW TREMENDOUS INSIGHT INTO
THE INROADS SPORT IS MAKING AROUND SUSTAINABILITY AND PURPOSE.

**On the frustration that the media does not seem to want to tell the story and
amplify the good that is being done in the sports space around greening:**
I believe it is partly because the media has not been shown the way. For the last
eight or nine years, it has been the sports leagues and teams in the main who have
been greening themselves, and they talk about it in their press releases, but they do
not tell the fans. It is their own doing. If they were really serious about it, they would
act differently and would include it in their negotiations with broadcast partners.
But no teams or leagues have put this kind of pressure on the networks.

**On the extent to which the coronavirus pandemic might inspire greater action in
the Purpose space:**
I do believe so, and that is why we launched a nonprofit called EcoAthletes at
this time to harness the cultural power of athletes to influence fans to take action
against climate change. We want to inspire, coach, and deploy athletes so that
they become experts on the climate crisis and can use their forums to speak out
about it. Athletes are the true power of sports. Launching our initiative now, during
the coronavirus pandemic, when sports calendars have been suspended, means
that athletes have time on their hands to educate themselves. They have also seen
how the coronavirus has required changes from everyone in a very short time,
which shows people that making climate-related changes is also doable. While the
greening initiatives undertaken by stadiums and arenas are good, the real power
of sport goes far beyond the people who come to the games because they are such
a tiny portion of the fanbase. The best way to reach fans is through athletes. The
challenge is to find athletes who can authentically align with our programs.

On the reasons for there being so few athlete activists on environmental issues:
It is a small group, but it is growing. I believe it is a function of a few things. It
involves science, and some athletes say they do not know enough about science to

feel comfortable speaking about it, some feel they will be criticized as a green washer for having a lavish lifestyle, and thirdly, there is the political aspect of it.

One high profile athlete who has engaged in climate change is Josh Rosen, the quarterback with the Miami Dolphins, also Kevin Anderson and Dominic Theim in tennis, and a handful in baseball and basketball. Then, of course, athletes in water sports and, even more so, in winter sports like skiing and snowboarding because their playing field has shrunk due to warming temperatures during their lifetime. They see the impact in real-time. There is an organization that has been training winter sports athletes for some time now to speak out on climate.

On what things will look like in the world of sports, greening, and sustainability in 2030:

I hope we have made the environment and climate part of the sports broadcasting and sports event fabric and that sports leagues, teams, and more athletes have taken on climate action as a cause and that fans have also moved in that direction as well.

KEVIN MARTINEZ   VP Corporate Citizenship at ESPN

ESPN IS A LEADING PROPONENT OF PURPOSE, AS IS EVIDENCED IN THE MULTIPLE PROGRAMS THE NETWORK IS INVOLVED WITH THAT CAPITALIZE ON THE POWER OF SPORT TO DO GOOD.

On the synergistic approach to corporate giving at ESPN:

Nurturing a culture of service and keeping it vibrant so that innovation can happen is crucial to what we do. The magic happens when everyone is aligned around a shared mission and a shared goal, and it is a democratized process at ESPN. This process is what is unique now versus ten years ago. Corporate social responsibility, from 15–20 years ago, when I first got into it, was very different—it was all happening transactionally in different spaces. Now it is looked at synergistically and in innovative ways. It is great to have a grantmaker. However, if they do not understand that there are ways to engage our volunteer force for service, our executives for Board development, and our reputation management for public affairs, then we have failed. I think that is the new iteration of CSR today.

On the move towards Purpose and where it is headed:
This commitment to Purpose is going to continue to be defined, but I do not think we should be so tight about what it means. We need to let people define Purpose and service for themselves, listen to them, and then transact and try to bring that definition back to them. We are going to have to think broadly about how people enter into the movement, whether it is technologically or physically.

On what the next ten years hold for ESPN in terms of engaging with the market through the lens of Sport for Good:
If we look at our mission statement of serving fans anytime, anywhere, it is pretty broad, so we are going to have to narrow things down a bit. Technology is going to be one of the big focus areas. We see it with gaming. I also think we are going to see the human dynamic of how the sports fan is unique. By this, I mean that when a game is over, and there are winners and losers, that regardless of who won, there is hope and generosity and moments of greatness left behind, and that gives you hope for the next game. We are going to have to look at ways to keep the sports fan and how to get more people involved in sport. We need to look at the next generation of athletes because they are going to be the next generation of leaders.

On the lessons sport can draw on to be more impactful:
The idea of Purpose is an interesting notion because right now, it has not been owned. It has been out there for a while as an iteration of corporate responsibility. Everyone is zoning in on the fact that we need to personify our brands, actions, and outcomes, and Purpose is the way to do that. It creates the road and the transmission to get there. It is not replacing your mission statement; it is the "why."

If we are going to establish credibility with the next generation of youth, we need to start thinking like them, and we need to recruit them. The youth are asking us what does your company stand for, not how many Emmys have you won, or am I going to learn new things from you, but rather am I going to be able to commit to my community through my work. Some of us are getting it wrong; we are calling it volunteerism, but they are looking to be part of a movement, to be part of a change, and companies need to provide that. When you do that and speak about volunteerism in a whole new way, then people will respond.

LUCIEN BOYER
Founder and Chairman of Global Sports Week

GLOBAL SPORTS WEEK SETS OUT TO ADDRESS THE BIGGEST GLOBAL
TRENDS AND TALKING POINTS IN SPORT TO GET LEADERS IN THEIR
RESPECTIVE FIELDS WORKING TOGETHER TO SHAPE A BETTER FUTURE.

On the evolution of sports marketing:
In the past, it was about visibility and exposure. Now there is a greater focus on
embracing Purpose through sport and investing in a legacy. Sport is a reflection
of what is going on in society, so, as the world evolves towards a more Purposeful
way of life, we see the same in sport. The difference for sport is that Purpose is in
its DNA, and it is genuine, unlike some other industries who are struggling to connect
and fill the gap because they are far away from Purpose. If you look back, there
have been many manifestations of Purpose in sport because athletes have always
been conscious of their place as role models and their obligation to give back. So,
the idea of Purpose in sport is not new. Even the Olympics spoke about solidarity
forty years ago. It is now about how to make Purpose more central to what is being
done in sport.

On whether the world of sport understands Purpose:
I think sport is gaining a better understanding of the role of Purpose. It takes time
because it is often not at the core and sometimes even conflicts with other priorities.
Sport is very dynamic and requires a single-minded focus a lot of the time. It is
about excellence, discipline, and hard work, and this often does not leave much
time to consider other things. A Purpose-driven approach requires you to be more
outward-looking. It is not only about doing something for yourself but others as well.

**On whether the world of sport understands that doing good can also result in
doing well, that Purpose is a business opportunity:**
There are always the early adopters, and then there are the followers. The
most advanced organizations are leading the way and embracing Purpose and
making it a central part of their strategy and communications, which makes a big
difference, rather than just doing Purpose to tick a box. Sport needs money, so
there is a focus on profit, and it takes time to realize that this can come at the same

time as being Purposeful. Some leaders have understood this already, but some see it as conflicting with their business model. I think that those businesses that take a more long-term view have realized that Purpose is good for business.

On the key insights from Global Sports Week:
Global Sports Week opened people's eyes to the responsibility of sport and made them realize that sport has influence. The biggest take-out was that sport needs to be proactive in accelerating change and not just the idea of change but real action. Across every element of the sports ecosystem, from sports brands to organizing committees, to athletes, fans, media, and sponsors, there is an acknowledgment that we all need to work together as a collective to bring about positive change.

Something else coming out of the conference was the importance of the new generation of young people who have different values and stronger expectations of the world, including sport. They are ready to say what they think and will call out untruths. They want actions, not just messages, and will pass judgment if the action does not come. They know how to use social media to good effect and are very impactful in how they tell a story and deliver a message, so they are vital to have on board because they are only going to become more important and more influential. For them, enjoying sports is not just about watching in the stadium; they want to be active fans.

CLAUDE ATCHER   CEO at Rugby World Cup France 2023

FRANCE HAS COMMITTED TO MAKING THE RUGBY WORLD CUP IN 2023
THE MOST SUSTAINABLE WORLD CUP EVER.

On how the France 2023 sustainability strategy is different from traditional CSR:
From the beginning, we set up a special division focusing on our sustainability strategy, and every action or project we embark on has to be run by this division. We have to think about how everything we are doing could be used to have a positive impact on the country, society, or the sport. This ambition drives every project, and it has dramatically changed the spirit and the meaning of what we are doing.

On the challenges of delivering a sustainable event:
One challenge is, of course, that it costs money. We want to showcase farmers, local producers, and chefs in each region so people can enjoy our local products. It will be a challenge for us, but we have decided to invest money in these types of projects, and we have received strong support from our first sponsors.

Rugby World Cup 2023 will take place in ten host cities. On how this is impacting their sustainability plans:
From the beginning, we have said that this is a global sporting event but that we need to look after the people living in France as well. So, if you look at the ten host cities, 80% of the French population live less than two hours from a stadium. Part of our thinking was to reduce the transportation impact of all the people who will be traveling for our event, and we are working with Total to come up with a clean mobility plan so that we can transport the 2.6 million fans with no negative impact.

On the opportunity of doing more than just reducing the environmental impact of the event but adopting a net positive model that focuses on doing more good:
We are responsible, in front of the country and the rest of the world. If we do not stop climate evolution in 2050, Samoa, Fiji, and Tonga will disappear, so it is impossible not to be responsible. We have to fight; we have to change, and the Rugby World Cup has to contribute. We are aiming to achieve 85–90% of our objectives but, if we can make 100%, we will do it. You cannot organize a big event these days without being environmentally conscious.

On the legacy of the Rugby World Cup 2023:
I prefer to talk about the positive impact. We have different goals that we would like to achieve in terms of our legacy. One is to show that France is a very welcoming country with some great tourist attractions and a strong historical culture. The second impact is the economic impact from the roughly 600,000 people that will come to France for the event and will experience French culture and food and drink. The third impact is a social impact, which means that we want to ensure that the event delivers a positive impact to people living in all regions in France—in terms of learning, work, and other areas.

On advice for executives considering embracing a more Purposeful approach to how they manage their investments in sport:

Globally, we have to change the business model of our clubs, competitions, and unions. We have to be more vigilant in terms of investment, for example, players' salaries. The second point is to take care of the social aspect of sports that we do not leave some people out. Sports events need to be accessible to all. Thirdly, we must be courageous in embracing Purpose. Clubs and unions who are scared because it requires money must be bold, and they will find people who are willing to give financial support.

JOHN BALKAM   Author, Sponsorship Practitioner, and Social Entrepreneur

JOHN IS A PASSIONATE BELIEVER IN THE POWER OF SPORTS TO BE A POSITIVE FORCE FOR GOOD IN THE WORLD.

On the current state of the Sports Marketing Industry:

What we have seen from brands that use sports to connect with consumers has not changed much in recent years. We are starting to see it slip a little bit, but only because consumers are demanding it. There is a big opportunity for brands to understand the power of social impact in their business and in their marketing message as a way of connecting with consumers. Brands can then use the platform of sports, where there is so much emotion tied up into it, to build a much more powerful marketing platform and drive a true impact in the community.

On how social impact does not seem to be ingrained within the business model of most sports teams and leagues to the same extent that it would be if they were run as social enterprises:

I think there has been a gap between the revenue department for sports leagues and teams and the community relations department or even the foundation. They are usually operating in different silos, and that is a missed opportunity. It should be about combining their efforts to deliver better value for brand partners. As a brand that is spending money in Sports Marketing, the first thing you should think about when you are approaching a league, team, or athlete, is what value you can provide to society or what message you can promote that will be inspiring. It is not about looking at the brand or the sports team; it is about what can be done when brands collaborate with consumers as well as their team or athlete of interest.

On what it will take to get sports to recognize that the world is changing around them and that the sponsors of tomorrow are going to have a different expectation of the value proposition they have with a sports property than they did yesterday:
Unfortunately, I think sports properties might have to bleed a little bit on the bottom line to realize that they have to change their approach. So, for example, if a team lost sponsorship revenue because they were not doing enough in the way of social impact, that would make the revenue office rethink how they are approaching sponsorship packages.

On whether it is conceivable that fans could begin to boycott teams and leagues that do not align with their values:
It is entirely possible. If things start to get more drastic regarding the climate crisis, natural disasters, people's jobs, or if a team or league is seen to be emitting too much carbon or not diverting waste, then I can see fans reacting and boycotting these sports events and organizations. If I were a business leader in sports, that would be a significant risk to think about, and I would ensure I was part of the solution because I am part of the problem and, if I do not do anything, then I risk losing my money.

On the need for professional sports teams or leagues to consider what their role is in social impact and how to use their brand as a force for good:
I think many properties get this; they realize that they are a convener in their community because they have fans who care and who have long-standing relationships with their team. As a team, you could think about how to amplify the good work of the nonprofits in your city. The property serves as the point person to give exposure to the great work of the local nonprofits. Community assets are going to become much more valuable sponsorship assets for teams and leagues.

On the idea of bringing the business of sport together around a common Purpose:

As we evolve and people start to push all businesses, whether in sports or not, to be driven by real societal peace and justice, sports businesses can be a platform to unite everyone around a common macro Purpose. I know that business is competitive by nature. However, imagine if we, as the sports industry as a whole, could agree on five Sustainable Development Goals to which we are all going to contribute, that are authentic to our business, and that we are going to go after for the next ten years. Imagine if we were to convene the sports business around a common Purpose so that everyone has a true north. Then you could tweak that on a micro-level from a team perspective to meet the different needs of each community.

DR. JOHN IZZO   Leading Author, Speaker, and Executive Coach

JOHN IS ONE OF THE MOST RESPECTED NAMES ON THE SUBJECT OF
LEADERSHIP AND PURPOSE AND THE BELIEF THAT DOING GOOD IN
BUSINESS CAN ALSO MEAN DOING WELL.

On whether Purpose can play a role in sport:

I think we underestimate the value of people wanting to be associated with good things. If we think about sports franchises themselves, they are businesses that are bigger than just what happens on the field or the court. I would argue that the people who care about Purpose in their life also care about it in sport. I am guessing that most sports franchises operate in the middle of the bell curve, i.e., they have got a couple of charities they support and do some good in the community, but they are not known for anything specific. Few sports franchises see the value in Purpose, and there are not many who have embraced it to the extent that they would attract the 34% of people who are deeply committed to Purpose, many of whom are likely to be sports fans. I am in that 34%, and I am a sports fan, but very few franchises have ever risen to the level that I would care about them.

CAROL CONE   Social Purpose pioneer and CEO at Carol Cone ON PURPOSE

CAROL IS KNOWN AND RESPECTED GLOBALLY FOR HELPING MANY
LEADING COMPANIES ACTIVATE THEIR PURPOSE BEYOND PROFIT.,
SOMETHING SHE HAS DONE FOR DECADES.

On sport being a platform for brands to activate around and use to amplify their Purpose messaging:

I think that as a platform, sport is phenomenal because it is reality TV every single game. In every single event, there is a tremendous amount of humanity in it. In the past, sports largely lived off of fandom, fan passion, and some of the outrageous athlete celebrities, but I think the shift today is coming from the athletes themselves, less from the owners. There is a recognition of the responsibility that they have been given. We need new heroes to emulate. The Colin Kaepernick situation with Nike was a great example of this. Being a hero needs to be more than just winning the game. It is how you got to the game, how you left the game, and how you conducted yourself?

What is disappointing to me is that there is so much money in a league, team, event, and venue, but they need help to understand how to incorporate Purpose more strategically and tie it into their brand. Sports will be so much more successful when they take a portion of every single ticket sale and every single ad and if athletes give a small portion of their salaries and put them towards things that are credible and meaningful. I think that is a challenge that I would put out to sport.

On whether the same value proposition around Purpose that applies in business applies equally to a sports franchise:

Absolutely, a sports franchise lives and breathes on the support of its fans in the community. Looking at it from a hard business perspective, if you want to have your Stadium renovated, you will need to look at your relationship with the regulators. If you are going to get some sort of tax concessions, questions will be asked about what you have given back to the community. Sport cannot live in a microcosm.

On her warning to sport if they do not embrace Purpose:

Purpose not only does positive things, but it also insulates you from crisis and reputational risk. I do not think consumers and fans will allow sports entities not to engage, so I believe there is a recognition in sports that it must be done. However, the question is, do you do it positively with innovation and excitement and lots of ideas, or do you do it begrudgingly? I think that sport and certain leagues, teams, and athletes could be demonized if they do not, and hopefully, the sport's owners recognize that it is more than just making money.

SPORT'S INITIAL RESPONSE TO THE COVID-19 PANDEMIC OF 2020

The COVID-19 pandemic that rocked the world in 2020 provided an opportunity for the sports sector to demonstrate Purpose and do its bit to help. From around mid-March, sports were shut down across the globe with tournaments and leagues having to be played in front of empty stadiums at first and then being postponed or canceled altogether. Even the IOC finally relented and postponed the 2020 Tokyo Olympic Games until 2021. The pandemic created so much uncertainty that many did not know how best to respond. However, the way that athletes and sports leagues across many categories stepped up was highly commendable.

By far, the biggest response came in the form of traditional sports philanthropy models such as donations and auctions. There were generous personal donations from countless athletes across several sports codes to support medical workers, hospitals, or vulnerable families affected by the coronavirus. Others agreed to pay cuts to support team employees or fellow players in lower leagues impacted by the cancellations. Others even created limited-edition merchandise lines to raise funds. For example, European soccer club Paris Saint-Germain launched a special edition "Tous Unis" (All Together) jersey, which was sold online with all proceeds going to healthcare staff and public hospitals in France.

The "Athletes for COVID-19 Relief" auction platform saw gear and other memorabilia from more than 100 athletes across most major professional sports auctioned to fans for a minimum bid of $25. And there was also the "All in Challenge" auction platform launched by Michael Rubin, the billionaire e-commerce CEO and co-owner of the Philadelphia 76ers and New Jersey Devils. Participants had the option of either buying tickets to enter a draw to win certain prizes or competing in an auction to buy many highly desirable experiences with sports stars and celebrities. These included things like the chance to throw the first pitch in the next World Series, to play in the 2021 NBA All-Stars Celebrity game, and to appear on the cover of Sports Illustrated magazine, many for a minimum of only $10. All money raised went to five US-based charities linked to keeping the hungry and vulnerable fed during the crisis.

Another line of response was more innovative in its thinking and saw parts of the sports industry leverage their technological expertise, transferring their skills from the sports world, to provide essential items and services needed by the health sector. The Mercedes-Benz Formula 1 team applied its engineering skills to manufacture much-needed ventilators. Bauer, the New Hampshire based hockey equipment manufacturer, took on the task of making protective face shields for medical workers instead of ice-hockey helmets.

Likewise, the live event industry pivoted their expertise from the event environment to help with the infrastructure set up for makeshift hospitals and testing centers in America. Sports brands, like Nike, New Balance, Under Armour and, MLB official kit manufacturer Fanatics, all switched from manufacturing sports kit and trainers to using the raw material to make masks and hospital gowns. There were also examples of teams, federations, and leagues making the space at their home stadiums available, either for coronavirus testing centers or as facilities to house and treat vulnerable patients or store medical supplies. For example, Manchester City offered its Etihad Stadium to the UK's NHS, as did Tottenham Hotspur. In Brazil, several stadiums, including the iconic Maracanã sports complex, were turned into temporary hospitals, as was the Billie Jean King National Tennis Center in New York, to name just a few.

There were several inspirational responses from the sports world too. Budweiser led the way with its One Team ad campaign that saw the brand redirect $5 million of its sports sponsorship budget to support the American Red Cross in setting up blood drives at empty stadiums and to assist those heroes working on the front line of the crisis.

With millions of people confined to their homes during the pandemic, sport looked to ways of keeping them entertained. Some athletes offered live online Q&A sessions with fans or challenged them to online fitness challenges as per Nike's "Living Room Cup." Cristiano Ronaldo was the first Nike athlete to set an online challenge, inviting fans and fellow soccer players to try and beat his abdominal crunch record of 142 crunches in 45 seconds. The post generated over 5.6 million likes on Instagram and a flurry of contenders. Red Bull launched a "What Does It Take" podcast series featuring interviews with Red Bull athletes from around the world, exploring what it takes to get to the top and stay there. GoPro initiated a #HomePro challenge, asking people to share the activities they were getting up to at home during the lockdown for the chance to win their latest performance camera.

In other attempts to engage fans, organizers of Formula 1, NASCAR, and La Liga all created video-game contests to replace canceled fixtures. The Formula 1 virtual Grand Prix streamed online versions of its events, using computer-generated circuits and simulators, on the same date and time that the events would have taken place in different cities. The eNASCAR series featured all of the sport's biggest names and drew impressive viewers right from the start. More than other sports, simulated motorsport events are in a very close parallel with the real world, which perhaps accounts for their success.

With fans starved of live sport, many turned to the world of esports for their fix of sporting entertainment. Esports were uniquely placed to thrive during the global pandemic, and it is believed its global audience of over 440 million people will have grown significantly in 2020. And many of these new fans are likely to remain fans even when live sport resumes. Esports did have to adapt during the coronavirus crisis, though, as its big events, where fans come to live arenas to see their favorite gamers compete in online games, had to be canceled. However, the difference for esports was that the nature of its competition did not change in any way when fans were limited to online viewing only.

The leading online gaming platform, Twitch, took advantage of the increased online traffic and initiated *Stream Aid* to raise money for the fight against coronavirus. The 12-hour livestream featured programming ranging from musical performances and games like Fortnite and UNO to appearances from celebrities and athletes and featured spots of Twitch streamers. Stream Aid was the start of a week's worth of fundraising opportunities on Twitch, and individuals were encouraged to continue to host their streams and help raise additional money for the WHO's Solidarity Relief Fund. Roughly $2.8 million was accumulated via the Twitch platform.

In perhaps the first sign of collective Purpose demonstrated by the gaming industry, a Gamers vs. COVID-19 pledge was established inviting gamers to sign up and thereby promise to take the necessary safety measures to help fight the virus. It was not much, but it was a start towards a more Purposeful journey in the world of esports. As esports continues to grow and gamers gain stature as role models, there is little doubt that they too will begin to feel the pressure from fans to stand up for good and use their influence for the service of humanity. More brands will look to the world of esports and its appealing viewer demographics as a platform off which to drive their Purposeful marketing messages.

There were many heartfelt responses to the crisis from sport, with many individuals and federations using their assets or influence to take care of people. Among them was an Italian international rugby player, Maxime Mbanda, who volunteered as an emergency ambulance driver in Parma during the pandemic. Sports leagues also stepped up, like Major League Soccer in the US, who created MLS Unites. This collaborative platform highlighted the efforts of the league and its players, coaches, and clubs to address the pandemic in ways that were informative, engaging, and inspiring. Across the Atlantic, the UK's Premier League used the #WeAreOneTeam hashtag as the driving force of its collective efforts. Its support included a $25 million donation to the NHS and vulnerable communities in the UK together with club-level support in local communities in the form of donations to food banks, food parcels to the vulnerable, telephone calls to the elderly, and a wide range of free resources to support wellbeing and education. Soccer's world governing body, FIFA, also played its part. It used its global muscle to good effect with an awareness campaign in partnership with the World Health Organization that featured world-renowned soccer players and was distributed across all 211 of its member associations to get the health & safety message out.

In addition, FIFA's $2 billion Emergency Relief Fund, akin to a federal bailout package, was the biggest response from any major sports governing body to help its members cope with the financial impact of the pandemic. Fortunately, FIFA was sitting on significant cash reserves to do this and could borrow against its future television and sponsorship income to raise the money required to support its members. It was a much-welcomed boon for many of its members.

The NFL was to be commended for its response to the pandemic. Staying true to the philosophy of using the league to "unite and inspire" people, the NFL created a three-day virtual fundraiser, the NFL Draft-a-Thon. Fans and communities were called on to donate during the 2020 NFL Draft to one central fund that helped to raise money for six national nonprofits in their efforts to support health care workers and first responders. After just four days, $6.6 million had been raised, contributing to the NFL's collective COVID relief contribution of $100 million, powerful proof of sport's supportive community.

San Francisco-based NBA team, the Golden State Warriors, was another standout for recognizing its role as a community asset and responding swiftly, with leadership and impact, during the crisis. Together with its partners, the team provided meals to local healthcare workers, donated $25,000 to the No Kid Hungry nonprofit, and committed a $1.4 million relief fund for Chase Center employees. Most encouraging here was the Warrior's keen understanding of its place at the heart of its community and its responsibility to be a powerful force for good therein.

One of the most comprehensive and humane responses to the crisis came from the NBA through its NBA Together platform, a social engagement campaign that aimed to support, engage, educate, and inspire youth, families, and fans in response to the pandemic. The campaign had four areas of focus—knowing the facts, acts of caring, expanding community, and NBA Together Live. It provided a centralized platform for basketball fans to stay informed about the virus, to tap into resources they might need to cope during the lockdown, to enjoy exclusive NBA content, and to connect with their favorite NBA players. The players contributed through the creation of public service announcements to share important health and safety information, and they also played a role in the creation of a series of virtual lessons that helped to make at-home learning fun while still being educational. The platform's "Acts of Caring" initiative encouraged fans and players to embrace a spirit of community and volunteerism by performing acts of kindness, whether big or small, to assist friends, families, and communities in need. The NBA also led a huge fundraising drive to provide cash to the areas of greatest need during the pandemic. Part of this included the manufacture of branded face masks featuring the logos of all 30 NBA and 12 WNBA teams, which were sold online with the proceeds going to feeding schemes in America and Canada.

In many instances, Sport for Good organizations were the real heroes during the crisis, showing commitment to supporting communities in need. Common Goal was one of these. Juan Mata, the founder of the movement, established the COVID Relief Fund and invited all football stakeholders to make a positive impact by contributing to the fund. The initiative also provided a "live match" platform for players to commit the 90 minutes they were no longer spending on the pitch to create positive outcomes. The Laureus Sport For Good Foundation used its website as a centralized hub for the sharing of information, toolkits, resources, and advice for the Laureus family and wider communities. And, Beyond Sport, who supports an array of sport-for-development organizations worldwide, used its community chats and network to provide support and connection to combat the effects of social distancing necessitated by the crisis.

The NBA's all-encompassing strategy in response to COVID-19 was perhaps the greatest indication that sport may finally be seeing its full potential as a leader in the force for good movement. And it is about time too. The fans are calling for it, and sport and its sponsors need to respond accordingly to remain relevant. Nielsen research conducted in the US during the coronavirus pandemic revealed that 70% of sports fans would support a sports league based on how they conducted themselves during the crisis, and 93% of them are somewhat or very likely to be loyal to brands that establish themselves as a leader in helping to fight the COVID-19 pandemic. We hope that the COVID crisis creates the impetus for the world of sport to take its rightful place in society as a community asset that is a powerful force for good. Only time will tell.

KEY INSIGHTS: SPORTS SHOWED UP DURING THE PANDEMIC BUT NOT ENOUGH TO BE CONSIDERED AN ESSENTIAL SERVICE

➤ The coronavirus pandemic that swept across the world in 2020 saw several sports organizations, leagues, and athletes stand up to make a difference.

➤ The most common response was in the form of personal cash donations and the auctioning of items and experiences or offering the use of stadiums as makeshift hospitals and testing centers.

➤ Other brands pivoted their business models to address urgent needs related to the crisis, such as the manufacture of ventilators and face masks.

➤ With live sports canceled across the globe, many sports organizations, such as F1 and NASCAR, turned to the online world and created virtual versions of their events. Esports also thrived.

➤ Sports organizing bodies had to come up with relief packages to ensure the economic survival of their members and players.

➤ The all-encompassing NBA Together campaign was perhaps the best collective response from the world of sport.

PART 3

BRINGING PURPOSE TO LIFE

N ow that we understand how the world of business has embraced Purpose as a management philosophy, and how the first movers within the business of sport have started to do the same, we shift our attention to how to embrace Purpose within your work.

WHAT PURPOSE IS, AND WHAT IT IS NOT

One of the biggest challenges in fully embracing the opportunities that Purpose presents is being able to mentally move beyond the traditional constructs within the capitalist system that we have applied to "doing good" for the last 100 years. Key to this is an acknowledgment and understanding that Purpose is not the same thing as philanthropy, charity, cause-related marketing, or corporate social responsibility. These practices all sit at the margins of how business has traditionally operated as opposed to being an organizing principle that sits as a management philosophy at the heart of everything that an organization does and does not do, which is Purpose.

To reinforce this definition of Purpose, and to better understand what Purpose is, let us take a look at the different forms of "doing good" that exist so that we can be clear on what Purpose is not.

"Philanthropy" derives from the Ancient Greek phrase philanthropia, meaning "to love people." Today, philanthropy centers around the practice of giving money to charities, foundations, or other nonprofit organizations whose mission it is to address a social or environmental issue, to help others concerning religion, medicine, health care, arts, and education. America has a strong philanthropic culture because giving has been part of the social contract for centuries. In contrast, other countries, for example, in Europe, have placed the responsibility for servicing society on Governments. In 2018, the 100 largest US charities generated $51.5 billion in donations, which equals 12% of the $427.7 billion in total contributions made across the country.

The philanthropic sector is not without its challenges. Mistrust in philanthropy is often based on doubts about the motives behind it, the limited transparency involved, and the real impact behind a donation. This mistrust has led to what we believe is an over-emphasis on the wrong metrics like how much money donated is allocated to administrative costs as opposed to the positive outcomes achieved. Prevailing charity models also limit charities from hiring the best people available to get a job done as charities paying their people market-related rates are generally frowned upon, which limits the potential of the sector to drive real change. Dan Palotta's epic book *Uncharitable* provides what we believe is a very convincing argument around what is wrong with the charity model, despite being written some ten years ago. We encourage you to read it if you are interested in gaining a deeper insight into what Dan believes is wrong with the sector.

In addition to the structural issues that Dan highlights, philanthropy faces greater competition from other forms of "doing good." Conscious consumption, or buying socially responsible goods, is increasingly being considered as a substitute for charitable giving, and there is increased interest in receiving a monetary return for doing good through vehicles like impact investing or providing capital to social enterprises.

"Philanthrocapitalism," on the other hand, is a new way of doing good that is emerging, which mirrors the way that business is done in the for-profit capitalist world but through a philanthropic lens. Examples include things like "venture philanthropy," which is a high-engagement approach whereby an investor for impact actively invests in social programs that would yield both a financial return on investment over the long term while also providing a social return.

The winners of capitalism increasingly see 'giving back' as an integral part of being wealthy. You cannot have one without the other. Capitalism makes philanthropy possible by creating a system that allows for both the creation of wealth and the disposing of it. Starbucks founder Howard

Schultz noted, "The price of admission to have a social impact agenda is to have financial performance."

There is also a growing recognition that big global problems cannot be left to governments alone to solve. Society is starting to change the way it solves its biggest problems by bringing together businesses, nonprofits, governments, social entrepreneurs, and philanthropists in innovative partnerships.

Critics of philanthrocapitalism, however, highlight that many of the billionaires preaching the value of philanthrocapitalism became billionaires by exacerbating social injustice, inequality, and disempowerment for millions of poor people in the first place. Whatever the rich give back through their philanthropy or philanthrocapitalism cannot compensate for the traditional way in which they have made their money. Fair point.

'Traditional Businesses' are organizations operating under an economic system called capitalism, whose primary goal is to make a profit, reach their financial goals, and maximize the profit to be shared only with shareholders. Owners, shareholders, and investors expect to maximize their returns on investment by receiving a portion of the company's profits in the form of dividends, options, shares, or other types of equity. The for-profit firm is so common that for most people, the term 'business' is synonymous with 'for-profit' or "shareholder capitalism."

Nonprofits, meanwhile, are a form of an organization dedicated to furthering a particular social cause, using their revenues to provide a service that people need rather than to make a profit. Nonprofit organizations are accountable to the donors, founders, volunteers, program recipients, and the public community. Can a nonprofit organization pursue both social impacts and business revenue? Traditionally, nonprofit organizations that wanted to increase their revenues tended to create commercial activities that were unrelated to their core social activities. However, new models of hybrid nonprofits have emerged. Nonprofit organizations have started to develop commercial activities and are learning how to integrate them deeply into their social mission. Great examples include Special Olympics, Red Cross, World Wildlife Fund, and The Nature Conservancy.

Social enterprise or social business is a new form of business with a social mission at its core. It combines the business acumen of a for-profit company with the purpose of a charity to solve social problems efficiently and sustainably. A Social Business is a hybrid company that either creates income for the poor or provides them with essential products and services like healthcare, safe water, or clean energy. They operate exactly like normal companies except for a few small differences. First, the primary aim of Social Business is to solve a social problem. Second, unlike a charity, a social business generates profit and aims to be financially self-sustaining in the long term and reinvest profits back into generating impact. Great examples include Kiva, Newman's Own, and Ten Thousand Villages.

Then, we have Mission-Driven For-Profit companies or Purpose-driven Companies, which are at the vanguard of the emergence of concepts like conscious capitalism, shared value capitalism, or triple bottom line. These organizations stand for and take action on something bigger than their products and services, in ways that create long-term value for their company, for society and the planet, and for all the people they serve.

Purpose-driven companies witness higher market share gains and grow faster on average than their competitors, all while achieving a higher workforce and customer satisfaction. According to the 2018 Cone/Porter Novelli Purpose report, 66% of people would switch to a Purpose-driven brand, and 91% of millennials would do the same. Also, 78% of consumers would encourage others to buy their products, 73% would defend these companies, and 68% want to work for them. Examples include the likes of Patagonia, Unilever, Warby Parker, Toms Shoes, Starbucks, and 17 Sport. If you have not already read the interview in Part 1 with Unilever Group PLC CEO Alan Jope, we suggest you do so now. Unilever is the quintessential Purpose-driven for-profit company and a great example of doing good while doing well with the welfare of all stakeholders in mind.

There is limited, if any, innovation happening in the business of sport right now when it comes to the types of organizations and business models that are used. While many professional sports properties do good on the fringes of their businesses through traditional Foundation or Community Relations departments, they almost all operate for the benefit of their owners. Most operate at the cutting edge of capitalism with more of a focus on financial engineering to reduce taxes and maximize capital gains for owners than on how to deliver maximum returns for all sport's stakeholders.

Governing bodies like the IOC and FIFA generally act like nation-states generating their revenues through the sale of commercial rights linked to their entertainment products and redistributing some of their profits to their member organizations around the world. These organizations have had more than their fair share of governance challenges over the years, and there is much skepticism around whether they exist to serve the interests of their member organizations or the individuals elected to run these organizations.

There is not a single example of a sports team or league that has registered as a B Corporation, and there are only a handful of examples in sports of true social businesses that exist to serve some higher ideal than just profits. One example comes from Lesotho in Africa, where Kick4Life has been established as the world's first soccer club exclusively dedicated to social change. Kick4Life's approach is based on the belief that soccer clubs do not always have to be run for private profit, and that we can more effectively leverage the enormous wealth and influence of the soccer industry for social development by becoming a part of it. They believe this new model, combining the soccer industry and the Sport for Development sector, is needed to uncap the power of sport for social change. Kick4Life is a registered charity and a social enterprise with offices in Lesotho, the UK, Luxembourg, and the USA.

Inspired by Kick4Life's Purpose-first model, Oakland Roots Sports Club, based in Oakland, California, was established in 2018 with a social Purpose at its core, that harnesses the magic of Oakland and the beautiful game of soccer as a force for positive social change. This higher Purpose drives everything that they do—whether on the pitch, in the stands, or within the community. Contrary to the traditional sports team business model where winning games and being commercially successful is all that matters, Oakland Roots applies a more balanced approach where performance on the field and their impact in the community matter as much as each other.

KEY INSIGHTS: PURPOSE IS NOT CSR OR PHILANTHROPY

➤ There are many different ways in which organizations and individuals can do good. These are linked to Purpose but are not Purpose in and of themselves.

➤ Philanthropy, cause-related marketing, and corporate social responsibility are not the same as Purpose as they operate at the fringes of a business.

➤ Purpose is when an organization stands for and takes action on something bigger than its products and services and places this as the core organizing philosophy around which it operates its entire business. In the process, it creates long-term value for the company, for society, the planet, and for all the people they serve.

➤ While there is an increasing number of examples of sports embracing Purpose as an organizing principle, the vast majority of sports organizations still operate as traditional "for-profit" businesses with capital appreciation of sports properties for the benefit of their owners being the primary objective.

➤ While there are over 3,500 companies in over 50 countries registered as B Corporations, there is not a single sports team, league, or property registered as a B Corporation.

LEADING THOUGHTS:
A SPORTS CLUB WITH PURPOSE AT ITS CORE

EDREECE ARGHANDIWAL   CMO & Co-founder at Oakland Roots

MIKE GEDDES   Chief Purpose Officer at Oakland Roots

OAKLAND ROOTS SPORTS CLUB IS COMMITTED TO PURPOSE BEYOND JUST WINNING GAMES AND MAKING MONEY AND SHOWS HOW OTHER PROFESSIONAL SPORTS TEAMS CAN MAKE THE JUMP TO PURPOSE.

On Oakland Roots' Purpose and why it is different from most traditional sports teams:
Our Purpose is to harness the magic of Oakland and the beautiful game of soccer as a force for positive social change. We are currently in the process of reviewing our Purpose statement. However, the fact that we have a higher Purpose beyond winning games and being commercially successful is the essence of it and always will be. It is the consistent thread that runs through everything we do. It is a challenge, and it is different, but if you look back on the success we have had in just one year, it was the right way to go.

On how the Oakland Root's approach is different from the way most traditional sports teams go about doing good:
A lot of sports organizations see Purpose as one arm of the organization, and that does not work in favor of the community because Purpose then takes a back seat to a lot of the business objectives. The misconception is that to make money, you have to detach yourself from the idea of Purpose, and this is fundamentally flawed. Impact, Purpose, and building a business are tremendously tied together, and they all contribute to positive financial outcomes. We have seen that within our first year of existence. To build proper movements, you have to think beyond just ideas and start thinking about how community and impact can be an integral part of everything that you do. We try to challenge assumptions and drive conversations further, which

can sometimes be quite uncomfortable. However, it is needed to break through the barriers of what most sports organizations in the United States have used.

On whether being Purpose-led means that Oakland Roots has to sacrifice the quality of the team and its aspirations:

We do not believe so. We believe that in a perfect world, these things operate together. If you look back at our performances on the field to date, they have not been the best, and yet the stadium has been packed to capacity at every single match, and that is a testament to the type of relationship the fans have with the team.

Sport is a very crowded landscape. There are very few opportunities to be the champion, and there are a lot of competing things out there for your fans' time, so you have to think about how to stay relevant and make people care about you. Winning games cannot be the only thing that defines your success; otherwise, there are going to be many times when that factor is not there. We are incredibly lucky to have a technical team that understands this process and is happy to align the team's success with our Purpose Mission, which ensures that Purpose is not put to one side.

On how the commitment to Purpose is helping to feed the bottom line and attract partners:

We have taken a different approach to the traditional sports advertising model. When we go to sponsors, we try to take them impactful stories, for example, our most recent partnership with GIG Car Share. We presented the idea of cardboard cut-outs that had already been done in Germany. However, we proposed that the campaign lives in various iconic locations in Oakland as an art mural rather than in the stadium, and to hire Black artists in our community to create the murals. GIG loved the idea and supported the concept. We have called the campaign "The Faces of Oakland," and the proceeds go to our Purpose partners. Our conversations happen through questions like how is this impacting the community, and does this put Oakland first as per our tagline.

On the outcomes of embarking on a Purpose-led strategy:

We wanted to build a club and a brand that Oakland was proud of, and, to do that, we had to represent Oakland in terms of what our team looks like, what our stadium experience is like, what our brand looks like, and how we show up in the community. We took the time to listen and learn how people would expect us to make a difference. Suppose you think about every aspect of how we operate as a team—what type of players we sign, what we ask them to do in the community, what type of purchasing decisions we make—all of these things are part of our Purpose. Part of our ongoing work is figuring out how we measure, track, and communicate that so that we can report on our impact. Success on the field is only one of several outcomes that we want to deliver to be able to demonstrate our success in terms of contributing to the city of Oakland. If we win a Title, then great, but if we do not, it is just one of our success metrics.

On the role of Purpose in terms of player recruitment and what is expected of them:

I'll answer by using the example of our current captain, Nana Attakora. He had a choice of several clubs, but he was captivated by the concept of a club doing positive things for the world, and that attracted him to us. As soccer teams and sports clubs begin to think about attractability, doing good in the world and having that as part of your function, does attract some of the best talents in the world.

Part of our selection, recruiting, and onboarding process is to instill in the players what our Purpose is. That is reflected in the work they do in the community and is part of the reason we have built a strong fan base so quickly because people identify with our players. Athletes are human beings, they have a holistic existence, and we think that by nurturing and investing in that side of it, you will produce better results on the field as well.

On how a traditional club who already has a long history should go about building Purpose into their organization:

My advice would be to flip the script and not be fearful. From day one, everything we have done has felt like a leap off a cliff, and we have been building our wings on the way down. Sports executives seem to be fixated on the way things should be done, but there are millions of different pathways to success and towards building a Purposeful organization. It is possible to reimagine your Purpose, but it requires authenticity, and you have to believe in it and commit to it at a foundational level. We have tried at Oakland Roots to think about the fact that we are here for Oakland rather than being here to be the most successful sports franchise in the world. That would be nice, but primarily we are here for the city, and we try to think about it through that lens.

DEFINING YOUR ORGANIZATIONAL PURPOSE

Before we dive into some suggestions on how to go about defining your organizational Purpose, let us make sure we understand the difference between some commonly used terms in business strategy.

Purpose — we love the French word for Purpose—Raison d'Etre. Translated, it means "reason for being," and that is what your Purpose statement should describe exactly, your WHY, what you stand for, the difference your organization makes in the world, what would be missed most if your organization suddenly ceased to exist. In other words, how does your organization make the world a better place socially or environmentally for the benefit of all stakeholders, not just shareholders?

adidas—Through sport, we have the power to change lives.

Vision — an organization's vision statement should best describe the type of world that your organization envisions in the future. The best vision statements are often associated with an almost unachievable scenario as they stretch the organization to think beyond the possible.

Microsoft—A computer on every desk and in every home.

Mission — it is important to set out clearly what business you are in as an organization—and importantly, what business you do not pursue. A mission statement should be easy to understand and be actionable by everyone involved in delivering the business every day. Your mission should make it clear what you do and how you do it.

Patagonia—We're in business to save our home planet.

Values or Guiding Principles — the rules of the game that everyone working at your organization is expected to follow. Values lead to organizational culture and act as a compass to guide decision making. Less is better than more when it comes to values. We always try to limit ourselves to just five core values.

Integrity, Accountability, Creativity, Resilience, Collaboration

Now that we are all on the same page, vis-à-vis the terminology we use, let us turn our attention to how one should go about defining an organizational Purpose statement.

To be effective, a Purpose Statement should ideally incorporate the following features:

1. Aspirational — it should inspire readers to want to join the fight, something they can relate to at a personal level.

2. Action-Oriented — words like change, awaken, inspire, enable are great words to include.

3. Outcome-Focused — with the end goal in mind.

4. Targeted — identify who or what the organization aims to serve.

REI's Purpose statement — *To awaken a life-long love of the outdoors*—is a good example of an organizational Purpose statement. It is aspirational, action-oriented, and clear on the outcome they want to achieve. It is, however, vague as to whom they aim to serve or who will benefit from this Purpose, although it could be implied that they are targeting everyone by not being specific. They could be relying on the implicit understanding of the value of the outdoors to society and individuals.

LEGO's Purpose — *To inspire and develop the builders of tomorrow*—is another good example. It is aspirational, action-oriented, clear on whom they are aiming to serve, but not on where this will lead. Again, it is implied that builders do positive things for the world, so that is good.

TESLA's Purpose — *We exist to accelerate the planet's transition to sustainable transport*—is not that aspirational. However, it is action-oriented, clear on the outcome, and very specific on the sector in which Tesla operates.

Developing a Purpose Statement is not an easy exercise and is as much an art as a science. With this in mind, we have found the principles of human-centered design thinking to be particularly effective in helping teams to define their organizational Purpose. Drawing on the inspiration provided by the likes of Google Ventures and impact agency, enso, we have developed our Design Sprint methodology at 17 Sport that effectively guides teams through a process of determining their organizational Purpose. What we like most about this approach is that it draws out the ideas and contributions of everyone in the team in a democratic way. The best Design Sprint processes draw on the insights of a broad cross-section of organizational stakeholders as this ensures that the views of others are considered and not just those in the marketing department. The saying "not for us without us" is as relevant as ever here as people love to follow things in which they feel a sense of ownership.

This process follows the following steps:

1. Share examples of Purpose Statements that you find inspiring and identify what it is about them that most relates to you. You can draw on these insights when designing your organizational Purpose.

2. Project fifty years ahead and imagine the headlines that are being written about your organization and the types of media in which

these headlines appear. These headlines will help you to identify the areas you will need to focus on to achieve your Purpose.

3. Identify how your organization will make the world a better place, socially or environmentally. Be specific about the impact you plan to have and how you will know whether you have been successful or not. Be clear on what it is that you stand for as an organization and what is required of your organization.

4. Identify the type of actions that you, as an organization, feel inspired to commit to and use these to settle on the role that you want to play as an organization in helping to deliver the impact identified in 3.

5. Identify whom your organization wishes to serve either geographically or by function.

Armed with these insights, you can set about the process of narrowing down the wording that best describes, in as few words as possible, what your organizational Purpose will be.

So, by way of example, let us apply the rules that we have set out above to the NFL and see what we can create. We could not find an organizational Purpose Statement for the NFL on their website, but we did find their Mission Statement, which reads:

> *We are all stewards of football. We unite people and inspire communities in the joy of the game by delivering the world's most exciting sports and entertainment experience.*

If we were to take this up a level, applying our Aspirational / Actionable / Outcome-Focussed / Targeted rules, we might come up with something like this for the NFL:

> *Bringing people together to build a resilient world.*

This statement is certainly aspirational—who does not want a more resilient world in the current challenging times in which we live? It is very actionable—"bringing people together to build." It is clear on the desired outcomes—"a resilient world." And, the target is also clear—people across the whole "world," which is in keeping with the NFL's status as a global brand.

Notice, nothing about football, nothing about putting on a great Super Bowl (or the one after that), nothing about money or the next player deal, nothing about sports and entertainment.

This Purpose Statement would also provide everyone involved with the NFL with a shining North Star that they could apply in all their decision making by asking these questions. Is this decision going to bring people together or draw them apart? Is this decision going to contribute towards building a more resilient world? Two simple questions that would drive behaviors that would make a HUGE impact on the world. That's Purpose.

KEY INSIGHTS: PURPOSE IS NOT ABOUT SPORT OR MONEY

➤ Your Purpose is not the same thing as your vision or mission.

➤ Your Purpose as a sports organization has nothing to do with sport or money and everything to do with what you stand for and how you make the world a better place.

➤ The best Purpose Statements are aspirational, action-oriented, outcome focussed, and targeted.

➤ The best Purpose Statements are designed through a collaborative process involving multiple stakeholders aligned around a shared Purpose.

CHAPTER 13

IDENTIFYING AND BUILDING COLLABORATIVE PARTNERSHIPS

There is a well-known Xhosa proverb in South Africa that says if you want to go quickly, go alone; if you want to go far, go together. Collaboration is the name of the game in the age of social good as more and more people realize that we can get more done together than we can alone.

Goal 17 of the United Nations Sustainable Development Goals is all about strengthening worldwide partnerships. It is also why we called our company 17 Sport because we believe that collaborative partnerships are a vital ingredient in any successful Purpose-driven undertaking.

When building a collaborative team around any Purpose-driven initiative in sport, we think it is important to consider involving a broad range of stakeholders. It is important that you identify people and organizations that are intentional, aligned around the power of Purpose, and committed to doing good while doing well—not just doing it because it is trendy or a way for them to hit their fee targets.

Your People — In short, people want to work for organizations that stand for something more than just profits. An organization's people are its most important asset. They are the living embodiment of your organization's true values and your Purpose ambassadors, and they want to be actively involved in helping the organizations they work for do good. Not only will the right people be drawn to work with your organization because of its stated Purpose and what it stands for, but also because it opens up opportunities to do good in their everyday work. For these reasons, Purpose can serve as a great staff retention tool.

One example of this that we love is Novelis' Recycle For Good initiative with Atlanta United FC. The staff at the Mercedes Benz Stadium are Recycle For Good's most vocal ambassadors and a huge part of its success. They help to collect used aluminum cans from fans that are then sold to raise funds to build houses with Habitat for Humanity in the Atlanta Westside Community alongside the stadium.

Athletes — Athletes are the influencers in the sports ecosystem and, therefore, a vital stakeholder if you want to amplify your impact and messaging. However, it is important that you only collaborate with athletes whose personal Purpose is aligned with social or environmental issues you are addressing and are therefore able to authentically and knowledgeably speak on the topic involved. In addition to having athletes endorse your initiative and promote it to your communities, you should also look to involve athletes in doing good. Purpose-led athlete endorsements are a lot more demanding than traditional endorsements but have the potential to deliver far more value.

We experienced this first-hand with Super Bowl 50 and our *Play Your Part* Campaign, where we tried hard to find NFL athletes that we could invite to become ambassadors for the program. Given the environmental focus of the campaign, we were particularly demanding in our screening to ensure that whichever players we ended up partnering with would be credible and walk the talk. We ended up deciding not to partner with anyone as we were unable to identify any NFL athletes at that time that met our stringent criteria.

Modern-day fans are quick to recognize inauthenticity. They will use their voice through social media to draw attention to any situations where they feel athletes have succumbed to the "show me the money" mantra.

Fans — Fans want to be actively involved in doing good, not just passive bystanders or observers. We learned this firsthand at Super Bowl 50 with the Play Your Part campaign, where we actively involved the fans in helping us to deliver a "net positive" event and rewarded them for doing so. Fans were asked to take one of four sustainability-related actions that Play Your Part Volunteers then recognized and rewarded. The level of fan engagement was very high, with participating fans commenting that they enjoyed having the opportunity to make a difference while also being recognized for this by the Host Committee and having the chance to win prizes for their efforts. This opportunity enabled us to put doing good while doing well in practice.

Another great example of Purposeful fan engagement comes from Brazilian Sport Club Recife and its Immortal Fans initiative, in which over 50,000 fans were mobilized to sign up for an organ donor program that reduced the waiting list for organ transplants in the city to zero and saved many lives.

We have learned through our work that the fans want to be actively involved in doing good alongside the sports properties and athletes that mean something to them. The days of treating fans as passive bystanders are over.

Impact Partners — Given its intrinsic values and engagement power, we believe that sport is the greatest platform available to society to deliver social and environmental impact. Nonprofit or impact organizations around the world understand this and continue to use sport as a platform to raise funding and awareness around social and environmental issues.

Sports properties also continue to leverage partnerships with nonprofit organizations as part of their community outreach or Foundation programs. A good example of this is the PGA Tour, which has built a symbiotic relationship with volunteers, its players, the fans, and local nonprofit organizations to both secure human resources to run its events and to contribute $3 billion in funding towards community charities.

We believe the best Purpose-led sports collaborations involve multiple impact organizations that are offered the opportunity to leverage the sports platform to drive their social or environmental mission. We did this successfully for the 34th America's Cup, where we created a bespoke collaboration of more than 20 impact partners around a shared mission, which we called the *Healthy Ocean Project,* to raise public awareness and action around ocean health issues.

In addition to delivering the social impact that they do, impact partners are also great influencers. They often have baked in communities that they can activate in support of the mission. Not only does this help to amplify the reach and impact, but it also adds tremendous credibility given how careful impact organizations are about deciding whom to work with and what projects to support.

Corporate Partners — More and more corporations are looking for ways to activate their sponsorships in a more Purposeful way, particularly those corporations that have already made the transition to Purpose at an organizational level. Corporate partners have so much value to add to any Purpose-led sports collaboration, whether it be their expertise, funding, resources, or increasing appetite to do good rather than just talk about doing good.

We have been fortunate enough to work with some amazing corporate partners over the years, including Danone and their 20-year-old Danone Nations Cup, the largest soccer tournament in the world, with over 2 million boys and girls from over 20 countries participating. Danone is now redesigning the competition with Purpose in mind and has set itself the lofty ambition of growing participation in the event 5X over the next ten years by leaning into the desire that young people today have to be actively involved in doing good. In the process, Danone intends that these boys and girls will become Global Citizens committed to both playing the beautiful game and leveraging it as a platform to do good in the world. We are working with Danone to help them identify other corporate partners that share their values and that they can collaborate with to help achieve their ambition. It is a great example of Purpose-driven thinking.

Sports Properties — While sports properties have traditionally supported external causes through their community affairs departments and Foundations, they increasingly recognize that they have the potential to take on issues in their own right and leverage their platforms directly for good.

A recent example of this is the stance that the NBA took around the COVID-19 pandemic and their decision to be the first league to postpone their season in the interests of the health and safety of the NBA Community. They followed this announcement with all facets of the NBA family joining forces to launch NBA Together—a global community and social engagement campaign to support, engage, educate, and inspire youth, families, and fans during the pandemic. Through its four pillars—Know the Facts, Acts of Caring, #NBATogetherLive, and Expand Your Community—NBA Together shared the latest health and safety information and used digital tools and virtual events to help keep communities connected during this time of social distancing. Just a month into the initiative, the league, teams, players, and owners had provided more than $76 million towards support and relief and nearly five million meals for food-insecure populations. The NBA is a great example of a league that understands that they are more than just an entertainment property and more akin to a community asset, which will only serve to reinforce their relevance as an organization to society as they navigate what comes post-COVID.

Impact Advisors — It is important to work with advisors who understand Purpose and what does and does not work in the context of sport. As Purpose starts to gain traction as a management philosophy, every agency has, overnight, become an expert in Purpose. However, they do not necessarily have the credibility, experience, or track record necessary to design, develop, and implement effective Purpose-led sports impact programs.

Purpose is an area in which we at 17 Sport believe we excel. Our senior team has been doing this work for the last ten years or more, working on some of the biggest Purpose-led initiatives that have happened in sports during this period. We are focussed on acting for good, not just talking about doing good, and will not work with clients that do not share our values and our commitment to using sport as a platform to build a more positive future for the world.

Make sure you do your due diligence when deciding which advisors to work alongside. There is a difference between traditional sports marketing and expertise in areas like Purpose strategy, operational sustainability (e.g., waste management, energy efficiency, and the like.), Purpose communications, Purpose event implementation, and Purpose measurement.

KEY INSIGHTS: COLLABORATIONS ARE THE CURRENCY IN THE AGE OF SOCIAL GOOD

➤ When building collaborative teams, ensure you pick people
   to partner with that are aligned around the same values and
   committed to doing good while doing well.

➤ The best results are achieved when you can build teams comprising
   multiple stakeholders, including your people, fans, athletes,
   corporate partners, impact partners, sports properties, and impact
   advisors.

ALIGNING YOUR PURPOSE WITH YOUR BUSINESS STRATEGY

Once you have fully developed your organizational Purpose, you will need to move on to thinking about HOW you are going to bring it to life. Key to your effectiveness will be the extent to which the leadership of your organization has bought into the philosophy of leading with Purpose. Purpose-led strategies need to be driven from the very top and then embraced at every level of the organization to be successful.

The best Purpose-led business strategies that we have seen place an organization's Purpose at the heart of the organization and leverage this as a central theme for everything that the business does. They create opportunities for the organization to positively impact the world beyond the products and services that they deliver and to provide all stakeholders, not just shareholders or owners, with outstanding returns.

Super Bowl 50 is a great example of this philosophy. Instead of adopting the traditional approach of focussing on the Super Bowl as an entertainment property and delivering Super Bowl as the year's biggest party—the second biggest day of consumption in the USA after Thanksgiving—the San Francisco Bay Area Super Bowl 50 Organizing Committee decided to organize the event around a Purpose of improving the lives of young people in the Bay Area, particularly those in underserved communities, IN ADDITION to delivering a great experience.

This Purpose drove EVERYTHING that the Host Committee did from how they communicated with their fans, how they went about staging the event itself, the value proposition offered to their corporate partners, and how they engaged with all stakeholders, including the nonprofit community. Also, it influenced how they recruited and managed their operational team and volunteer corp, how they motivated the appropriate behaviors, and how they measured their success with both financial and impact KPI's. (Disclosure: Neill Duffy was deeply involved in Super Bowl 50 as Co-Chair of the Host Committee's Sustainability Committee and Lead Sustainability Advisor to the Host Committee).

A key factor in the success of Super Bowl 50 was that the leadership of the Host Committee, under the Chair of Daniel Lurie and CEO Keith Bruce, truly believed that leading with Purpose would deliver the best results. This commitment filtered down throughout the organization to every member of the team, including the thousands of volunteers, who made it their business to ensure that the event lived up to its Purpose even when the going got tough, and it may have been tempting to default to the traditional way of doing things.

CASE STUDY
SUPER BOWL 50

How San Francisco embedded Purpose as a central organizing theme into every part of Super Bowl 50 and delivered the most commercially successful, shared, sustainable, and giving Super Bowl in history:

The Super Bowl is the world's single biggest one-day sports event, watched by over 160 million people and with in-stadium attendance of 60,000. However, it is more than just a football game; it is an American cultural showpiece. In 2016, the host city, San Francisco, capitalized on its high visibility by using the event as a platform to demonstrate the city's dedication to positive social impact, specifically to improve the lives of young people living in the Bay Area. Purpose was embedded into the heart of the Host Committee plan from the beginning, both as a core strategic business advantage and as a way to leave a lasting impact of positive good for the region.

The Host Committee adopted a "Net Positive" strategy with four sustainability objectives:

1. Reduce the impact on climate change by delivering a low emissions event
2. Responsible use of resources and materials during and after the event
3. Create ways for fans and guests at the event to personally participate in sustainable practices
4. Leave a lasting legacy for the entire Bay Area

By adopting this unique approach, the Host Committee created new opportunities for businesses, vendors, public and private partners, and fans to take sustainable and environmentally friendly event practices to an entirely new level. Simple, consumer-friendly sustainability programs were initiated so that both residents and event partners could grasp the full potential of sustainability as an advantageous business and personal practice.

While the main event is the NFL's championship game on Super Bowl Sunday, several other activities take place in celebration of the Super Bowl. In 2016, these included a free-to-the-public fan village, Super Bowl City, that spanned nine days and offered fans interactive games, autograph sessions with past and present NFL players, a history of the game display, and an event merchandise outlet. Community, engaging with, and giving back to local communities, was a key element of the host committee's strategy. To this end, the Host Committee staged various community celebration events that attracted nearly two million residents, including The 50 Tour, a roadshow fan experience that visited 25 communities over three months leading up to Super Bowl Sunday.

The **impact on climate change was reduced** in several ways. Fans were encouraged to make use of the bike valet station at Super Bowl City or the charter bus system provided by the event organizers to limit car emissions. Thanks to PG&E, the Official Clean Energy Partner, Super Bowl City was able to run on cleaner power with reduced emissions and noise. Hydrogen Fuel Cell generators were also used at Super Bowl City to supplement the renewable diesel generators and showcase technology of the future. Terra Pass, the event's Sustainability Partner, made it possible to offset 300mT of residual emissions and developed a unique offset product that allowed fans to offset their emissions. The NFL also came to the party with its urban forestry grant program that facilitated the planting of trees in the Bay area. A total of 28,500 trees were planted through this donation.

The Host Committee ensured the **responsible use of materials and resources** by mandating that all food served was locally sourced and presented in 100% recycled or compostable materials. Excess food was donated to local food banks to prevent wastage. Free water stations were located throughout Super Bowl City and resulted in the elimination of 14,580 single-use plastic bottles from landfills. The #BringYourOwn Campaign, whereby fans were encouraged to bring reusable containers and water bottles to the event, also helped to reduce waste significantly.

To inspire fans and residents to **live more sustainably** in their personal lives and to demonstrate how they could also play their part in delivering a Net Positive event, the Host Committee created the Play Your Part campaign. This campaign rewarded fans for their Net Positive behavior—either a pledge to take a sustainable action on the Play Your Part website or a sustainable action in Super Bowl City—which then rewarded them with 50 Good Coins that they could donate to a Bay Area nonprofit of their choice. Fans who participated in the campaign also stood a chance to win one of nine daily Super Bowl 50 related prizes, including tickets to Super Bowl Sunday. The campaign inspired social consciousness and was a huge success with almost 24,000 Net Positive pledges being made, which resulted in a donation of $200,000 to local nonprofits.

Youth-focused campaigns, aimed at educating the younger generation and inspiring them to embrace a sustainable future, were another area of focus for the Host Committee. One such campaign was the Super Kids Super Sharing campaign, whereby schools from across the Bay Area donated books, sports equipment, and school supplies to children in need. There was also a YES Youth Conference, which was attended by 300 youth leaders to equip them with the knowledge to spread the sustainability message to their peer group. Work experience opportunities were created via the event's volunteer program, which saw 5,500 volunteers providing 100,000 volunteer hours in return for training on the Host Committee's Net Positive sustainability program.

It was critical to the event strategy that it left a **lasting legacy,** the most obvious of which was the upgraded Levi's® Stadium—the first professional football stadium to have achieved LEED Gold Certification at the time of its opening. More importantly, though, were the lasting economic and social benefits to residents, particularly children, youth, and families living in low-income communities. Through the 50 Fund, the philanthropic arm of the Host Committee, together with event Partners and the NFL, $13 million was raised and distributed to local nonprofit organizations. There was also a concerted effort to link local businesses with contracting opportunities with the NFL and the Host Committee. This effort proved successful as $5.5 million was spent with diverse local businesses.

Super Bowl 50 was a success on many levels. It delivered a $240 million boost to the Bay Area economy and raised $13 million for the 50 Fund, which benefited 537,000 Bay Area youth and 141 Bay Area nonprofit organizations. This success was pleasing, not only for the residents of San Francisco but also for the corporations who had partnered the Host Committee in the staging of the event. Eighty percent of corporates that funded the Host Committee were not already NFL or 49ers sponsors. They cited the Host Committee's promise to give back as a major influencer in their decision to support the event. Emissions were lowered, partly thanks to 10,987 people using public transit on Super Bowl Sunday and Neste supplying 36,674 gallons of renewable diesel, which diverted 242.51MT of carbon dioxide equivalent emissions from the atmosphere. From a participatory perspective, over 1 million fans experienced Super Bowl City, 1.9 million attended at least one Super Bowl 50 related event in the region, and a further 550,000 were reached via the 50 Tour roadshow. The roadshow also generated 57 million media impressions. In terms of social media, the reach was prolific—a 4.3 billion twitter audience on game day as well as 141 million fans reached via Facebook during Super Bowl week, not to mention the 3.96 million live stream viewers on game day.

Super Bowl 50 demonstrates how sport can be a powerful force for good, that a Purposeful sports event can outperform the traditional sports business model. By leading with Purpose, the city of San Francisco showed how the world's biggest one-day sports event became the most shared, most participatory, most giving, most sustainable, and most commercially successful Super Bowl in history—an achievement that still stands today. ∎

KEY INSIGHTS: PURPOSE AT THE CENTER

➤ Purpose-led strategies need to be led from the very top and then embraced at every level of the organization.

➤ The best Purpose-led business strategies that we have seen place an organization's Purpose at the heart of the organization and leverage it as a central theme for everything that the business does, e.g., Super Bowl 50.

MEASURING WHAT MATTERS

Measuring the ROI (Return On Investment) on traditional sponsorships has become pretty commonplace these days, and there are as many measurement models as there are sports marketing agencies, like Octagon and GMR, and research agencies like IEG and Nielsen. These models have evolved in sophistication over time and are used for the pre-acquisition valuation of sponsorships as well as the post-evaluation assessment of sponsorship performance.

With the evolution of social media, promotion via social media channels has become as important—if not more important—than in-event activation. This evolution has given rise, more recently, to technology and AI-powered sponsorship analytics and valuation services, like Hookit and Gum Gum, which have done a good job of further developing the science and rigor around sponsorship valuation.

While these types of services play an important role in improving the efficiency of traditional sponsorships, we are critical of them to the extent that they are very 'output' as opposed to 'outcome' focussed. For example, they tell you what kind of reach you attained through your sponsorship but not what the outcome of achieving that reach was. Further, while these models may measure traditional benefits like media values and other equivalencies, none of them do justice to the true value that Purpose-driven activations deliver. The closest we have seen any of the traditional models come to measuring the social impact connected with a particular sponsorship are those that apply some arbitrary pre-mium to the conventional media and equivalency valuation metrics to try and factor this in. In our opinion, this approach does not cut it and only serves to undermine the huge value of Purpose-driven activations.

Other attempts that we have seen to measure social impact associated with social good activations also miss the point in that they focus on outputs as opposed to outcomes, e.g., Our Foundation made it possible for 10,000 kids to participate in our program. So what? Ten thousand kids are an output metric, not an outcome. What matters more is what impact the program had on the 10,000 kids—how did they benefit, and how did society benefit as a result of the intervention? Outcomes are what count.

The main reason for this disconnect is that the people driving the tra-ditional valuation methodologies in sport simply do not understand the world of social and environmental impact and the complexities involved. However, one person who does understand both the world of traditional sponsorship valuation—because she pioneered it at IEG—and the world of social impact is Lesa Ukman. She has, together with her partners, Bill Doyle and Jed Pearsall at *Performance Research,* developed a social capital valuation service to measure the return on Purpose associated with a Purpose-driven activation. Called PSV (Pro-Social Valuation), this ser-vice uses the power of big data and evidence-based research to go beyond output and measure outcomes to mathematically translate each unit of social capital into a dollar value based on income or savings to the public and benefits to individuals or society. This service is great as it not only allows for the valuation of social capital around a specific project, but it also allows for comparison between one or more initiatives.

For the avoidance of doubt, Social Capital is not referring to the value created through social media but rather the value created for society through an intervention. PSV defines social capital as the currency cre-ated by ProSocial organizations, programs, and partnerships that enrich the well-being of people and the planet. Unlike personal property, which enhances individual economic success, the acquisition of social capital delivers a common good and serves the public interest. Types of social capital that PSV measures and values include things like human capital, natural capital, community capital, and civic capital.

The Homeless World Cup, which takes place annually in different cities around the world, is a great example of how PSV shines a light on the true worth of the competition to society, a value that traditional sponsorship valuation models do not capture. PSV calculated that the $1.5 million spent on staging the event in 2016 in Glasgow, Scotland, translated into over $12 million in social capital being directly created for society. This metric is hugely important as it tells sponsors and funders of the event that for every dollar they spent on the event, $8.62 in Social ROI was created. And this excludes any of the traditional media and other equivalents generated around the event and through sponsor-driven activations. Social capital was generated in areas such as behavior shifts, capacity building, advocacy, and awareness, which all reduce the cost on society of managing the consequences of homelessness.

The ProSocial Valuation Map for Homeless World Cup sets out the basic framework that PSV used in valuing the social capital created by the event. We understand that on the back of this valuation, the Homeless World Cup was able to renew a sponsorship with a partner that had, before seeing the data, been considering not renewing their partnership.

Armed with this PSV service, it is now, for the first time, possible to develop a full ROI calculation, which takes into account the value of both the traditional media and other equivalents as well as the social capital to understand the true value created through a Purpose-driven sponsorship.

At 17 Sport, we recognize how difficult it is to measure the benefits of sponsorship marketing, Purpose-led or not. However, we are, none-theless, thinking through how to take the science and art of sponsorship valuation a step further, to factor in the full range of outcomes that we believe are attached to a Purpose-driven sponsorship. Our ROI formula looks something like this:

ROI = FINANCIAL RETURN + IMPACT RETURN

Financial Return consists of measures like new and incremental revenues, enhanced brand equity, greater relevance, deeper engagement, new audiences, reduced costs/improved efficiencies, and traditional sponsorship metrics. In contrast, Impact Return consists of measures like the social, environmental, and economic benefits that a service like PSV provides.

KEY INSIGHTS: OUTCOMES NOT OUTPUTS

➤ Traditional sponsorship valuation models do not factor in the true value of social capital created through Purpose-led sponsorships.

➤ The sports industry is far too focussed on outputs as opposed to outcomes, which are much more useful indicators of success.

➤ ProSocial Valuation Service is the first measurement model to quantify in dollar terms the value of social capital created.

➤ 17 Sport is working towards developing an integrated measurement model which factors in the financial and social outcomes of a Purpose-driven sponsorship for the first time.

L E A D I N G   T H O U G H T :
MEASURE WHAT MATTERS

LESA UKMAN   Founder of ProSocial Valuation Service

LESA IS A PIONEER IN ASSIGNING VALUE TO MARKETING COLLABORATIONS
AND DEVELOPED THE FIRST MODEL TO MEASURE THE SOCIAL OUTCOMES
OF PURPOSE-DRIVEN CAMPAIGNS.

On the transition from IEG and the move towards measuring social good:
One of our clients at IEG included the FIFA World Cup, and they have done an
excellent job of generating revenue through sponsorship. I was at a conference in
the Middle East, where I met Mel Young, who started the Homeless World Cup.
He shared with me that he had no sponsors, and not only did he have no sponsors,
but his hands were tied because FIFA had forbidden him from approaching any of
the official World Cup sponsors. That got me upset because if I were FIFA, I would
have bought Homeless World Cup and made it part of the FIFA offering and used
it to build a halo of goodwill around the brand, which FIFA sorely needed at the
time. It was also a great brand extension that FIFA's partners would have loved to
activate. It made me think that there was something wrong with the IEG valuation
model if it was just based on the point of view of the sponsor and did not take into
account the point of view of people and the planet. I realized it was time, not just
for an alternative to IEG, but a whole new way of thinking about value. What is the
value created by an initiative for people and the planet, and who is at the table
speaking up for them? At the time, there was nothing. I sold IEG and started thinking
about social good and the need to build a consistent lexicon to talk about it and
consistent standards of measuring it.

I started ProSocial Valuation four years ago, and, honestly, I never thought it
was going to take so long to figure it all out, but we finally finished our model at
the end of last year. We now have clients, some of whom are even corporations,
which I never anticipated when we created this. It was to help people like the
Homeless World Cup get money from foundations and philanthropy because so

many of the dollars were going to the best marketers. We wanted to level the playing field and help tell the story for those people doing the most good.

On the kind of metrics used to measure social good using Homeless World Cup as an example:
Part of the issue is that nonprofits are not measuring outcomes. When I started, I assumed they had those metrics in place already, and we could just put them into some algorithms and spit out some valuation statements. But it turns out, nonprofits are great at defining their mission, but they do not have budgets or people specialized in tracking metrics. So, with the Homeless World Cup, there was some primary research tracking participants and whether they were still homeless two years after participating or not. We then also looked at a few other primary outcomes like Healthcare usage and arrests and things like that because homeless people tend to get arrested at higher rates than others. The Homeless World Cup is a global project across 80 countries, so when assessing the dollar value of the outcomes, we had to consider the value, to the public, not to the sponsors, of not being homeless again across all the different countries. For example, in Nordic countries where they spend a lot of money on homeless people, the average value of getting someone off the street might be $32,000.

In contrast, in Russia, they denied that they even had any homeless people, so the value was zero. We had to create this global weighted average to reflect all the markets where the Homeless World Cup existed. Once we had done this across all the countries, we looked at the value to the public in the sense of saving taxpayers and then looked at other primary outcomes. It took a long time, but the results were great.

Everything we do is transparent. Every number is backed by research, and there is a link to a digital file with every single research report if you want to see the raw data in there, so it is all very transparent and understandable. We do not use any multipliers, and we also look at costs. So, for example, the Homeless World Cup brings people from around the world to one site to compete every year in the event. We look at how much fossil fuel is burnt flying all these people in, and we subtract that from the ultimate value. So, we look at the benefits and costs to people and the planet.

The default response when you start to interrogate how to analyze the return from these kinds of social programs is that it is a long-term thing, and you need to look ten years from now. However, listening to you, it sounds like you have figured out a way of actually doing something on more of a short term basis: We are building all the technologies so that it is more automated and getting quicker. One of the issues is coming up with the right taxonomy because many of the standard metrics used for sport draw a blank when valuing the outcomes for people and the planet. We have embedded research into the valuation process for every property type website so that we do not have to create that from scratch.

On looking ahead to 2030 and whether sport is going to start embracing social capital and making it part and parcel for its existence in the world: I think they already have. Athletes are incredibly charitable, giving people as a group, and they are leading the way. And every sports team, from 15 years ago, has had a community relations department. They have now added on to that, not just a foundation but a CSR version two within sports. The sports owners understand that they need to get buy-in from governments and all kinds of other people. Sport needs to be not just great value, but have great values too, and they have to be adding something of benefit to the world. I think concepts are there, but maybe they are not all measuring it yet. They are looking more at outputs as opposed to outcomes, but I think they will get there.

I see the future role of sports as being to help make the cities they operate in more livable in really important ways. Sport has a platform that no one else has to influence and reach so many people, so it is what they can do as an entity and the behavior that they, their athletes, and sponsors can influence and change. When you start measuring that, the future looks interesting.

BRINGING IT ALL TOGETHER

Now that we have helped you to understand (1) what Purpose is and what it is not, (2) the difference between an organization's Purpose, vision, mission, and values, (3) how to collaborate with multiple stakeholders, (4) how you should move from outputs to outcomes, and (5) how to align your organization's business strategy around your Purpose as a central organizing theme, we thought we would bring it all together and provide you with a template that you can use to develop your strategic Purpose framework.

This template will work at a macro organizational level, e.g., for a sports team or property, or equally well at a micro level, e.g., for sponsorship activation.

SPORTS PURPOSE FRAMEWORK QUESTIONNAIRE

1. What is your vision for the world?

. . . .

2. What is your organizational Purpose? How do you intend to contribute towards achieving this vision? How will you make the world a better place beyond the products and services you provide?

. . . .

3. What is your mission? What is it that you do as an organization, and how do you go about doing it?

....

4. What is your organizational strategy? What are the actions that you will take as an organization to live up to your Purpose and deliver your mission?

....

5. What are your organizational values and guiding principles? What commitments will you make to everyone inside and outside the organization in terms of how you will behave?

....

6. What are your organizational goals? What outcomes do you intend to deliver through your efforts? How will you measure and manage your performance?

....

7. Who will collaborate with you?

....

8. What value will you provide to each of your stakeholders—owners, employees, suppliers, volunteers, community, and environment?

....

CASE STUDY

THE DANONE NATIONS CUP – A FORCE FOR GOOD IN THE WORLD

Here is an example of a Purpose Framework that was developed for the Danone Nations Cup using this approach. The Danone Nations Cup, an event that was started by Danone over 20 years ago, is an event that has grown into the largest soccer tournament in the world for U12 boys and girls with over 2 million participants each year. Danone recently decided to reposition the event in line with their corporate commitment to act as a Purpose-led organization and their ambition to leverage the event as a force for good in the world. As you read, pay special attention to where the event itself appears as part of the Framework—as part of the HOW, not the WHY. (Disclosure: 17 Sport is working with Danone to help build the ecosystem of partners that will help bring this vision to life).

The Danone Nations Cup
Play Football, Change the Game.

Our Purpose
We exist to improve the lives of children around the world.

Our Mission
To leverage the passion and reach of soccer to inspire and empower 12-year-old boys and girls to become world citizens and to act in service of good.

Our Strategy

1. Host and promote the world's largest annual soccer tournament for U12 boys and girls as a model world-class responsible event.

2. Collaborate with players, corporations, nonprofits, ambassadors, and sports properties that share our values and vision to amplify our reach and impact.

3. Focus on supporting initiatives linked to issues that boys and girls care most about—ending poverty, gender equity, life below water, and climate change—and create pathways that make it easy for them to act in support of these issues.

4. Take bold actions in support of our mission.

5. Promote the value of healthy lifestyles by educating girls and boys on healthy eating and drinking habits and the importance of a balanced diet.

Our 2030 Goals

1. Directly improve the lives of 10 million kids.

2. Achieve equal participation of boys and girls in everything we do.

3. Grow the reach of the tournament globally.

4. Deliver a positive financial, social, and environmental ROI for our collaborators.

Our Value Proposition for Our Collaborators

1. Build brand affinity with the "Next Generation" of consumers—Gen Alpha.

2. Act in alignment with your organization's corporate Purpose.

3. Associate with brands that share your organization's values.

4. Amplify the value of Sport for Good as a platform to drive real impact at scale. ∎

LEADING THOUGHT:
ACTING ON PURPOSE

FLORENCE DARQUIE-BOSSARD   Global Marketing Director
at Danone

DANONE HAS TRANSFORMED THE DANONE NATIONS CUP INTO A HIGHLY
EFFECTIVE PLATFORM TO DRIVE THE BRAND'S PURPOSE AGENDA.

How Purpose plays out in the way Danone is run:
Today, the company's vision is reflected in its "One Planet. One Health" byline. We
know that people's health is strongly linked to the health of the planet. The way
we produce and grow products, the way we conduct ourselves, and the way we
manage our people is done with this vision in mind. From a marketing perspective,
we know that sustainability drives brand preference amongst people today, so it is
strongly anchored in all of our brands. Likewise, in procurement, our decisions about
which suppliers and partners to use are determined with sustainability in mind.
Lastly, we are mindful of the need to be inclusive in that we must produce goods
that are affordable to the population, and we must run the business inclusively by
practicing gender equality.

**On the way Danone's Purpose philosophy impacts the way it runs its sports
sponsorships and what it expects out of them:**
Sport for us serves as a touchpoint with consumers. We know that there is a strong
relationship between sports performance and healthy eating and drinking, so
we use our sports sponsorships and our partnerships with athletes to convey this
message. Water is an important component of sports performance and sports
recovery. For instance, using our Evian brand, we have partnerships with Maria
Sharapova, Stan Wawrinka, and Madison Keys, and we partner with tennis
tournaments like Wimbledon and the US Open. All of these drive the message of
the importance of hydration in sport.

But we also have events and assets that we own, like the Danone Nations Cup
that targets kids aged 10 -12 years. We must connect with the youth as they are

the ones who can shift the world and change food consumption habits. We have decided to move beyond it being just a soccer competition and want it to become a lifetime experience for the two million kids that participate, helping them to play soccer, but also helping them to become better citizens of the world. We now use the event to drive messages about the ability these kids have to positively impact the world and the planet through their healthy habits of drinking and eating.

On using the platform of the Danone Nations Cup to activate two million 10–12-year-old kids to act for good:

Our starting point was that the Danone Nations Cup is an amazing asset and so it must be used to bring the company's mission to life. But this was not enough. So we looked at all the initiatives we have to provide water access to people in need, and that, together with the participating kids and the passion point of soccer, and the kids' mindset that nothing is impossible, created something special. So, with water as our first battle, we got the kids to act for other kids who did not have access to water, and they reacted very well to this challenge. We then thought it would be a good idea to unleash these kids' voices and for them to decide on the future they wanted to see in the world. We adapted the UN's Sustainable Development Goals to make them easily understandable to the kids, and we asked them to vote on which of the 17 goals were the most important for them. At our last Danone Nations Cup final in Barcelona, back in October 2019, the kids voted. It was amazing and very emotional to see because the kids took their duty to vote for a better world seriously. We are incredibly proud of the kids and are committed to acting on their voice and their votes.

On the like-minded collaborations that make up the Danone Nations Cup:

We wanted to have an impact at scale, but we realized that on our own, we would never be able to do this, so we joined Common Goal and streetfootballworld. These organizations are already doing something meaningful on the ground. We are very proud to be associated with these movements because we strongly believe that, through them and the scale that they have, there is now momentum for sports to act as a powerful force for good. There is money. There is passion. And there are many people involved to initiate the movement towards shaping a better tomorrow and a better planet, and better people being able to live together and act together so that we can move the needle towards a better world.

On the corporate partners that have been inspired by Danone's values:
When we first embarked on this journey of being Purposeful through our
sponsorships, we realized that we needed others to help us. We were excited to
have Decathlon join us, not only to get kids to play soccer but for the opportunity
for those kids to join a worldwide competition and to play for a better tomorrow.
Decathlon was one of the first partners to join us, and their Purpose is to get as
many people as possible practicing sport. Their Purpose aligned perfectly with our
mission to bring healthy food to as many people as possible, so there was a strong
connection.

On the Decathlon "Laces for Change" initiative:
"Laces for Change" was our first joint campaign with Decathlon. We made laces
from recycled plastic bottles, and each purchase of a pair of laces provided safe
water for a year for one child in India. Laces were offered to the communities
around the Danone Nations Cup or could be bought online and in stores. This
initiative was a great communications tool and allowed us to engage further than
the food community. Many influencers joined the movement and carried the laces as
a sign of pride because they were happy to be part of it. The campaign was really
special and impactful because it was a cause that mattered to the kids.

On the future and what it holds for the Danone Nations Cup:
My wish is that the Danone Nations Cup becomes the perfect platform for brands
that want to make an impact and believe in sport as a force for good. I would
like for us to have more partners joining forces with us to make these kids' dreams
come true and to extend the event's footprint. The two million kids who participate
today are a lot, but this is small compared to the number of kids on earth. With the
evolution of technology, we should look at creating opportunities for a connection
online in addition to getting the kids together physically. I would like the event to be
a pioneer in connecting kids from all around the world and to reach out with strong
positive messages about the future for these kids and the role they can play in
creating it. Finally, my dream is for the Danone Nations Cup to become as powerful,
at kid level, as the Olympic Games, not only from a sporting standpoint but from an
ability to act collectively for a better tomorrow.

WHAT SPORT SHOULD DO TO BECOME AN ESSENTIAL SERVICE

We finish writing *Legacy Sport* just as the global COVID-19 pandemic starts to take hold.

Sport has been furloughed as authorities around the world deem it a non-essential service, even worse, a risk factor to be managed in efforts to keep people apart and "flatten the curve." If this is not a huge wakeup call that sport needs to reinvent itself to remain relevant in a post-COVID-19 world, I do not know what else could be.

Organizations have had to respond to external threats before. We believe that the organizations that thrive in these circumstances are the ones that grasp the opportunity to innovate to remain relevant. The ones that fail, in a natural selection like system, are those that focus on trying to maintain the status quo, simply try to survive.

The business of sport is not immune to all of this. Unless governments step up and bail them out—which they might still do—there will be many sports organizations that focused on survival, by doing what they have always done, that will go out of business in the coming months and years as a result of the pandemic. But there will also be those, led by visionary leaders, that recognize that they need to redesign their value proposition beyond being only an entertainment product, towards something more relevant to what fans around the world want and need today.

The survival mentality is very evident in sports during the pandemic as its actors make laudable efforts, albeit with only marginal impact, to help address the fallout from the Crisis. Sebastian Buck, founder and strategic lead at leading impact agency enso and fellow collaborator, commented on 17 Sport's webinar Purposefull Stories, "It is sad that, at a time of elevated need for togetherness to take on the challenges we are facing, sport has not played a bigger role than it has. This probably stems from a lack of investment historically by sport in community building." In short, the pandemic has revealed that sport as we know it is just not designed with Purpose in mind.

The discussion amongst sports business executives during the early weeks of the pandemic sent out strong signs of a survival mentality with most focusing on economics and sport as an entertainment product—how do we restart our competitions or move our product to an online environment? Everyone is talking about playing their games in front of empty stadiums, and every day we read about traditional sports migrating their product to the virtual world.

As such, it seems that the prevailing response from sport to the Crisis is to try and reboot its old operating system, a system in which COVID has already proved to be redundant. What happens if we do manage to get our live events going again only to fall victim to a resurgence in the COVID Virus that forces us all to practice extreme social distancing again? What happens if bad actors hack into and close down the world of virtual sport. Sports will be out of business again.

It is clear to us that what we need right now is a radically different approach, one that takes a hard look at what value sport has to offer to the world beyond and in addition to its entertainment product. But to realize this value, it is also clear that we will need a radically different mindset from sports leaders, one that takes an infinite view on the role that sport can play in building a resilient society as opposed to the finite, traditional, shareholder first mindset that has ruled the sector for the last 40 years.

In short, sport needs a just cause—a Purpose beyond just entertainment and dollars—that it can rally around and leverage to fuel the birth of Sport 2.0 as an essential service. As Sebastian Buck says, "In order to be successful in the future, sport needs to clearly identify and understand how it builds value for the world beyond its product and how to bring people together around this proposition as participants and not just as consumers."

While the business of sport, intoxicated by the trappings of the success of its 40-year-old business model, clearly has not been paying attention, several opportunities are lying in plain view that sport just has not embraced. One such prospect is the latent power that exists within sports to build community and bring people together, despite their differences. I hear it over and over again from people I speak with right now. "We so miss the sense of community that sport provides, the sense of belonging, the sense of pride."

Unsurprisingly, the NBA was one of the first to identify this opportunity with its COVID inspired NBA Together platform aimed at supporting, engaging, educating, and inspiring youth, families, and fans in response to the pandemic. And another basketball property, the Golden State Warriors, also showed signs that they were leaning into this opportunity with their activations with partners highlighting their vision of becoming a community asset. Mike Kitts, SVP Partnerships at the Warriors, clearly demonstrated this when he said, "In the eye of this challenge comes the opportunity to innovate. It has the potential to be a real area of growth."

The other cultural phenomenon that sport should be leaning into but is not yet is people's—aka Fans'—increasing desire to do good beyond just making donations, and their rapidly evolving expectations that organizations stand for something more than just profits. People today are okay with businesses making a profit just as long as they do it in a way that is good for their customers, employees, communities, and the environment at large. And they want to buy from, work for, invest in, advocate for, and support the organizations that take this position. In short, we now live in the age of Social Good, and sport needs to adjust accordingly.

Nielsen research conducted during the height of the COVID pandemic confirmed that this sentiment is alive and well amongst sports fans, with 70% of those surveyed saying they would support a sports league based on how they conducted themselves during the crisis. Further, 78% of sports fans agreed that brands that lead during times of crisis are stronger than those that follow, and 57% of sports fans would try watching a new sport or sports league based on how they conducted themselves during the pandemic.

Imagine if we could redesign sport's value proposition in such a way that, beyond just being positioned as an entertainment product, sport could tap into these evolving fan expectations, and sport's latent power to build community, and turn this into a core value proposition for sport. Imagine if sport was designed with the long game in mind and in such a way that it could rapidly activate and mobilize its fan community in service of good and in the name of the teams that they passionately follow—whether their team was playing or not. Brazilian Sports Club Recife did this in 2012 with their "Immortal Fans" initiative in which they mobilized over 50,000 of their fans to sign up for an organ donor program that reduced the organ transplant waiting list in the city to zero and saved many lives.

And there are many other embedded value-adds that sport offers that are just waiting to be brought to life. Quoting Sebastian Buck again, "Being the most-loved organization in your city isn't just about entertainment anymore, it's about being relevant every day. And being the most-loved organization unlocks all kinds of business opportunities: from high sales of existing products and services, to new business lines that serve the community in new ways." This idea is not about pivoting from a for-profit model to a nonprofit model; it is about finding ways of creating more value for your community, which in turn unlocks more brand and business value, while still delivering a great entertainment product. It is a classic example of a brand extension.

At this time of crisis, it has become clear to us that sport needs to embrace Purpose more so than ever before. The work that we do, and the message in this book, will, we hope, inspire, educate, and enable people to do good while doing well through sport.

Yes, we will one day soon hopefully be able to watch and attend live sports events again the way we used to pre-COVID. But our wish is that sport will not waste the opportunity it has to reinvent itself and that, post-COVID, we will see sport taking its rightful place in society as a community asset that is deemed an essential service that the authorities cannot simply switch off. It is up to all of us to make sure this happens.

Sport's journey towards Purpose is a continuously evolving story that we look forward to following and contributing to in the coming months and years both through the work we do at 17 Sport and through subsequent editions of this book.

LEGACY SPORT PODCAST SERIES

The Leading Thoughts that are featured throughout Legacy Sport are excerpts from in-person interviews that we conducted with the various thought leaders who were kind enough to share their insights with you and us.

Given the quality of these interviews and the information shared in them, we decided to create The Legacy Sport Podcast Series as a companion resource to *Legacy Sport*. Each Podcast includes a 30-minute interview and provides an additional layer of insights to those already covered in this book.

The Legacy Sport Podcast Series includes interviews with:

Alan Jope (Unilever)
Allen Hershkowitz (Sport & Sustainability International)
Anna Isaacson (NFL)
Anne-Cecile Turner (The Ocean Race)
Ben Astin (Lionsraw)
Benita Fitzgerald-Mosley (Laureus Sport for Good USA)
Carol Cone (Carol Cone ON PURPOSE)
Claude Atcher (RWC France 2023)
Clementine Painter (adidas)
Dean Kamen (FIRST)
Edreece Arghandiwal (Oakland Roots)

Florence Darquie-Bossard (Danone)
Hubert Joly (Best Buy)
Joanne Pasternack (Warriors and 49ers)
John Balkam (3-Win Sponsorship)
John Izzo (drjohnizzo.com)
Julia Palle (Formula E)
Kevin Anderson (ATP tennis player)
Kevin Martinez (ESPN)
Kely Nascimento-DeLuca Kirk Souder (enso)
Lesa Ukman (ProSocial Valuation)
Lew Blaustein (Green Sports Blog)
Lisa Arie (Vista Caballo)
Lisa Zimouche (freestyle footballer)
Lucien Boyer (Global Sports Week)
Marie Sallois (IOC)
Matthew Campelli (The Sustainability Report)
Mike Geddes (Oakland Roots)
Olga Harvey (Women's Sports Foundation)
Ricardo Fort (Coca-Cola)
Scott Jenkins (Green Sports Alliance and Mercedes-Benz Stadium)
Sebastian Buck (enso)
Tania Braga (IOC)
Tim Shriver (Special Olympics)

Please subscribe to The Legacy Sport Podcast Series wherever you normally get your podcasts from, or you can visit the *Legacy Sport* website at www.legacysport.org.

17 SPORT
RAISE THE GAME

We are excited to be able to practice what we preach here in *Legacy Sport* through our company 17 Sport, the world's first integrated sports impact company operating at the intersection of sport, business, and Purpose.

17 Sport exists to use the power of sport to build a positive future for the world, which we do by collaborating with the pioneers and thought leaders of the sports world to inspire, educate, and enable the business of sport to do good while doing well. We provide Purpose-led business solutions—advisory, commercial, and management—to brands, sports properties, athletes, and sports-based nonprofits to help them manage their investments in sport in a more meaningful way, and through initiatives like *Legacy Sport*—the book and the Podcast.

Our name, 17 Sport, is inspired by the United Nations Sustainable Development Goals, of which there are 17, including Goal 17, which is about partnerships. Partnerships are a central tenet of our guiding principles as an organization.

100% of the net profits from the sale of *Legacy Sport* are being directed towards organizations committed to building a positive future for the world through sport.

You can learn more about 17 Sport on our website www.17-sport.com or by contacting us at legacysport@17-sport.com.

REFERENCES

PART 1: THE PURPOSE REVOLUTION AND WHY IT MATTERS

Chapter 1: The ever-evolving relationship between them and us

"Accenture Strategy." 2018. *To Affinity and Beyond: From Me to We, The Rise of the Purpose-Led Brand.* https://www.accenture.com/_acnmedia/thought-leadership -assets/pdf/accenture-competitive-agility-gcpr-pov.pdf.

Anchor, Shawn, Andrew Reece, Gabriella Rosen Kellerman, and Alexi Robichaux. 2018. *"9 Out of 10 People are Willing to Earn Less Money to Do More Meaningful Work"* Harvard Business Review, November 6, 2018. https://hbr.org/2018/11/9| -out-of-10-people-are-willing-to-earn-less-money-to-do-more-meaningful-work/.

Denning, Steve. 2017. "Making Sense Of Shareholder Value: The World's Dumbest Idea." *Forbes,* July17, 2017. https://www.forbes.com/sites/stevedenning/2017/07/17 /making-sense-of-shareholder-value-the-worlds-dumbest-idea/.

Friedman, Milton. 1962. *Capitalism and Freedom.* University of Chicago Press.

Howe, Neill. 2019. "Millennials and the Loneliness Epidemic." *Forbes,* May 3, 2019. https://www.google.com/search?q=millenials+and+the+loneliness+epidemic+ forbes+2018&rlz=1C1JZAP_enZA772ZA772&oq=millenials+and+t&aqs= chrome.2.69i57j0j69i59j0l5.5785.

Porter, Michael and Michael Kramer. 2011. *Creating Shared Value* Harvard Business Review. January/February 2011. https://hbr.org/2011/01/the-big-idea-creating -shared-value/.

Reece, Andrew, Andria Kellerman, and Alexi Robichaux. 2018. "Meaning and Purpose at Work." *Better Up,* file:///C:/Users/Test/Downloads/BetterUp-Meaning &Purpose-FINAL_sm.pdf.

Sinek, Simon. 2009. *Start with Why* Portfolio.

Unilever Sustainable Living Plan. n.d. https://www.unilever.com/sustainable-living/.

Chapter 2: How Business is responding to the shifting moral landscape

Benioff, Marc. 2018. "The Social Responsibility of Business" *New York Times,* October 24, 2018. https://www.nytimes.com/2018/10/24/opinion/business-social-respon sibility-proposition-c.html.

Cone, Carol. 2020. "7 Lessons from Davos: It's Time to Act." *Real Leaders,* February 5, 2020. https://real-leaders.com/7-lessons-from-davos-2020-its-time-to-act.

Deloitte. 2019. *The Deloitte Global Millennial Survey.* https://www2.deloitte.com/za/en/pages/about-deloitte/articles/millennialsurvey.html.

Edelman. 2020. *Edelman Trust Barometer.* https://www.edelman.com/trustbarometer.

"Havas Group. 2017. *Meaningful Brands* https://dk.havas.com/wp-content/uploads/sites/37/2017/02/mb17_brochure_final_web.pdf.

"Kantar Consulting". 2020. *Igniting Purpose-Led Growth.* https://consulting.kantar.com/wp-content/uploads/2019/06/Purpose-2020-PDF-Presentation.pdf.

Millard, Drew. 2019. "Jamie Dimon wants a kinder, gentler capitalism. Shut up Jamie." *The Outline,* April 11, 2019. https://theoutline.com/post/7300/jpmorgan-chase-ceo-jamie-dimon-wants-a-kinder-gentler-capitalism-shut-up-jamie.

Phenix Capital Impact Summit 2020 n.d. https://www.phenixcapital.nl/impact-summit-europe-2020.

Skapinker, Michael. 2018 "Unilever's Paul Polman was a standout CEO of the past decade" F*inancial Times,* December 11, 2018. https://www.ft.com/content/e7040df4-fa19-11e8-8b7c-6fa24bd5409c.

Chapter 4: Personal Purpose—You are more than what you may have become

Crowe, Cameron. 2016. "Jerry Maguire Mission Statement." *The Uncool,* April 25, 2016. http:// www.theuncool. com/2016/04/25/jerry-maguire-mission-statement.

Enso. 2018. *World Value Index.* https://www.enso.co/wp-content/uploads/2018/09/World-Value-Index-2018-Brand-Report-enso.pdf.

Jacobs, Katie. 2016. "The Importance of Work with Purpose for Gen Y" *HR Magazine,* February 23, 2016. https://hrmagazine.co.uk/article-details/the-importance-of-work-with-Purpose-for-gen-y.

MacLeod, David and Nita Clarke. 2009. *Engaging for Success: enhancing performance through employee engagement.* Crown Copyright, July 2009. https://engagefor success.org/engaging-for-success.

PART 2: DOING GOOD WHILE DOING WELL IN SPORT

Chapter 5: Athletes—A mirror on society

Biography. 2019. "Colin Kaepernick." November 18, 2019. https://www.biography.com/athlete/colin-kaepernick.

George, Sarah. 2018. "ATP unveils sweeping plastic phase-outs for Nitto tennis finals in London" *Edie,* November 8, 2018. https://www.edie.net/news/5/ATP-unveils-sweeping-plastic-phase-outs-for-Nitto-Tennis-Finals-in-London/.

Mules, Ineke. 2019. "Meet the athletes taking action on climate change." *Deutsche Welle,* May 17, 2019. https://www.dw.com/en/meet-the-athletes-taking-action-on-climate-change/a-48660770.

Perelman, Richard. 2020. "Edwin Moses is Right When he says Protests Can't be Stopped, but Neither can the Blowback." *The Sports Examiner,* February 9, 2020. http://www.thesportsexaminer.com/lane-one-edwin-moses-is-right-when-he-says-protests-cant-be-stopped-but-neither-can-the-blowback.

Rhoden, William C. 2013. "In Ali's Voice From the Past, a Stand for the Ages." *The New York Times,* June 20, 2013. https://www.nytimes.com/2013/06/21/sports/in-alis-voice-from-the-past-a-stand-for-the-ages.html

Weinrib, Ben. 2019. "Michael Jordan applauds athletes for using their platform for activism." *Yahoo Sports,* October 18, 2019. https://sports.yahoo.com/michael-jordan-applauds-athletes-platform-activism-172643722.htmlwww.yahoo.com

Chapter 6: The Olympic Movement—From Los Angeles and back again

Campelli, Matthew. 2020. "IOC preparing 'more ambitious' sustainability targets for 2021–2024 cycle." *The Sustainability Report,* March 12, 2020. https://sustainabilityreport.com/2020/03/12/ioc-preparing-more-ambitious-sustainability-targets-for-2021-2024-cycle/.

Young, Georgina. 2020. "Legacy and the Olympic Games."

Chapter 7: Stories from the frontline of Purpose and Sport

Casey, Michael. 2015. "9 ways professional sports are going green." *CBS News,* January 28, 2015. https://www.cbsnews.com/news/9-ways-professional-sports-are-going-green.

Chadband, Ian. 2019. "Why winning the Rugby World Cup isn't Enough for Siya Kolisi." *Red Bull,* December 13, 2019. https://www.redbull.com/za-en/siya-kolisi-interview.

IOC. 2020. "Vancouver 2010: Setting the Standard for Sport, Sustainability and Social Legacy." *CSR Wire,* March 9, 2020. https://www.csrwire.com/press_releases/43625-Vancouver-2010-Setting-the-Standard-for-Sport-Sustainability-and-Social-Legacy.

Lew, Josh. 2010. "Vancouver 2010: The Greenest Olympics?" *Mother Nature Network,* January 28, 2010. https://www.mnn.com/lifestyle/eco-tourism/stories/vancouver-2010-the-greenest-olympics.

Mann, Colin. 2019. "Formula E, Record audience figures, revenue." *Advanced Television,* September 13, 2019.https://advanced-television.com/2019/09/13/formula-e-record-audience-figures-revenue/.

Ridley, Louise. 2012. "Olympic sustainability report: key findings." *Campaign,* December 13, 2012. https://www.campaignlive.co.uk/article/olympic-sustainability-report-key-findings/1164193.

Chapter 9: Where Sport and Purpose are heading and why it matters. What's next?

Performance Research. 2017. *Sponsorship Decision Makers Survey 2017.* http://www .sponsorship.com/ieg/files/7f/7fd3bb31-2c81-4fe9-8f5d-1c9d7cab1232.pdf

PART 3: BRINGING PURPOSE TO LIFE

Chapter 11: What Purpose is and what it is not

Barrett, William P. 2018. "The Largest Charities for 2018." *Forbes,* December 11, 2018. https://www.forbes.com/sites/williampbarrett/2018/12/11/largest-charities -2018/#5a06c78f2022
Cone/Porter Novelli Purpose Report. 2018.
Pallotta, Dan. 2010. *Uncharitable: How Restraints on Nonprofits Undermine Their Potential.* University Press of New England.

Chapter 15: Measuring what matters

Pro Social Valuation n.d. "What We Do, Why We Do It." https://www.prosocial valuation.com/what-we-do/.

Chapter 16: Bringing it all together

Danone Nations Cup n.d. "About Danone Nations Cup." https://www.danonenations cup.com/en/.

SPORT FOR GOOD USEFUL WEBSITES

Beyond Sport – www.beyondsport.org
Laureus Sport For Good Foundation – www.laureus.com
Peace and Sport – www.peace-sport.org
Streetfootballworld – www.streetfootballworld.org
Women's Sports Foundation – www.womenssportsfoundation.org

ABOUT THE AUTHORS

NEILL DUFFY has, for 20 years, enabled global brands, international sports properties, and high-performing nonprofits to do good while doing well through sport. He has achieved a number of world firsts like helping the 34th America's Cup become the first major international sports events to go zero waste and carbon neutral, and as Chair of the Sustainability Committee, delivered Super Bowl 50 as the "most shared, participatory, giving, and sustainable Super Bowl in history." Neill is the Co-Founder and CEO of 17 Sport as well as a published author and sought-after speaker.

FABIEN PAGET, a former semi-professional tennis player, has more than 15 years experience in the sports industry with previous tenures at Nike and the acclaimed Mouratoglou Tennis Academy. In 2012, Fabien created O2 Management, a boutique sport management agency that represented world-class athletes and rising stars across a variety of sports—tennis, soccer, sailing, surfing, swimming, and more. During this time, Fabien also worked with Serena Williams to deliver mission-aligned partnerships that highlighted her commitment to women's empowerment. Fabien is the Co-Founder of 17 Sport and was recently named #37 among the Top #100 Sport business leaders Under 40.

JO RAMSAY has over 20 years experience in the sports industry, working at leading agencies, including Octagon, as the head of strategy and sponsorship measurement. She has developed industry leading tools to manage and measure sponsorship investments and has designed and activated purposeful sponsorship programs across diverse categories. Jo has witnessed firsthand the transformative power of sport in her home country, South Africa, and, as Strategy Director for 17 Sport, is a firm believer that sport needs to fully embrace Purpose if it is to thrive in the years to come.

Made in USA - Crawfordsville, IN
99706_9781620064030
10.21.2020 1335